Rudolf Agstner

One week in Ethiopia, forever with God

Rudolf Agstner

One week in Ethiopia, forever with God

Guidebook to the Foreigners' Cemeteries in Addis Ababa, Ethiopia

LIT

Umschlagbilder: © Rudolf Agstner

∞

Gedruckt auf alterungsbeständigem Werkdruckpapier entsprechend
ANSI Z3948 DIN ISO 9706

Bibliographic information published by the Deutsche Nationalbibliothek
The Deutsche Nationalbibliothek lists this publication in the Deutsche Nationalbibliografie; detailed bibliographic data are available in the Internet at http://dnb.d-nb.de.

ISBN 978-3-643-50091-5

A catalogue record for this book is available from the British Library

Krotenthallergasse 10/8
A-1080 Wien
Tel. +43 (0) 1-409 56 61
Fax +43 (0) 1-409 56 97
e-Mail: wien@lit-verlag.at
http://www.lit-verlag.at

LIT VERLAG Dr. W. Hopf
Berlin 2009
Fresnostr. 2
D-48159 Münster
Tel. +49 (0) 2 51-620 32 22
Fax +49 (0) 2 51-922 60 99
e-Mail: lit@lit-verlag.de
http://www.lit-verlag.de

Distribution:
In Germany: LIT Verlag Fresnostr. 2, D-48159 Münster
Tel. +49 (0) 2 51-620 32 22, Fax +49 (0) 2 51-922 60 99, e-Mail: vertrieb@lit-verlag.de

In Austria: Medienlogistik Pichler-ÖBZ GmbH & Co KG
IZ-NÖ, Süd, Straße 1, Objekt 34, A-2355 Wiener Neudorf
Tel. +43 (0) 22 36-63 53 52 90, Fax +43 (0) 22 36-63 53 52 43, e-Mail: mlo@medien-logistik.at

In Switzerland: B + M Buch- und Medienvertriebs AG
Hochstr. 357, CH-8200 Schaffhausen
Tel. +41 (0) 52-643 54 30, Fax +41 (0) 52-643 54 35, e-Mail: order@buch-medien.ch

In the UK by: Global Book Marketing, 99B Wallis Rd, London, E9 5LN
Phone: +44 (0) 20 8533 5800 – Fax: +44 (0) 1600 775 663
http://www.centralbooks.co.uk/html

In North America by:

Transaction Publishers
New Brunswick (U.S.A.) and London (U.K.)

Transaction Publishers
Rutgers University
35 Berrue Circle
Piscataway, NJ 08854

Phone: +1 (732) 445 - 2280
Fax: + 1 (732) 445 - 3138
for orders (U. S. only):
toll free (888) 999 - 6778
e-mail: orders@transactionpub.com

"A Perenne Ricordo… Tu Spociva V Kristu Panu … Ici Repose en Paix … Known unto God … Pax … May His Soul Rest Eternally … Odpocivej V Pokoji … Regrets Eternels … Gestorben im Dreissigsten Jahre seines hoffnungsvollen Lebens… Rest in Peace until the Day Breaks and the Shadows flee away… En Vecka I Etiopien för Evigt Hos Gud (One week in Ethiopia, for ever with God) … Die Wond is Diep en Saar Maar God is Lief de Hy Reg'aar"

To the Hospitality and Friendship of the Ethiopian People

TABLE OF CONTENTS

Text in Italics signifies data from sources other than the tombstone

1. INTRODUCTION

A week after arriving in Ethiopia in October of 2006 as ambassador of Austria, my wife Brigitte and I asked the embassy's driver Negatu Assefa Kebede to take us to the foreigners' cemetery in Gulele on the outskirts of Addis Ababa of whose existence I had learned while researching relations between Austria and Ethiopia. While unable to locate the tomb of the Austrian SS war – criminal turned hospital-director I was looking for in connection with a project on the Austrians in Ethiopia, we soon realized that the cemetery in Gulele was an oasis of peace and quiet. Not only that, it turned out to be a source of Ethiopia's history of the 20th century, an open book reminding the rare visitors of the role of the large Armenian, Greek and Italian communities and several smaller ones. Some of them came in search of business, 40 Armenian orphans in Jerusalem were offered a safe haven in 1924 by Haile Selassie, while many Italians came as colonizers – and were allowed to stay on after "il Duce's" dream of an "Africa Orientale Italiano" had collapsed in 1941. Italian soldiers who invaded Ethiopia in 1935/36 and Commonwealth soldiers fighting them in 1940/1941 during World War II were buried in the beautifully kept military cemeteries in Gulele. Others too found a safe haven in Ethiopia after World War II – German and Austrian Nazis. The cemetery, where citizens of many nations rest in peace alongside each other is also a sign of the hospitality extended by Ethiopia and its people to foreigners, which in our modern times with its xenophobic tendencies deserves due appreciation. Although the cemetery is only one of at present 77 active cemeteries in Addis Ababa (among them 51 Orthodox, eight Muslim, seven municipal and two church-based community organizations) it should be the most appealing to tourists.

After looking for any information on the cemetery, it turned out that there was none. This interesting cemetery, revealing the presence of thousands of foreigners in Ethiopia and their contribution to the development of the country, was not mentioned in any of the guide books on Ethiopia[1] nor in guide books dealing with Addis Ababa only, as Milena Batistoni and Gian Paolo Chiari's "Old Tracks in the New Flower – A Historical Guide to Addis Ababa"[2] or the official guide books of the Addis Ababa Tourism Commission. No photos of the cemetery are reproduced in books with historical views of Addis Ababa.

It does not even figure on the most recent map of Addis Ababa, produced by GTZ – German Technical Cooperation, the Ethiopian Mapping Authority and the German Embassy Addis Ababa, released in December 2008[3]; while showing a "Catholic Church" and a "Greek Church" in sector 5 B, both of them actually inaccessible and normally closed funeral chapels, no mentioning is made of the cemetery surrounding them.

Today, the cemetery today faces several challenges, which prevent its further expansion. It is on one side surrounded by the road to Ambo, presently being wid-

---

[1] Lonely Planet – Ethiopia and Eritrea; Bradt – Ethiopia; Jumbo Guide – Äthiopien; Reise Know-How „Äthiopien“; John GRAHAM, Ethiopia off the Beaten Trail, Addis Ababa 2001.

[2] Arada Press, Addis Ababa 2004.

[3] Addis Ababa City Map, Ethiopia 1:20.000, 1st edition 2008, cartography by geo3 Institute for Geo Research, TFH Berlin.

ened, on the other side by encroaching settlements; to its North is the new ring road around Addis Ababa. So far, it was able to avoid the problems of several other cemeteries in Addis Ababa, which became victims of the construction of the ring road around Addis Ababa or several street-widening projects.

Change is taking place within the cemetery walls - more and more tombs of Italians, buried in Gulele in Campo I during the 1940s and 1950s are being removed to make way for new tombs of Ethiopian Catholics.

Visitors to the cemetery will appreciate the quiet and peaceful atmosphere and the view to the wooded mountains surrounding Addis Ababa, letting them forget that they are actually not far from a bustling metropolis of 2.7 million inhabitants according to the latest census of May 2007. When leaving, visitors should not forget to give the guard at the entrance a generous "schai" (tea-money or baksheesh); a 10 Birr banknote (roughly 60 Eurocents) will be much appreciated.

Whoever wants to see Gulele cemetery as a multi-national and multi-denominational civilian cemetery, reflecting through its tombstones the presence of a large foreign community in Addis Ababa in the 20th century should not loose time, as increasingly older Italian tombs are replaced by Ethiopian Catholic tombstones, which are of a completely different style. It will not take long, and the cemetery in Gulele will look like any other Ethiopian Orthodox cemetery.

Considering that numerous well-researched and illustrated books exist about the cemeteries of my hometown Vienna[4] I decided to gather information about those Addis Ababa cemeteries, where foreigners had found their last resting place.

This work could not have been undertaken without the valuable support of Reverend Chrisostomos Barberis (Greek-Orthodox Church) and Reverend Martin Gossens (German Protestant Church), who allowed access to the death registers of the Greek-Orthodox Church and the German Protestant Church. These registers, which as of 1928 indicate the cause of death, are a valuable source of information on living conditions of foreigners in Addis Ababa. The register of burials kept by the Protestant Lutheran Church[5] of Addis Ababa reveals amongst other things that in the 1930s many children died before reaching the age of one, and other entries of the pre WW II – times tell us of death by suicide, influenza, pneumonia or murder by shiftas (highwaymen) as e.g. in 1935/36 some Germans were taken for Italians.

Two entries in the Greek Orthodox burial register are rather tragic - *"killed with an axe by his servant"* or *"drowned in Aqaqi River"*. Around 1955, the first deaths due to "car accidents" appear in the registers, and later, in the 1970s death by car accidents prevail, as increasingly "Ferendjis" were killed in accidents on the way to Lake Langano, where the Addis Ababa upper class spent their weekends on the shores of the only Ethiopian lake where it is safe to swim. They were however not buried in Gulele, but transferred to Germany for burial.

The computerized death ledger of the Armenian community, which was generously made available to the author by Mr. Vartkes Nalbandian, gives a similar picture – deaths by influenza, pneumonia, malaria, meningitis, hepatitis, typhoid and

[4] Peter PLEYEL, Friedhöfe in Wien vom Mittelalter bis Heute, Vienna 1999; Patricia STEINES, Hunderttausend Steine – Grabstellen großer Österreicher jüdischer Konfession auf dem Wiener Zentralfriedhof Tor I und Tor V, Vienna 1993; Tina WALZER, Der Jüdische Friedhof in Währing, Vienna 2009; Martha KEIL, Von Baronen und Branntweinern – Ein jüdischer Friedhof erzählt, Vienna 2009; Traude VERAN, Das steinerne Archiv – Der Wiener jüdische Friedhof in der Rossau, Vienna 2009.

[5] Verzeichnis der Begrabenen der Parochie der ev. luth. Christuskirche in Adis Abeba (gegr. 12. Februar 1930) für die Zeit vom 12. Februar 1928 bis …

tuberculosis, car accidents, falling from a horse, drowning in Lake Hora near Debre Zeyt / Bishoftu or suicide.

Others who provided valuable information include Mr. Charalambos N. Tsimas ("Mr. Bambis") and Mr. Manoli Mesfin, driver of H.E. the Greek ambassador, on the Greeks in Addis Ababa. Mr. Vartkes Nalbandian, Mr. Vahak Karibian and Mrs. Sevan Aslanian were valuable sources of information on the Armenian community. Dr. Carlo Iori, Mr. Guido Checchin and Nadia Mini made available information on the Italian community and Colonel Ottavio Silitti (Italian Embassy) on the military cemetery. Ms. Kersti Karlsson, local representative of the Church of Sweden, allowed a look at the data she had on Danish, Finnish, Norwegian and Swedish nationals[6]. Dr. Wolbert Smidt, University of Hamburg, made valuable suggestions.

This book would however never have been written without extensive research on the ground, clearing overgrown tombs, recording barely legible inscriptions, taking hundreds of photos – in all of these activities the author was, in morning and afternoon hours, weekdays and weekends, in sunshine and rain, untiringly assisted by the Austrian Embassy's driver and liason officer Negatu Assefa.

The reader will find in the guidebook a total of 3716 names of persons buried in the cemetery at Gulele (International Cemetery 225; Greek Orthodox Cemetery: 603; Catholic Cemetery "San Pietro e Paolo": 1001; Old Armenian Cemetery: 447, New Armenian Cemetery: 245; Cimitero Militare Italiano: 833, Commonwealth War Graves Cemetery: 352 (291 soldiers, 61 in civilian part). In most cases, where access to death registers was not available, it was impossible to establish the profession or other biographical data of those buried, in other cases data of persons buried in long abandoned graves were readily available.

The guidebook is neither intended as a study of the various foreign communities in Addis Ababa nor as a biographical lexicon of foreigners who once lived in Addis Ababa. This topic would be an interesting subject for further in-depth research. The author however hopes that it will one day serve as basis for a comprehensive history of the "Ferendjis" in Ethiopia and their contribution to the development of Ethiopia in the 20th century.

Rudolf Agstner — Addis Ababa, 11 September 2009

---

[6] Two Swedish citizens are buried in the cemtery of Nekempt: Dr. Ulla Marklund * 6 VIII 1932 + 15 VIII 1962 and Ingrid Karlsson * V 1934 + V 1935.

2. THE FOREIGN COMMUNITIES IN ADDIS ABABA AND THE ORIGINS OF THE CEMETERY AT GULELE

In 1881 Menelik, King of Shoa, moved his capital from Ankober to the Entotto Mountain. In 1886 Emperor Menelik and Empress Taitu had a house built near the Filawoha springs, and in 1889 the Emperor chose a hill North - East of the Filawoha hot springs as the site of his new Gebbi. The place was renamed Addis Ababa – "New Flower" – and became the capital of Ethiopia in 1891.

The new capital of the expanding empire soon attracted Ethiopians from all parts of the country as well as numerous foreigners – Armenians, Greeks, Italians, Indians, Russians, French, Swedes, Norwegians, Germans, Austrians and Hungarians. Contrary to today, when most foreigners in Addis Ababa stay for a few years only and return home or proceed to other countries, the foreigners who had come at the beginning of the 20th century intended to stay. Some of them died in Addis Ababa, which eventually raised the question of a separate burial. On 10 August 1908 the first Austrian citizen, who had died in Addis Ababa, a carpenter by name of Karl Hilfer from Jungbunzlau in Bohemia (Mlada Boleslav, Czech Republic) was buried at the Abyssinian cemetery, as there was no cemetery for Europeans in the Ethiopian capital at the time.[7]

In 1912 a "European" cemetery was established *"dans un vaste terrain plat accordé [...] par le Gouvernement Ethiopien et amenagé à cette époque pour la sépulture des morts étrangers."* The cemetery was apparently divided into a Catholic, an Armenian, a Greek-Orthodox, a Protestant and a Jewish part. The situation changed after World War II, when an Italian and a Commonwealth military cemetery were added, whereas a separate Jewish cemetery was established around 1950 in today's Burkina Faso Street. The Indian community maintained their cemetery opposite the Jewish cemetery.

So far, the only description of foreign communities is contained in the chapter *"Les Étrangers en Éthiopie"* of Adrien Zervos[8] book "L'Empire d'Éthiopie"[9], published in 1936 after the Italian occupation.

Zervos in 1935 lists 14,580 foreigners in Ethiopia, 6000 of them in Addis Ababa, 800 in Dire Dawa, 6780 in Harar and 1000 in other parts of Ethiopia. The figures for individual countries were as follows:

Americans (US)	103	
Germans	230	
British (and Dominions)	75	
Armenians	2800	(under French, Greek and Turkish protection)
Arabs	4000	(under British, French and Italian protection)
Austrians	50	(under German protection)
Belgians	28	

[7] Friedrich Freiherr von KULMER, Im Reiche Kaiser Meneliks – Tagebuch einer Abessinischen Reise, edited by Emanuela Baronin MATTL-LÖWENKREUZ, Leipzig 1910, pp. 220-221.

[8] See Encyclopaedia Aethiopica (EAE), vol. 5, entry Zervos, Adrien.

[9] Adrien ZERVOS, L'Empire d'Ethiopie. Le miroir de l'Ethiopie moderne 1906-1935, Alexandria 1936.

Bulgarians	3	(under Italian protection)
Egyptians	60	
French	350	
Greeks	3140	
Hungarians	30	(under Italian protection)
Italians	350	
Japanese	4	
Jews	125	(under German and other protection)
Lebanese – Syrians	40	(under French protection)
Lituanians	1	
Polish	2	(under French protection)
Swedes	55	
Swiss	30	(under French and German protection)
Turks	20	
Russians	28	(under French and Greek protection)
Dutch	2	(under German protection)
Chinese	2	(under French protection)
Indians	3000	(under British protection)
Estonians	2	(under German protection)

Zervos[10] was the first to mention "Le Cimetière Européen" : *"Le cimetière européen est situé a Goullalé (extrémité Nord-Ouest d'Addis-Abeba), dans un vaste terrain plat accordé en 1912 par le Gouvernement Ethiopien et aménagé à cette époque pour la sépulture des morts étrangers. Hélas ! De nombreuses tombes, la plupart sont dotées de monuments de regrets et de souvenirs, occupent un grand espace de terrain. Le cimetière européen est divisé en plusieurs parties dont chacune est réservée, à un rite religieux. Les sépultures catholiques sont séparées des sépultures grecques-orthodoxes, arméniennes, protestantes et juives."*

Two years later, the situation had changed dramatically: there were 17,301 Italians in Addis Ababa, 4214 of them women. On 31 March 1938, 2443 other foreigners were living in Addis Ababa, including 830 Armenians, 800 Greeks, 245 British, 83 Germans including Austrians, 55 Turks, 46 Americans and 31 French.[11]

In the same year, the cemetery is mentioned ort he first – and probably last – time in a tourist-guide book. The first-ever guide book on Ethiopia, published in 1938 by the Italians, in ist chapter on Addis Ababa *"dalla piazza dell Littorio* (near the old post office) *a Gullele*" mentions that *"piu lontano, a destra, il Cimitero Cattolico, su una collinetta pianegiante* (nearly flat), *all ombra degli eucalipti..."* is located.[12]

[10] ZERVOS, ibid, p. 502.

[11] Guida d'Italia della Consociazione Turistica Italiana – Africa Orientale Italiana, Milano 1938, p. 479.

[12] Guida d'Italia della Consociazione Turistica Italiana – Africa Orientale Italiana, Milano 1938, p. 486.

General view of the Catholic Cemetery

This book takes you on a stroll through these two cemeteries in Gulele at the outskirts of Addis Ababa, and to the small cemetery in the British Embassy Compound, which is not open to the public. Sadly many tombstones do not tell the story of the person buried there. A walk through the Gulele Cemetry is also a reminder of the foreign presence in Addis Ababa and ist gradual disappearance. Today, there are probably ten times more tomb stones of Greeks and Armenians in the Gulele Cemetery as Greeks and Armenians are living in Ethiopia's capital of 2.7 million inhabitants. The number of Italian civilians buried in Gulele and of those living in Addis Ababa – around 1200 – seems to be roughly equal. It is a far cry from the days when the Italian community numbered around 25,000.

Under the rule of Emperor Menelik II, Empress Zawditu and Emperor Haile Selassie I. Ethiopia was attracting foreigners. The decline of the foreign communities can be pinpointed to the fall of Haile Selassie I and the rise to power of the Derg in 1974.

The history of the Armenian community in Addis Ababa is well documented in Rev. Myron Sarkissian's book "Armenians towards Ethiopia",[13] which contains reprints of three extensinve papers of Professor Richard Pankhurst on this subject.[14] The first Armenians began to settle in Harar around 1875; after the massacres of Armenians in the Ottoman Empire (1894-1896) more Armenians settled in Harar, bringing their number to 50. The 1915 massacres of Armenians marked the second phase of Armenian immigration to Ethiopia. In 1928 the Armenian community

[13] Myron SARKISSIAN, Armenians towards Ethiopia, Addis Ababa 2007 (in Armenian).

[14] Richard PANKHURST, The History of Ethiopian-Armenian Relations, in: Revue des Études Arméniennes 1977 XII, pp. 273-345; "The History of Ethiopian-Armenian Relations (II)", in: Revue des Études Arméniennes 1978-1979, XIII, pp. 259-312; "The History of Ethiopian-Armenian Relations (III) The Late Nineteenth and Early Twentieth Centuries", in: Revue des Études Arméniennes 1981, XV, pp. 355-400.

began construction of the church “Sourp Kevork” (St. Georges); it was finished in 1930. In 1935, of the 2800 Armenians in Ethiopia, 1200 lived in the capital, where construction of the Armenian school had just been finished.

By 1974, when Emperor Haile Selassie I. was the deposed and arrested by the Derg rulers, the Armenian community in Addis Ababa had reached 1500. With the nationalisation of private business their numbers began to decline, Armenians leaving ort he United States, Canada, Europe and Australia. In 2009 the Armenian community in Ethiopia’s capital – including children – is made up of a mere 90 persons. The community already lost ist school and a five-storey apartment building under the Derg regime, but still owns a church and a club, as well as two cemeteries described below. The question arises as to what will happen to this valuable real estate once the Armenian community has vanished.

The same also holds true for the Greek community, which in 1960 had built a club, designed by a Greek architect, with sports facilities on an area of 3 hectares at the outskirts of Addis Ababa. Now situated in the center of the capital, it will – when the Greek community will have gone – become property of the Greek Embassy.

The international part of the Gulele Cemetery is also testimony to a strong White Russian presence in Ethiopia after the October Revolution of 1917, as well as a small royalist Yougoslav presence in Addis Ababa.

The fate of the Czechoslovak community is even more telling: between 1920 and 1935 around 200 Czechs had immigrated to Ethiopia, roughly 80 settling in Dire-Dawa, the other 120 in Addis Ababa. Today only three Czechs are living in Addis Ababa.

Unlike in Idi Amin’s Uganda at about the same time, no foreign communities were expelled by the Derg regime; many foreigners did however leave, due to economic pressures.

3. THE FOREIGNERS' CEMETERY

The foreigners' cemetery, usually referred to by Ethiopians as "Petros we Paulos" in the northern environs of the Ethiopian capital Addis Ababa, or as it is known by foreigners "San Pietro e Paolo" in Gulele, is located on Arbanyoch (Patriots) Street circa 4,5 km from Abuna Paulos Square at the city's outskirts on the road to Ambo.[15] The cemetery, open daily from 6 a.m. to 6 p.m. is not easy to find. It used to be marked at its main gate by a small marble plaque with a barely legible inscription "Ethiopian Catholic Cemetery" in Amharic and Geez, which was on the one hand correct and on the other hand completely misleading, as there are several distinctly different cemeteries behind the gate, of which only one is named after the two apostles "Peter and Paul". The plaque has apparently been lost to the widening of the road which has started in February 2009.

Aerial View of the Foreigners' Cemetery at Gulele[16]

Today's main entrance to this highly interesting cemetery is located at N 09 ° 03.340' E 038° 42.975'.[17] The entrance to the Greek Orthodox cemetery of St. George is 100 m further on the road, and the old entrance dating back to 1912 lea-

[15] See Rudolf AGSTNER, The Stories Gravestones Tell – The Ferenji Cemetery at Gulele, Addis Ababa, in: The Anglo-Ethiopian Society News File, Winter 2008, London 2008, p. 12-15.

[16] The Roman Catholic Church of St. Peter and Paul can been clearly seen in the center of the cemetery, as can the St. George Chapel (Velissariou Mausoleum) in the Greek Orthodox Cemetery at the lower corner. The Commonwealth War Graves Cemetery is easily recognizable at the top, bordered by the Cimitero Militare Italiano adjacent to it. The many trees in the lower part indicate the International Cemetery. The long narrow cemetery parallel to the ring road, which can be seen at the left, is the New Armenian Cemetery.

[17] GPS data were taken on 9 February 2009 by Nicolaus Keller, counsellor at the Austrian Permanent Mission to the African Union Addis Ababa, using a Garmin GPS Map 60 CSX.

ding to the "International Cemetery" and the "Old Armenian Cemetery" is another 80 m uphill. Near the next gate uphill, which leads to the Catholic, the International, the Old and New Armenian and the two Military Cemeteries, you might spot piles of old tombstones – a telltale sign that the Catholic cemetery is undergoing rapid changes.

Italian tombstones from the former Campo N. 1 of the Catholic Cemetery

The cemetery covers an area of 110,000 m2, stretched on the slope of a hill from an altitude of 2537 m at the main gate to 2552 m at its highest point in the NE corner of the new Armenian cemetery (N 09° 03.488' E 039° 42.879'), probably making it one of the highest Catholic-Protestant-Armenian-Greek Orthodox cemeteries in the world. Documents referring to the cemetery are supposed to be kept in "Gulele Sub-City, Kebele 35"; as most of area of the cemetery is made up of various imperial donations, there are however no title deeds, which makes researching the cemetery's history rather difficult.

When entering the cemetery, one sees uphill the "Chiesa Santi Pietro e Paolo", in the centre of the "Peter and Paul Cemetery", a gift from Ragionere Pietro Tringali, an accountant living in Addis Ababa whose grave is located in this church, situated at an altitude of 2512 m (N 09° 03.385' E 038° 42.905').

The length from main gate to the upper wall of the new Armenian cemetery is 300 m, the width from the – usually locked – side-gate, which had been the original entrance (N 09° 03.295' E 038° 42.863') to the corner of the Commonwealth Cemetery (N 09° 03.449' E 038° 42.943') slightly less.

The oldest part of the cemetery is situated to the left, above the Greek Orthodox Cemetery. Here we find the grave of Dr. A. Chaiban, "medecin particulier de S.A. Imp. Ras Taffari" (* 13 IV 1883 + 17 IX 1918), a victim of the Spanish influenza pandemic of 1918, which also struck the future emperor. His tomb is probably the oldest surviving in the cemetery. The oldest *Ferenji* tombs in the not clearly marked area of the "international cemetery" could be that of German Oskar Reich (* 25 XI 1918) and of Karl Cederquist[18], a Swedish missionary who had arrived in 1904 and probably fell victim to Spanish influenza pandemic of 1918/19.

[18] See Gustav AREN, Evangelical Pioneers in Ethiopia, Stockholm 1978; G. AREN, Envoys of the Gospel in Ethiopia, Stockholm 1999.

Tomb of Karl Cederquist

The most recent tomb in the international cemetery is of Peta Philo (* 24 IV 1953 + 6 II 2009), in the Catholic cemetery the latest grave, that of Marco Morandi (* 1916 + 2009) is located in Campo XIX (old numbering) close to the main gate.

The cemetery consists of several independently owned and administered parts, some of them walled like the Greek Orthodox and the New Armenian cemetery, others not. Five are civilian and two are military cemeteries, the latter administered by the British and Italian embassies in Addis Ababa.[19]

[19]There are no tombs of German World War II soldiers in Gulele; there are however four graves of German soldiers from WW II in Agordat and Asmara (Eritrea); communication by Volksbund Deutsche Kriegsgräberfürsorge to the author, 25 II 2009.

3.1. CIVILIAN CEMETERIES

3.1.1 International Cemetery

Location: N 09° 03.299' E 038° 42.869'
Altitude: 2537 m
Administered by: Ethiopian Catholic Archbishop, represented by Abba Gebre Mariam Amente Abeya, Catholic Cathedral Church of the Holy Nativity (Santa Nativita della Beata Maria Virgine), Arada Kifle Ketema, Kebele 14, House 371 (office and residence; opposite Café Tomoka), Tel. 00251 11 112457

The International Cemetery goes back to 1912 and is at the same time the most romantic and dilapidated part of the cemetery; many headstones are missing, making it difficult to draw up an inventory. Visitors should be careful when walking around in this part.
Here we find tombs of Americans, Austrians, Belgians, Czechs, French, Germans, Russians, Swedes, Yougoslavs and many others. Most of those buried here seem to have been Protestants, as Catholics had their own Catholic cemetery after 1930; in addition, Russian Orthodox and several Jews found their last resting place here. The first person registered in the Greek-Orthodox register of burials concerns an Armenian buried on 15 X 1912 in the "International Cemetery".

Tomb of Czechoslovak Alois Heligr

Using the old entrance, we find to our right many graves of Ethiopian Catholics, among them Major-General Wolde-Tsadik Gebre-Meskal (1909 EC – 26 XII 1992 EC). This area with Ethiopian Catholic graves extends up to an abandoned Italian campo further on and to the wall of the Greek Orthodox cemetery. At the wall, next to a little unmarked mausoleum, we find the impressive art-deco grave of renowned French Africa explorer Alphonse Fondere, “membre du conseil supérieur des colonies” (* Marseille 26 VIII 1863 + Addis Ababa 26 XI 1930).

The impressive art-deco tomb of Henri Fondere

Before we reach the "Irish Cross" one can see the on the right side the probably oldest grave, that of Dr. A. Chaiban, "medecin particulier de S.A. Imp. Ras Taffari" (* 13 IV 1883 + 17 IX 1918), who died as "victime de son devoir"during the Spanish Influenza influenza pandemic of 1918, referred to in Amharic as "Hedar Beshita".[20] In his autobiography, Emperor Haile Selassie (in 1918 Ras Tafari Makonnen) states that he had been "seriously ill", but survived "by God's goodness"

[20] Richard PANKHURST, An Introduction to the medical history of Ethiopia, Addis Ababa 1990.

New Ethiopian Catholic tombs

To the left is the Old Armenian Cemetery, with some very impressive graves. The historic International Cemetery is located between the Old Armenian and the expanding Ethiopian Catholic Cemetery. It today covers an area of probably less than 2000 m2, and also contains some older graves of Ethiopian Catholics.

Coming from the other side, walking from the Catholic Cemetery towards the old entrance, we see at the right the pyramid tomb of the first Imperial Russian minister to Ethiopia, K.N. Lighine (* 19 II 1854 + 15 I 1906), who was originally buried in the Imperial Russian legation compound. The present monument located at N 09° 03.353' E 038° 42.887' was erected decades after the his death by his grandson who was living in Germany.

Tomb of the Imperial Russian minister to Ethiopia, K.N. Lighine, with wreath laid down by the ambassador of the Russian Federation (2008); in front of the pyramid the tomb of Austrian SS surgeon Dr. Karl Babor

There are 21 more graves of Russians in this sector, most of who apparently stayed on in Addis Ababa after the October Revolution of 1917. The Russian graves are in notably good order; due to the initiative of Russian ambassador Mikhail Y. Afanasiev they are annually cleaned and their inscriptions renewed by students of the Russian school on "Russian Foreign Service Day", celebrated on 10 February[21].

[21] On 10 II 1549 Tsar Ivan the Terrible has established a Russian Foreign Service.

Tomb of Russian Konstantin Michailovich Tichomirov

It is an irony of history, that the tomb directly adjacent at the foot of the pyramid is the last resting place of an Austrian SS-surgeon who was wanted by German and Austrian authorities for allegedly killing 900 Soviet POWs. The tomb used to be overgrown and barely legible; thanks to the initiative of the Russian ambassador however it has now been cleared and cleaned. SS - Hauptscharführer (Master Sergeant) Dr. Karl Babor (* Vienna 23 VIII 1918 + near Addis Ababa-Jimma road 16 I 1964?)[22] was buried here after having committed suicide[23]. He had served in 2nd SS-Division "Das Reich" in 1940 and 3rd SS-Division "Totenkopf" in 1943 and as physician of KZ Groß-Rosen in Silesia from 1941 to 1945. Having finished his medical studies after WW II he left Austria and was director of a hospital in Addis

[22] NSDAP Nr. 6242838, SS Nr. 296670; National Archive Washington File Nr. A 3343 SSO-023; served in 2nd SS-Division "Das Reich" 1940 and 3rd SS-Division "Totenkopf" 1943; Iron Cross 1st Class.

[23] Communication by H.E. Ato Girma Wolde-Giorgis, President of the Federal Democratic Republic of Ethiopia, to the author, 14 V 2008; the version that Babor was killed by Mossad agents can be discounted.

Ababa from 1952 to 1964. His grave is a grim reminder that Ethiopia after 1950 became a small scale haven for German and Austrian SS and Wehrmacht physicians, some of them wanted by German and Austrian justice authorities. Babor's wife Helga, née Babo (* Vienna 6 III 1921 + Addis Ababa 20 III 1960), who had died after a car accident in Debre Zeyt / Bishoftu hitting a donkey with her VW, is buried a few steps away.

The international cemetery is increasingly endangered by tombs of Ethiopian Catholics

Bertha Wöss-Weinzinger (* Vienna 1856 + Addis Ababa 1924), mother of Dr. Erich Weinzinger (* Vienna 31 VII 1888 + Vienna 17 VIII 1960), honorary consul of Austria in Addis Ababa from 1923 to 1927, and editor of "Correspondence d' Ethiopie", is buried at N 09° 03.314' W 038° 42.883'. Willi (Wilhelm) Holländer (* Czernovitz, Bukovina / Cernovci, Ukraine 3 XII 1896 + Addis Ababa 13 VI 1970) was a businessman, dealing in Volkswagens.

Several French citizens are buried here as well. On the Western wall, south of the old entrance, we find the tomb of Adolphe Gerbal (* 1884 + 1947), Administrateur de la Compagnie du Chemin de Fer Franco-Ethiopien, located at N 09° 03.288' E 038° 42.888'.

Numerous tombs remind us of the rather sizeable German community in Addis Ababa, the second oldest grave being that of Oskar Reich, who died in Addis Ababa on 29 XI 1918 "in the thirtieth year of a promising life". The three graves of the Hildebrandt family are located behind the pyramid tomb of the Russian minister. Kurt Hildebrandt (* Tempelhof / Berlin 21 VI 1900 + Addis Ababa 26 IX 1980), a chemist and pharmacist, settled in Addis Ababa and in 1954 established the Lion's Pharmacy in Eden Street.

Hildegard Hildebrandt née Berner (* Klütz, Mecklenburg-Vorpommern 12 IV 1906 + Addis Ababa 15 II 1979) was his wife. Next to them is the grave of their son Christian Hildebrandt (* Wandlitz / Berlin 3 XI 1931 + near Dessie 17 XI 1952), an engineer with the Ethiopian Highways Authority, who died in a car accident near Dessie together with Hans-Siegfried Bartsch (* 1 III 1916). Bartsch owned an Engineering Service on Patriots Street in the early 1950s.

The graves of the Hildebrandt family

There are more graves of Germans killed in car accidents. Ursula Borkhoff née Trautmann (* 4 IX 1932 + Addis Ababa 25 I 1961) died after a car accident near Modjo on the way to Lake Langano, Gerhard Schirrmacher (* 21 VI 1911) and his wife Hildegard (* 1 III 1915) died in a car accident on 7 January 1970, as did carpenter Ernst Zirpitz (Zirpins according to his tombstone), * Ridszen, East Prussia 22 IX 1908 + Nile Valley 11 I 1976.

Emil Loeb (* 3 I 1879 ? + 5 IV 1948) was a leather and hides merchant, who from 1928 to 1936 was the honorary consul of Turkey in Ethiopia. Otto Hertling (* Strasbourg, Alsace 9 III 1910 + Addis Ababa 5 X 1993) was a structural engineer, who had come to Addis Ababa in 1961. He, amongst other things, supervised the construction of the Addis Ababa City Hall (finished in 1965), the Hilton Hotel (opened 3 XI 1969) and designed the German Protestant Parish house (1966).

Dietrich Wassman (* 28 X 1897 + Addis Ababa 7 I 1954) was a missionary of the German Hermannsburg Mission in Aira, Western Wollega, Ethiopia from 1927 to 1935, 1938 to 1941 and 1951 to 1954. In 1935 he had sent his new-born daughter Helene Maria Line Fride (* Aira, Ethiopia 16 IX 1934) back to Germany because of the danger of war and bandits; she died in Khartoum, Sudan on 20 X 1935, where she was buried.

The latest German who found his final resting place in Gulele is Gunter Alfred Joachim Korp (* Sonneburg 12 IV 1920 + Addis Ababa 2 IX 2008), a former employee of the German Embassy Addis Ababa, who had settled in Ethiopia.

Comparing the register of burials of the German Protestant Church (Kreuzkirche Addis Ababa) with the situation on the ground, it becomes obvious that many graves of Germans once buried there no longer exist.

Since the 1960s, the remains of many Germans who have died in Ethiopia have been returned to Germany for burial. Dr. Martin Joseph Dietz (* Bonn 14 XII 1944 + Lufthansa flight Addis Ababa – Frankfurt 21 VI 2008) however presents a particular case. Having lived in Addis Ababa since 1984 and well known as the head of "Sunshine Higher Clinic" and the "German Doctor" in Ethiopia's capital, he died en route to Germany and found his final resting place not in Addis Ababa - Gulele as he had wished but in Königswinter on the Rhine.

Turning uphill, a rusty iron grille protects the gravestones of the Hall family.

The graves of the Hall family

Inscription on Katharina Hall's grave

The grave of Katharina Hall (* Gondär 30 I 1850 + Addis Ababa 15 VIII 1932) is located at N 09° 03.335 E 038° 42.863'. Her Ethiopian name was "Wälätta-Iyäsus". She was a daughter of Eduard Zander (* Gröbzig near Köthen, Anhalt-Dessau 22 X 1813 + Imkullo near Massaua, Eritrea 25 IX 1868) and Isätä-Wärq Mäqado[24]. Katharina Hall was married to Moritz Hall of Cracow, Austria in 1863, she is the great-grandmother of the late Sir Peter Ustinov and was lady in waiting to Empress Taytu.[25] Jakob G. Hall (* 9 XI 1865 + 3 VI 1919) was the son of Jacob and Katharina Hall. He was advisor to Emperor Menelik II, school director in Addis Ababa, and a diplomatic delegate of Emperor Menelik II. Paul Robert Hall (* 3 IX 1922 + 27 VIII 1974) was the son of David Hall[26], an Ethiopian national buried in the Holy Trinity Church cemetery (see chapter 4). Christine Hall (* 2 XII 1874 + 9 XI 1964) was a sister of David Hall, a teacher and lady in waiting to Empress Mänän II. The graves are in a dilapidated state and offer a rather depressing sight.

Another prominent person buried right next to Lighine's pyramid is Carl Gustav von Rosen (* 19 VIII 1909 +13 VII 1977), at N 09° 03.359' E 038° 42.887'. Rosen was a Swedish pioneer aviator – his sister Karin was married to German Marshal Hermann Göring. In 1935/36 he joined a relief mission in Ethiopia, flying food and supplies for the Red Cross, and after 1945 he was an instructor for the Imperial Ethiopian Air Force. During the Biafra war, he founded the Biafran Air Force, and in 1977, during the Ogaden war between Ethiopia and Somalia, Rosen was again flying relief for refugees. He was killed during a Somali attack on Gode.

Tomb of Carl Gustav von Rosen

Dan Anderson (* Stockholm 18 II 1936 + Ethiopia 30 VIII 1976) is another Swedish pilot buried here, who died when his plane crashed at take off in Awassa.

[24] Lady in waiting of Empress Mänän I (mother of Ras Ali) in 1849.
[25] Her daughter Christine Hall was lady in waiting to Empress Mänän II.
[26] See EAE, vol 2, entry Hall, David.

One of the oldest graves is that of Karl Cederquist (* 1854 + 1919), who since 1904 was with the Swedish Evangelical Mission in Addis Ababa. Professor Edgar Mannheimer (* 2 III 1904 + 9 IV 1965) had started a paediatric clinic in Addis Ababa; he died in a car accident in Uganda. Jan Egil Ofstad (* 13 X 1918 + 26 XI 1974) was a Norwegian missionary with the "Evangelic Church Mekhane Jesus".

Behind the "Russian pyramid" we find the tomb of an Ethiopian Catholic, Dr. Adanech Kidane-Maryam (* 19 XII 1943 + Addis Ababa 3 V 2006). She was assistant professor at Addis Ababa University from 1991 – 1994 and was the first woman to become a minister in Ethiopia (Minister of Health).

Three officers of the Royal Yugoslav Army, who had found their way to Ethiopia via Egypt in World War II, are buried in the international cemetery, like Pavlje F. Grujic (* Ujasku, Yu. 28 XI 1906 + Addis Ababa 6 VIII 1960), formerly a major in the Royal Yugoslav Guards.

Several Swiss are buried here. Edouard Evalet (* 2 XII 1874 + 21 X 1942) ran a saw-mill near Addis Alem[27]. His son André Evalet was married to Edith Annemarie Desta, née Haertel, the daughter of German architect Carl Haertel in Addis Ababa on 30 XI 1940.[28] Other members of the family buried here include Monique-Eve Evalet and Jeanne Evalet-Roth.

Three graves are of the Hess family. Friedrich Hess (* Amriswil / Zürich 26 VII 1884 + Addis Ababa 17 I 1967) came to Ethiopia via Egypt and Djibouti in 1902. He worked for a Swiss company exporting wood from Harar via Djibouti to Marseille, which would seem hardly possible today. In 1916 or 1918 he married Alice Spinner (* Zürich 11 VIII 1896 + Addis Ababa 23 IV 1985). When the company went bankrupt he settled in Jimma and began exporting coffee, accompanying caravans all the way from Jimma to Djibouti, while importing hunting-rifles from Belgium for Ethiopia's nobility. Their son Walter Hess (* Addis Ababa * 22 II 1933 + Addis Ababa 18 VIII 1957) was a mechanic with Seferian at Mexico Square, who represented VW, Magirus and Hanomag in Ethiopia.[29] Today the family is known to tourists because of "Hess Travel Ethiopia".

Only few citizens of the Benelux-States are buried in Gulele, among them Roger Schneider (* Luxembourg 29 IV 1917 + Addis Ababa 4 IV 2002), or Belgians Ernest Auguste Baijeot (* Belgique 13 II 1884 + Ethiopie 28 XI 1961) and the couple Hubert Leopold (* Gentbrugge 20 II 1901 + Addis Ababa 3 II 1946) and Josephine Comhaie Bleys (* Gent 11 V 1893 + 10 VIII 1956) who had run a farm in Wondo, as well as Dutchman Jan Willem den Hertog (+ 1 I 1962). However other Dutch , who most probably were working at the Wonji Sugar Estate, are buried in the Catholic Cemetery.

It is interesting to see that also some Greeks are buried in the international part of the cemetery, and not in the Greek-Orthodox cemetery.

The grave of Monsignore Theodore Monnens, (* 1881 + 1956), Special Envoy of the Holy See in Ethiopia 1948-1956 is to be found here next to the graves of Abuna Ser'atemaryam Yemeru, Arch-Bishop of the Ethiopian Catholic Church (4 IV 1904 + 9 X 1990) and the latter's successor Cardinal Paulos Tsadwa[30] (29 VIII 1921 + 8 XII 2004).

---

[27] See EAE, vol. 2, entry Evalet, Edouard.

[28] André EVALET, "De Ménélik à Mengistu. Un Suisse en Éthiopie, Geneva 1999

[29] Communication to the author by Mr. Hermann Hess, 16 II 2009.

[30] See EAE, vol. 4, entry Paulos Tsadua. Cardinal Tsadua's niece, Ethiopia Habte-Mariam, was married to Swiss architect Edouard Perret (Perret-Habtemariam).

Tomb of Theodore Monnens, S.J.

In this area there are graves of a number of mostly Italian missionary sisters and other missionaries from Europe, mostly Consolata Missionary Sisters, Camboni Missionaries, Franciscan Missionary Sisters of Christ and others. Among them are also Piet Overheyden (* 20 VIII 1929 + 10 III 1986) and father Denis Corkery (* 23 VI 1925 + 19 VII 1989) as well as numerous Ethiopian Catholic clergy.

A sign of decay

Dr. Zoltan Fabo, M.D. (* Hungary 30 VII 1904 + Ethiopia 18 I 1969) was a Hungarian doctor who lived in Russia Street as did his compatriot Otto Conrad (* 27 II 1904 + 30 XII 1960).

At least eight apparently Roman Catholic Indians are buried here, two of them originating from Goa and three from Kerala.

The gravestone of Wilfred Courtenay Barber (* New York 15 IX 1903 + Addis Ababa 6 X 1935), correspondent of "The Chicago Tribune", reporting on the beginning war between Italy and Ethiopia, reminds us of the dangers of journalism – and lack of medical care as well - in times of war. Barber, a son, grandson, great grandson and great-great grandson of war correspondents, had in September 1935 undertaken a 10 day trip to the Ogaden front, the only US journalist allowed to do so. After his return to Addis Ababa he fell ill and died of malaria. He was posthumously awarded the Pulitzer Prize in 1936 (N 09° 03.329' E 038° 42.885').

AUSTRIA

BABOR Helga née BABO * Vienna 6 III 1921 + AA 20 III 1960
wife of Dr. Karl Babor; died after car accident in Debre Zeyt hitting a donkey with her VW.

BABOR Dr. Karl * Vienna 23 VIII 1918 + nearAA-Jimmaroad1611964 ?
(directly next to the tomb pyramid of first Imperial Russian Minister to Ethiopia)
Cause of death uncertain; was found dead on the banks of the Omo River (VBev)SS-Hauptscharführer (Master Sergeant), served as physician of KZ Groß-Rosen in Silesia from 1941 to 1945. In the 1950s and early 1960s German and Austrian justice charged Dr. Babor with murder in at least 250 cases and war crimes, as he was believed to have administered lethal injections of hydrocyanic acid to Russian POWs and Jewish KZ inmates. After WW II, he served 4 years of medical internship in Gmunden, qualifying as medical practitioner. In January 1952 he went to Ethiopia, where he became head of a hospital in Addis Ababa. After the accidental death of his wife in Bishoftu, where she hit a disabled truck on the road with her VW, Babor became mentally unstable. Babor was last seen on 15 January 1964 in Addis Ababa and reported missing. He had driven to a crocodile pond roughly 173 kms South-West of Addis Ababa which he knew, where he shot himself with a gun. On 21 January, his body was found by American tourists in a river valley near the Addis Ababa-Jimma road, according to one version not ravaged by his beloved crocodiles, according to another ravaged by crocodiles. (Communication by H.E. Ato Girma Wolde-Giorgis, President of the F.D.R. of Ethiopia to the author, 14 May 2008). Another story has it that Babor was liquidated by agents of the Mossad once Simon Wiesenthal who had followed his trail had established his whereabouts.

DIALER Werner * Addis Ababa 27 III 1966 + Addis Ababa 5 IV 1966
son of Dr. med Lothar Dialer (Gmunden, Upper Austria 3 VII 1914 + Kufstein/Tyrol 17 I 1977, member NSDAP since 1938, SS-Obersturmführer /*
1 st Lieutenant, chief surgeon at the Imperial Body Guard Hospital, and director of the Police Hospital between 1954 and 1967)

HOLLÄNDER Willi (Wilhelm) * Czernovitz, Bukovina/ Cernovci, Ukraine 3 XII 1896 + Addis Ababa 13 VI 1970
businessman (Volkswagen)

WINARZ Herbert * 17 V 1917 + 6 VII 1942

WÖSS – WEINZINGER Bertha[31] * Vienna 1856 + AA 1924
N 09° 03.314' W 038° 42.883'

BELGIUM

BAIJEOT Ernest Auguste * Belgique 13 II 1884 + Ethiopie 28 XI 1961

BLEYS Hubert Leopold * Gentbrugge 20 II 1901 + Addis Ababa 3 II 1946
Planteur à Wondo

COMHAIE Josephine *Johanna Auguste*
veuve BLEYS * Gent 11 V 1893 + Addis Ababa 10 VIII 1956

DOOLAEGE-BUN Luc * 17 VIII 1964 + 18 VIII 1964

[31] See EAE, vol. 4, entry Weinzinger, Erich.

CANADA

BEAUDRY Paul *Jesuit*	* 25 VI 1916	+ 12 I 1970

CHINA

YING Wang Kiang Mrs.	* 22 VII 1933	+ 22 IX 1966

CZECHOSLOVAKIA

FRANZ Josef	* Böhmen 11 VIII 1890	+ 3 V 1941
HELIGR ? Mother of Alois	* 1898 ?	+ 5 XII 1942
HELIGR Alois	* 1916 ?	+ 5 VII 1941
HOUDEK Vita J.	* 27 IX 1920	+ Addis Ababa 20 XI 1965
KODYTEK Joseph F.	* 1 II 1908	+10 VIII 1967
MEZNIK Franta	* ?	+ 21 V 1937
SABADKA Jozef	* 18 II 1908	+ Addis Ababa 19 I 1961
SUCHY Karel	* ?	+ 28 IX 1920

DENMARK

LODAHL Inger Marie * Skjern, Denmark 8 X 1931 + Asella 10 VII 1962
nurse, working at Tafari Makonnen hospital in Asella, died of meningitis

NILSEN Gunnar Boysen * 14 I 1915 + 24 II 1983
Danish consul

FINLAND

MATTSSON Sanfrid *Pedersöre, Finl. 23 V 1895 + Addis Ababa 17 VII 1976
Missionary, came to Ethiopia in 1951 with his wife Anna-Liisa founded a mission of the Pentecostal Kaikille Luoduille ("To All Creatures") organisation in Addis Ababa; in 1955 established a missionary school and clinic on 80 hectares in Volmera 35 kms from Addis Ababa.[32] *It became the predecessor of the "Full Gospel Church". His wife founded the "International Women's Association."*

[32] See Päivi COLLANDER (editor), Four Decades – History of Finnish-Ethiopian Relations, Helsinki 2006, p. 21-22; the author thanks H.E. Kirsti Aarnio, Ambassador of Finland to Ethiopia, for a copy of this book.

FRANCE

AGIUS Marie Therese	* 4 X 1946	+ 10 I 1947
ANGOT Fernand	* 1886	+ 1974
BAOUMWALD Sophie	* 2 XII 1863	+ AA 29 III 1949
BLANC Alice	* 13 VI 1907	+ 14 I 1975
BRAS Zoete née BOURILLON	* 1882 ?	+ 23 XI 1918[33]
DETRY Henri	* 1 V 1893	+ 28 XI 1918
DETRY – SAVOWE Yvonne	* 7 I 1896	+ 27 IV 1941

Tomb of Adolphe Gerbal

GERBAL Adolphe Administrateur de la Compagnie du Chemin de Fer Franco-Ethiopien N 09° 03.288' E 038° 42.888'	* 1884	+ 1947
GOYON René Edouard	* ?	+ 16 VI 1930
JUBIN Jean	* Lorient 5 XII 1920	+ Addis Ababa 29 VIII 1993
LE BARON Jules Legion d'honneur	* 31 XII 1872	+ 30 XI 1938
LEVY Laurent	* ?	+ 19 VIII 1927

[33] Most probably victim of Spanish influenza.

LOURIE Michael Ethingoff	* ?	+ 14 IX 1955
MERAB Jeanne née Le Mere	* Lourdeac 1884	+ Addis Ababa 1927[34]
MOUSSA Louis	* 1938	+ July 1998
PALEOLOGUE Michel	* 1894	+ 1961
TARDY Marcel	* Ajaccio 1913	+ Addis Ababa 1983
WALARE Marie Therese Fontana	* 18 II 1903	+ 15 X 1954

GERMANY

BARTSCH Siegfried * 1 III 1916 + near Dessie 17 XI 1952
died in a car accident near Dessie (together with Christian Hildebrandt) (VBen)

BOOG née SOMMER **14 IX 1934* *+ Addis Ababa VIII 1956*
Marianne Clara Mathilde
Died after a car accident on the road to Shashemene; tomb no longer existing (VBev)

BORINSKI Hans * 18 VII 1901 + 13 VIII 1943

BORKHOFF Ursula * 4 IX 1932 + Addis Ababa 25 I 1961
née TRAUTMANN
died after a car accident near Modjo on the way to Lake Langano (VBev)

*BYRON Ottilie, wid. SMUNDEL * Dresden 1896? + Addis Ababa III 1938*
née PITSCH
tomb no longer existing (VBev)

*CONRAD Otto * 27 II 1904 + Addis Ababa XII 1960*
tomb no longer existing (VBev)

*DENNER Hans Dieter * AddisAbaba 18 VIII 1929? + Addis Ababa XII 1929*
tomb no longer existing (VBev)

DENNER Rolf * Addis Ababa 12 XII 1931 ? *+ Addis Ababa II 1932*
tomb no longer existing (VBev)

EHM Friedrich A. * 20 VII 1913 + 4 II 1985

*EHM Therese * Dillingen/Donau 1 II 1883 + Modjo 15 XII 1940*
attacked and stabbed by robbers and murderers in her farm, where she had lived alone fearlessly, on 15 XII 1940 at noon; tomb no longer existing (VBev)

*ENGELBREDSTEN Arnold von * 13 XI 1932 + Lake Langano I 1976*
died in a car accident near Lake Langano; buried in Germany (VBev)

FROESE Gundula * 8 XII 1929 + 7 IX 1968

*GEHRKE Paul * ? + Addis Ababa VI 1960*
Carpenter; tomb no longer existing (VBev)

---

[34] See EAE, vol. 3, entry Mérab, Paul.

GERKE Paul Karl August ** 14 IV 1933 ?* *+ Addis Ababa I 1934*
tomb no longer existing (VBev)

GEORGI Christian ** 13 IX 1943* *+ near Kobo V 1978*
Died in a car accident; buried in Germany (VBev)

GÖTZ Hermannn ("Opa Götz") ** Schwäbisch-Gmünd 21 VIII 1878*
+ Addis Ababa – Haile Selassie Hospital 2 IX 1970
Immigrated to Ethiopia in 1902; arrived in Addis Ababa in 1904 after staying in Harar. Having been donated land near Adaamii Tulluu by Emperor Menelik II, he established an ostrich farm. After World War I he switched to cattle breeding, which brought him into conflict with the local Oromos, later switching to the production of butter, which was shipped to Addis Ababa. From 1946 to 1955 Veterinary at the State Farm near bei Adaamii Tulluu; buried in an unmarked grave.[35]

GROTERJAHN Walter **Austria* *+ Addis Ababa 23 III 1930*
Coming from Arussi with a camel caravan, was attacked in his camp not far from Aqaqi at the outskirts of Addis Ababa in the night of 21 to 22 March, shot and robbed and the following night succumbed in Bethsaida – Hospital to the injuries suffered; tomb no longer existing (VBev)

HALL Christine ** Jaffa 2 XII 1874* + 9 XI 1964

HALL Jakob Gottlieb ** Däbrä Tabor 9 XI 1865* + 3 VI 1919
Son of Moritz and Katharina Hall; advisor to Emperor Menelik II, school director in Addis Ababa; diplomatic delegate of Emperor Menelik II

HALL Katharina * Gondar 30 I 1850 + Addis Ababa 15 VIII 1932
N 09° 03.335 E 038° 42.863'
Ethiopian name "Wälätta-Iyäsus"; daughter of Eduard Zander (Gröbzig near Köthen, Anhalt-Dessau 22 X 1813 + Imkullo near Massaua, Eritrea 25 IX 1868) and Woyzero Isätä-Wärq Mäqado, Lady in waiting of Itege Mänän I; married to Moritz Hall of Cracow, Austria in 1863; great-grandmother of Sir Peter Ustinov; according to VBev née HOWSEPIJAN after her Armenian adoptive parents.*

HALL Paul Robert ** Addis Ababa 3 IX 1922* + 27 VIII 1974
Son of David Hall; Ethiopian national

HEINI Ernst ** 24 XII 1899* *+ Addis Ababa V 1960*
tomb no longer existing (VBev)

HERTLING Otto K.F. * Straßburg, Alsace 9 III 1910 + Addis Ababa 5 X 1993
Structural engineer; supervised i.a. construction of City Hall (1965) and Hilton Hotel (opened 3 XI 1969) in Addis Ababa; built German Protestant Parish House (1966)

HILDEBRANDT Christian * Wandlitz/Berlin 3 XI 1931 + near Dessie 17 XI 1952
Engineer with the Ethiopian Highways Authority; died in a car accident near Dessie (together with Hans-Siegfried Bartsch) (VBev)

HILDEBRANDT Hildegard * Klütz, Mecklenburg-Vorpommern 12 IV 1906
née BERNER + Addis Ababa 15 II 1979

---

[35] See EAE, vol. 2, entry Götz, Hermann.

HILDEBRANDT Kurt * Tempelhof/Berlin 21 VI 1900 + Addis Ababa 26 IX 1980
Chemist and Pharmacist, owner of Lion's Pharmacy

HINTZ Dora née PIETSCH * 12 XII 1891 + 11 IV 1927

*JACOBS Ewald * 10 XII 1900 + Addis Ababa II 1984*
tomb no longer existing (VBev)

*KARNVANSKA Dora née MATZ * 6 III 1904 ? + Addis Ababa VIII 1929*
suicide; tomb no longer existing (VBev)

KIEFER Ursula geb. WITTE * 12 VII 1922 + 16 X 1953

KINSKY Erich * 30 VI 1880 + 17 VI 1940

KINSKY Vali Y. * 22 XII 1880 + 31 I 1956
Dentist, Dr. med Walter Kinsky, Duke of Harrar street

*KÖNIG Ruth Margarethe * Addis Ababa 29 IV 1928 + Addis Ababa 18 VIII 1928*
Katharina El.
tomb no longer existing (VBev)

KORP Gunter Alfred Joachim * Sonneburg, D 12 IV 1920 + Addis Ababa 2 IX 2008
employee of German Embassy Addis Ababa

*KROSSIGK Anton von * 18 XI 1960 + Lake Langano I 1976*
Died in a car accident near Lake Langano; buried in Germany (VBev)

*KROSSIGK Eberhard von * 4 VI 1962 + Lake Langano I 1976*
Died in a car accident near Lake Langano; buried in Germany (VBev)

*KUNZE *? + Addis Ababa VIII 1929*
suicide, tomb no longer existing (VBev)

LOEB Emil * 3 I 1879 ? + 5 IV 1948
Leader and hides merchant, Turkish honorary consul for Ethiopia 1928 -1936

LOEB Erna born TEWS, w. HINTZ * 18 XII 1987 + 21 V 1981

*LUTHER née WOHLGEMUTH * 4 VI 1929 + Addis Ababa VIII 1954*
Anneliese Erna
tomb no longer existing (VBev)

*MÜLLER Adolf * 26 XII 1906 ? + Addis Ababa V 1936*
tomb in Kella Belesda on Didessa (Wollega, Oromyia) en route from Bedella to Addis Ababa During the disturbances in Abyssinia shot on 11 May by Lij Abebe, leader of a group of bandits while sitting under a Warqa tree (wild fig) at the camp near Kella Belesda, murdered, while holding his youngest daughter in his arms (VBev)

NADIR Carl Alfred *stateless* * Kattowitz 10 III 1894 + Addis Ababa 3 IX 1971

*NIXDORF Otto * 23 VII 1909? + Addis Ababa IV 1933*
tomb no longer existing (VBev)

*PFEFFER Anna Luise Helma * Thuringia 1876 ? + Addis Ababa I 1937*
died of pneumonia in Filawoha-Hospital, tomb no longer existing (VBev)

PIEN Dr. Lina * 10 VIII 1965 + 28 VIII 1996

PIETSCH Alwine, née HAUMER * 13 XII 1869 + 6 III 1927

PLATZER Victor * ? + *Dessie ? 1958*
tomb no longer existing (VBev)
RANZI Karl * 28 III 19?? + 24 VIII 1929

The oldest tomb of a German buried in Gulele

REICH Oskar * 1889 ? + Addis Ababa 25 XI 1918
„Gestorben im Dreissigsten Jahre seines hoffnungsvollen Lebens“, victim of Spanish Influenza

*ROHDE Heinz * Gellihausen 2 XI 1912 + Debre Berhan 27 IV 1938*
buried in Debre Berhan; attacked by bandits and fatally hit on 27 IV 1938 leading a caravan with goods, in the service of Mr. Hess, on the road between Debre Berhan to Ankober (VBev)

SCHILLER Rudolf M. Baron de * 19 VII 1911 + 21 XI 1973

SCHIRRMACHER Gerhard * 21 VI 1911 + 7 I 1970
died in a car accident (VBev)

SCHIRRMACHER Hildegard died * 1 III 1915 + 7 I 1970
in a car accident (VBev)

*SCHUMACHER Alfred Jakob Friedrich * Jaffa 29 XI 1884 + Addis Ababa XII 1959*
tomb no longer existing (VBev)

SOLTECK Gabriele * ? + *Addis Ababa XI 1952*
died of malaria tropica; tomb no longer existing (VBev)

*UHLEMANN August Paul Heinrich * 28 II 1935 ? + Addis Ababa V 1935*
tomb no longer existing (VBev)

*UMBACH Stefan * 9 XI 1953 + Addis Ababa X 1975*
tomb no longer existing (VBev)

WASSMANN Dietrich *(Heinrich)*[36] * 28 X 1897 + Addis Ababa 7 I 1954
German Hermannsburg Mission (GHM) in Aira, Western Wollega, Ethiopia 1927-1935, 1938-1941, 1951-1954 (VBev)

*WASSMANN Helene Marie Line Frida * Aira, Ethiopia 16 IX 1934 + Khartoum 20 X 1935*
on the way back to Germany because of danger of war and bandits; buried in Khartoum (VBev)

*WEIDNER – BOHNENBERGER Bernhard * Munich 7 II 1900 + AA 24 III 1933*
On his honeymoon voyage came to Addis Ababa in 1933, where his brothers Hans Bernhard Walter Bohnenberger (in AA 1927-1935) and Bernhard Werner Bohnenberger (in AA 1931-1941) lived; fell ill with typhoid fever and died in Addis Ababa. Tomb no longer existing (VBev), buried in the family tomb in Stuttgart.

WITTE Elli geb. DIETSCH * 28 II 1891 + 12 IV 1964

WOLKAN Hans * 28 VIII 1904 + Addis Ababa 13 III 1930
(VBev)

ZIRPITZ (ZIRPINS) Ernst * Ridszen, East Pr. 22 IX 1908 + Nile Valley 11 I 1976
carpenter; died in a car accident (VBev)

*ZÜLOW Fritz von * 7 II 1890 ? + Addis Ababa III 1933*
tomb no longer existing (VBev)

GREAT BRITAIN

MAUNSELL Rev. Colin * 29 X 1933 + 8 IX 2005

SOLOMON Jacob Alexander * 24 II 1934 + 11 XI 1976

STREET Alfred Charles * 1887 + 1962
Chevalier de la Légion d'' honneur

YOUNG John Cameron * Glasgow + 2 II 1926

GREECE

ARVANTOPOULOS E.M.T. * 1906 + 1936

ARVANTOPOULOS Marica * 1927 + 1969

TRAGE Konstantinos * 27 XI 1899 + 1 I 1942

TRAGE Margherita * 1907 + 1956

HOLY SEE

MONNENS Theodore Mons., S.-J. * 1881 + 1956
Dean of the Faculty of Missiology at the Gregoriana University in Rome, Special Envoy of the Holy See in Ethiopia and Apostolic Vicar for Addis Ababa 18 VIII 1948 - 1956

---

[36] See EAE, vol. 3, entry Hermannsburger Mission.

HUNGARY

FABO Dr. Zoltan, M.D.	* Hungary 30 VII 1904	+ Ethiopia 18 I 1969
CONRAD Ing. Otto	* 27 II 1904	+ 30 XII 1960

INDIA

FERNANDES Raimondo	* Goa 15 II 1902	+ Addis Ababa 16 VII 1968
GONSALVES Edwin Martin	* 4 III 1912	+ 15 XI 1972
GOSH Dr. Rosh Behari	* India 1920	+ Ethiopia 17 I 1967
MATTHEW Simi G.	* Kerala 18 VI 1974	+ 3 VII 1985
MODI OUSTADJEE Khan Sahib Jehengir Jee *Photographer*	* Indore, India 22 III 1880	+ Addis Ababa 31 X 1959
RAO Paul	* 27 IV 1946	+ 4 I 1976
SEGUEIRA John A.	* Goa, India 1 XII 1896	+ Addis Ababa 6 IX 1921
THANCKACHAN Edicula	* Kerala, India 11 I 1934	+ AddisAbaba 27 May 1966
WARUGHESE Thomas	* Kerala, India 10XI1918	+ 22 III 1969

ITALY (civilians not buried in Campos I to XVIII)

ALLOATTI Margherita – Tille	* 1888	+ 1945 ?
BOVOLENTA Ing. Carlo	* 20 V 1901	+ ?
BRUSONI Andrea *Capo Ufficio della Banca d'Italia*	* 23 I 1995	+ 17 V 1995
CARBONARO Cav. Salvatore	* Ispica 27 VII 1912	+ Addis Ababa 20 1 2000
CARBONARO Regina Supelsa in	* Halai, Eritrea 23 VI 1923	+ Addis Ababa 8 XI 1981
DAMIANI Antonia	* Addis Ababa 11 VI 1948	+ Italy 4 III 1995
FOSCHIN de LEO Emma	* 21 X 1916	+ 26 XI 1943
FRANCO Nini	* 1 I 1940	+ 20 X 1941 child
MARTINAZZO Antonio	* Massawa 18 XII 1962	+ Addis Ababa 5 IV 1946
MORELLI Dottore Emanuele	* 24 III 1886	+ 22 VII 1936
SALVI Rosa	* 1918	+ 1959
VOLBERT Giorgio	* 1901	+ 1974

LUXEMBOURG

SCHNEIDER Roger	* Luxembourg 29 IV 1917	+ Addis Ababa 4 IV 2002

NETHERLANDS

HARTOG Jan Wieelm den		+ 1 I 1962
VERSLUYS Vanessa	* ?	+ 12 I 1971

NIGERIA

IYALLA Opuwele baby 1 year 4 months old		+ 11 IX 1965

NORWAY

AAGEDAL Karin	* 19 XI 1974	+ 10 XII 1974

daughter of Norwegian Lutheran missionaries

AASE Ragnar	* 26 VII 1915	+ 18 X 1981

Architect, lived in Ethiopia

NEERGARD Ingebjörg	* 16 II 1975	+ 18 II 1975

daughter of Norwegian missionaries Hans-Birger and Ase Neergard

OFSTAD Jan Egil	* 13 X 1918	+ 26 XI 1974

Director of radio "Voice of the Gospel" of The Evangelic Church Mekhane Jesus1970 - 1973; in September 1974 appointed head of information department of Mekhane Yesus Church; died of heart problems.

POLAND

SKOCZEK Dr. Kazimiercz

RUSSIA

CHROSTOV Ivan Sergejevitch	* February 1889	+ 27 III 1955
CHROSTOVA Natalia Vladimirnova	* 5 VII 1892	+ 25 I 1975
DOBROVOLSKAJA Tatjana Doliva	* 7 XI 1895	+ 8 VII 1956
KARTASCHEV Sergej Michailowitch	* 15 VII 1896	* 9 VII 1945
KHROSTOFF Jean S.		
KHROSTOFF Nathalie V. née Comtesse TATISTCHEFF		
KONOVALOVA Maria Dimitrievna	* 22 VI 1891	+ 25 III 1937
KOROSTOVETZ Nicolas	* Ekaterinoslav, Ru. 12 V 1897	+ 30 VII 1971

LIGHINE K.N. * 19 II 1854 + 15 I 1906
General, Imperial Russian Minister to Ethiopia; originally buried in the Imperial Russian Legation Compound, grave transferred in the 1950s to Gulele
N 09° 03.353' E 038° 42.887'

PETROW Dr. Georges	* Kislowodskaja 1900	+ Addis Ababa 1967
PROSKURIAKOFF Dr. Nicolas	* 5 V 1892	+ 12 IX 1959
SCHAULI Dr. med. Sava	* 1897	+ 1966
SITNIKOV Dr. Ing. Michael	* Russie 1899	+ Addis Ababa 1963
SKOURIDINE Colonel Alexis	* ?	+ 23 XII 1964
SPDOVA Alexandra Alexandrovna	* 15 IV 1885	+ 5 XII 1963
TATISTCHEFF Comte Pierre	* 5 I 1911	+ 21 VI 1956
TICHOMIROV Konstantin Michailov.	* 28 X 1898	+ 16 IV 1951
TURTSCHANINOFF Gergij Alexandr. *Engineer*	* 28 II 1889	+ 25 I 1977
VLASENKO Elena C.	* ?	+ 18 VI 1957
VORONOVSKY Ing. Boris	* 4 III 1901	+ 17 XII 1958
VORONOVSKY Pawel	* 19 IX 1867	+ 4 VII 1938

SPAIN

ALMEIDA Maria Helena Jorge de	* 11 X 1922	+ 27 III 1956
ARIS Ledesma Adelina	* 12 VIII 1967	+ 11 X 2003
CANTARELL de GÜELL Isabel	* Barcelona 14 V 1937	+ Addis Ababa 15 X 1966
SOARES Filomena	* 18 VII 1908	+ 30 XII 1980
SOARES Robert	* 25 IX 1907	+ 17 VII 1956

SWEDEN

ANDERSON Dan * Stockholm 18 II 1936 + *Awassa* 30 VIII 1976
Pilot, had planned to set up hot-air ballooning company for flights above Addis Ababa; killed when his plane's engine was hit by big bird and crashed at take-off in Awassa

CEDERQUIST Karl * 1854 + 11 XI 1919
Swedish missionary, arrived in Ethiopia in 1893 coming from Kenya as member of a "Galla mission"; first Swede to enter Ethiopia; since 1904 with Swedish Evangelical Mission in Addis Ababa

DAHL Carin + 1968
Daughter of Swedish Pentecostal missionaries in Awassa

DAHL Hans Gustav * Addis Ababa 2 IX 1956 + 2 IX 1956
Son of a Swedish Air Force pilot

JOHNSSON Hirut * 1986 + 24 II 1987
Ethiopian child, adopted by Swedish family; died before having been taken to Sweden

KARLENBORG Gunnar * 25 X 1918 + *Awash River* 6 X 1946
Air Force pilot, trainer of Ethiopian Air Force, drowned in Awash River while hunting a crocodile

LARSSON Vivan * *Örnskjöldsvik 1919* + 11 June 1946
Wife of an electrician; died on Swedish National Day

MANNHEIMER Edgar Prof. * Gothenburg 2 III 1904 + near Murchinson's Falls *Uganda* 9 IV 1965
Of a Jewish family from Denmark that immigrated in the middle of the 19th century to Sweden; internationally known children's heart specialist, arrived in Addis Ababa in November 1957 and started ther Ethio-Swedish Paediatric out-patient clinic in Princess Tsehay Memorial Hospital (today Armed Forces General Hospital); died in a car accident on the road from Kampala (where he hgad organized a paediatric cinference) to Murchinson's Falls in Uganda.

ROSEN Carl Gustav Erich Count von * *Rockelstad, Södermanland 19 VIII 1909*
+ *Gode, Ethiopia 13 VII 1977*
N 09° 03.359' E 038° 42.887' directly adjacent to pyramid tomb of Russian minister Lighine
Swedish pioneer aviator; in 1935 - 1936 joined a relief mission in Ethiopia, flying food and supplies for the Red Cross; then left for the Netherlands and joined KLM. In 1940 volunteered for service in Finnish Air Force during the Winter War; then left for London, flying KLM's route London-Lisbon during World War II. After 1945 instructor for the Imperial Ethiopian Air Force, later pilot of UN Secretary General Dag Hammarskjöld. During the Biafra war, he flew relief missions. In 1969, he imported 5 Saab MFI-9B planes, and in May attacked and destroyed numerous Nigerian fighter planes in surprise attacks. At the outset of the Ogaden war between Ethiopia and Somalia, Rosen was flying relief for refugees in the Ogaden who had fled flooding. On the first day of the war, on 13 July 1977, Somalia attacked the Imperial Palace in Gode. Rosen chose to stay in the palace, sought shelter near a pillar, when the ceiling collapsed killing him[37].

SANDLUND Gemechu * 2 IX 1991 + 17 V 1991
Adoptive Ethiopian child

STJÄRNE Anna-Greta * Skone 6 III 1926 + near Merib River 6 IX 1958
Teacher, first in Debre Zeyt, later at teachers training college in Adua; shot by bandits near Merib River Bridge

WALLSTROM Doris * 14 XII 1938 + *Awassa* 30 VIII 1976
Working for Swedish Pentecostal Mission hostel at Entotto; died in a plane accident together with Dan Anderson, when his plane's engine was hit by big bird and crashed at take-off in Awassa

SWITZERLAND

BÄCHINGER Albert * Hohenthannen, *TH* 21 VI 1908 + 5 I 1985
Technical engineer, Darmar Tannery Aqaqi

BÄCHINGER Fany * Addis A. 20 V 1941 + AA 10 VI 1957
Daughter of Albert Bächinger

[37] Communication by H.E. Ato Girma Wolde-Giorgis, President of the F.D.R. of Ethiopia to the author, 31 January 2009.

EVALET Edouard	* *La Heutte, Jura* 2 XII 1874	+ 21 X 1942
EVALET Monique-Eve	* 18 IV 1943	+ 17 VIII 1966
EVALET-ROTH Jeanne	* 21 VI 1887	+ 14 I 1973
FANKHAUSER Doris	* 3 VI 1909	+ 15 VIII 1969
FANKHAUSER Fritz		+ 5 I 1971
HESS *née SPINNER* Alice	* *Zürich 11 VIII 1896*	+ *Addis Ababa 23 IV 1985*

HESS Friedrich * *Amriswil/Zürich 26 VII 1884* + *Addis Ababa 17 I 1967*
came to Ethiopia via Egypt and Djibouti in 1902, worked for a Swiss company exporting wood from Harar via Djibouti to Marseille. In 1916 or 1918 he married Alice Spinner. When the company went bankrupt he settled in Jimma and began exporting coffee, accompanying caravans all the way from Jimma to Djibouti, while importing hunting-rifles from Belgium for Ethiopia's nobility.

HESS Walter * *Addis Ababa 22 II 1933* + *Addis Ababa 18 VIII 1957*
Mechanic with Seferian at Mexico Square, who represented VW, Magirus and Hanomag in Ethiopia

NÄGELI Née SUHNER Hedy Emma * *22 V 1929* + *Addis Ababa VI 1956*
tomb no longer existing (VBev)

PERRET HABTEMARIAM Edouard * 13 VIII 1919 + Addis Ababa 21 XII 1992
Architect of the Emperor Haile Selassie, arrived in Ethiopia in 1947, built Jubilee Palace, Clock Tower of Ethiopian Parliament, Mitchell Cotts Building, Moenco-Building.

PILLOND Robert * *Yverdon 1896?* + *Addis Ababa 27 XI 1936?*
Site engineer; died of pneumonia in Filawoha-Hospital after an illness of 4 to 5 days; had walked from Sudan to Addis Ababa; tomb no longer existing (VBev).

UNITED STATES

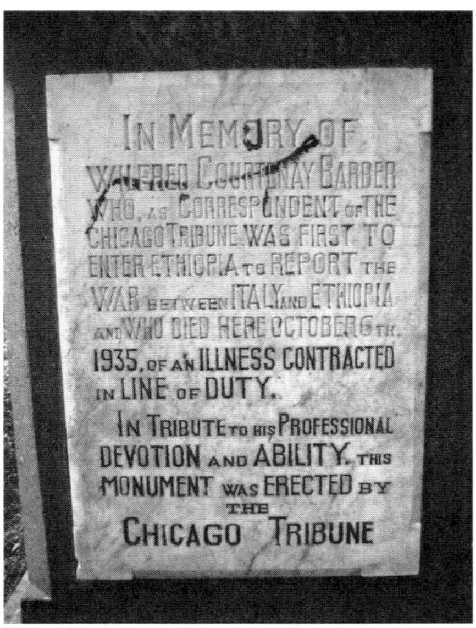

Tomb of Pulitzer-Prize Winner Wilfred Courtenay Barber

'BARBER Wilfred Courtenay * *New York* 15 IX 1903 + *Addis Ababa 6 X 1935*
Correspondent of The Chicago Tribune, reporting on the war between Italy and Ethiopia; died after his return from Ogaden front of Malaria; posthumously awarded Pulitzer Prize 1936

BRANDT Patricia Lynn ? * I 1947 + I 1951

CHERIAN George *Second Officer; died in car accident* * 8 I 1948 + 30 I 1972

CHERIAN George * 17 VI 1908 + 11 II 1972
Second Officer; died in car accident

ESHLEMAN Ellen Keener * 1924 + 1953

FERM Eroy Lucas * 12 III 1924 + 28 III 1957

HANSON Herbert Martin * Chokio, Minnes. 10 III 1884 + 27 X 1966
Missionary, Seventh Day Adventist Church, Akaki

HORST William S. * 1904 + 1966

OWEN Smiles A. * 6 IV 1932 + 12 II 1973

PETERSON Camille * 5 V 1919 + 6 VI 1959

POLLOCK Alexander Wilson * 1875 + 1935

WESTFALL Don Lloyd * Texas 4 X 1930 + Addis Ababa 25 X 1971

YOUGOSLAVIA

GRUJIC Pavlje F. * Ujasku, Yu. 28 XI 1906 + Addis Ababa 6 VIII 1960
Major in the Royal Yougoslav Garde

TANASIJEVIC Dr. jur. Sava D. * Cacak ? 1900 + 1966
Sreski Nacelnik

TRBOJEVIC Ing. Svetislav M. * 1907 + 1961

ZIVANCEVIC Budimir * 1900 + 1960
Katasterski Inspektor

RELIGIOUS ORDERS

Sister Brigitte * 20 I 1931 + 14 IV 2008
Sister of Jesus

Pater Mario BOTTA MdC + 1923

Sister Fede CAVALOTTI MdC * 1906 + 1932

Sister Theofana BERBENN MdC * 1906 + 1936

Sister Maria Elena BIFTU *Consolata Missionary Sister* * 1923 + 2004

Sister Maria Marta LATA * 1922 + 2009

Sister Agatangela Predieri LILIANA * 29 XI 1924 + 27 XII 2007

Sister M. Elda (Anna) BELLOLI	* Castel Rozzono 28 III 1918	+ Addis Ababa 15 VIII 2006
Fr. Denis CORKERY	* 23 VI 1925	+ 19 VII 1989
Piet OVERHEYDEN C.M.	* 20 VIII 1929	+ 10 III 1986

NATIONALITY UNCERTAIN

ABRAHA Michelina	* 20 I 1981	+ 3 VII 1985
ADAMS Alessandra Grace		+ 1 IX 2003
BOL Thokriel K.	* 17 IV 1881	+ 29 IV 1985
CHAIBAN Dr. A.	* 13 IV 1883	+ Addis Ababa 17 IX 1918
Medecin particulier de S.A. Imp. Ras Taffari, victim of Spanish influenza		
ETIANG (twins)		+ 27 III 1979
KOSHY George	* 15 IX 1945	+ 15 IX 1992
KIRBA V.S.	* 24 X 1941	+ 17 VI 1995
PHILO Peta	* 24 IV 1953	+ 6 II 2009
RASCHKE Harry	* 11 V 1954	+ 12 V 1954
TÜKROSSY Richard	* 25 VII 1917	+ 16 VIII 1955

3.2. GREEK ORTHODOX CEMETERY "ST. GEORGE"

Location: N 09° 03.276' E 038° 42.908'
Altitude: 2535 m
Administered by: Archimandrit Reverend Chrisostomos Barberis, Tel. 00 251 911-660381, Greek-Orthodox St. Frumentius Cathedral, P.O.Box 14069, Addis Ababa; depending from the Greek Orthodox Patriarchate of Alexandria and all Africa / Greek Orthodox Archbishopric of Aksum

Reverend Chrisostomos Barberis, since 1988 priest of the Greek-Orthodox St. Frumentius Cathedral, keeps the two death registers of the church, listing all Greek-Orthodox who died in Ethiopia, and to the extent possible in Eritrea and Djibouti since 15 October 1912 and who are buried in Addis Ababa-Gulele, Asmara, Dembi Dolo and Dire Dawa as well as possibly Djibouti. Death Register No. 1 covers the period from 1912 to 1941, listing 253 persons, whereas Death Register No. 2 covers the period from 1942 until present, registering 645 persons, which adds up to 898 Greek Orthodox having been buried in St. George cemetery. However, not all burials in the cemetery can be found in the death register, whereas there are roughly two dozen graves with headstones missing or no legible inscription.

As Greek data protection law prevents obtaining detailed information from death registers, it was only possible to obtain global data on the 893 deceased members of the Greek community in Ethiopia – which from 1940 to 1970 amounted to about 3500 and has since, as a result of the Derg-Regime, dwindled to around 150 in 2009, to which figure roughly 1000 mixeed race would have to be added.

Beginning in 1928, the death register shows the causes of death; and is particularly revealing. As in the death register of the German Protestant Church, causes of death included sickness, influenza, tuberculosis, pneumonia, (e.g. a 32 year man on 16 XI 1932), suicide, drowning in Aqaqi River; or criminal acts like an Armenian who was killed close to the German legation by a fellow Armenian, or another Armenian by name of Karazian who was killed by his servant with a stroke of an axe on his head.

The numbers of burials were as follows:

15 X 1912 – 1941: 253; 1942: 10; 1943: 15; 1944: 14; 1945: 13; 1946: 14; 1947: 12; 1948 – 1952:57; 1953 – 1954: 13; 1955: 13; 1956: 13; 1957: 20; 1958: 8; 1959: 15; 1960: 12; 1961: 17; 1962: 18; 1963: 8; 1964: 8; 1965: 11; 1966: 14; 1967: 14; 1968: 12; 1969: 12; 1970: 14; 1971: 18; 1972: 17; 1973: 17; 1974: 23; 1975: 17; 1976: 11; 1977: 11; 1978: 6; 1979: 10; 1980: 9; 1981: 7; 1982: 7; 1983: 6; 1984: 6; 1985: 3; 1986: 1; 1987: 4; 1988: 3; 1989: 3; 1990: 4; 1991: 4; 1992: 13; 1993: 5; 1994: 1; 1995: 6; 1996: 3; 1997: 4; 1998: 4; 1999: 8; 2000: 4; 2001: 5; 2002: 5; 2003: 10; 2004: 1; 2005: 5; 2006: 11; 2007: 8; 2008: 6, until 1 VIII 2009: 3 (total: 898)

The Greek Orthodox cemetery is situated to the left of the main gate in the lowest part of the cemetery area; it is walled in. According to tradition the land had been donated to the Greek community by Emperor Menelik II in 1912. The oldest tomb, in the second row rougly 20 m from the entrance, is the tomb of Andromache Papavasiliadou, born in Aithinioti in 1822, who died in Addis Ababa in 1916.

Within the cemetery there is the chapel of St. George, which gave the name to the cemetery: It serves as the mausoleum of Velissarios I. Velissariou and is property of the Velissariou family. The other building was donated by Dr. Zervos[38], the private doctor of Emperor Haile Selassie, whose funeral was attended by the Emperor.

St. George Chapel, Mausoleum of Velissarios I. Velissariou (1893 – 1954)

The first person registered in the Greek-Orthodox death register and buried on 15 X 1912 was actually an Armenian, who was laid to rest in the "International Cemetery", probably one of the first foreigners to be buried there. The Death Register of the Greek-Orthodox St. Frumentius Church includes Armenians, as until 1923 Armenians were attended to by the Greek Orthodox priest; surprisingly, Armenians are also registered after 1923.

Most of the graves are still intact, although there seems to have been vandalism in the time of Emperor Haile Selassie, as many photos and their bronze frames are missing.

The cemetery has two vacant plots of land as a reserve, which would probably last for another ten years, given the present number of annual burials.

[38] * Kephalonia 1883 + Addis Ababa 10 VI 1956

List of existing graves (as of 1 August 2009) by alphabetical order; the place of death, if not otherwise indicated, is Addis Ababa

Nicolaos * Nazareth 1891 + 1967

Greek-Orthodox Archbishop of Aksum (Ethiopia, Eritrea, Djibouti, Somalia) 1942-1967

AGAPITOS Emmanuel	* 1880	+ 1975
ALEXANDRIDIS George	* 1900	+ 1967
ALKATORAS Gebriel	* 10 IX 1975	+ 10 IV 1977
ALMPIRIS Emilius		+ VII 1919
ANASTASIADIOU Stella A.	*1902	+ 1957
ANASTASIADIS Anastatos F.	* 1896	+ 1971
ANASTASIADI Fiellosa	* 1923	+ 1930
ANASTASIADIS Grigorios K.	* 1896	+ 6 I 1966
ANNITSA E. Lapad	* 20 VII 1935	+ 23 I 1937
ANTIPAS Kostas	* 27 II 1921	+ 9 IV 2006
ANTONIOU Michael	* *Karpathos*	+ 5 VIII 1957
ANTONOPOULOS Chr.		+ aged 68
ANTIPA Aliki	* 13 X 1930	+ 2 II 2000
APNIAS Konstantinos D.M.	* 1900	+ 1987
ARAKERIMIOTES Nicola A.	* 1 VIII 1916	+ 16 VI 1978
ARAPOGLOU Dimitrios A.	* 1881 (75)	+ 12 VII 1956
ARAPOGLOU Dimitrios A.	* 1896 (39)	+ 17 VII 1935
ARBANITOPOULOS Demetrios L.	* 1887	+ 1933
ASGIRIADOU Georgia Th.		+ 8 VI 2005
ASIMAKOPOULOU Maria	* 1956	+ ?
ASLANIADIOU Evthimia V.	* 15 VI 1892	+ 17 XI 1957
ASLANIDES Antonios	* Karpassos 23 XII 1900	+ 5 VIII 1939
ASLANIDIS Antonios	* 5 VIII 1890	+ 19 IX 1957
ASLANIDIS Nicolos Antonios	* 7 XI 1934	+ 26 IX 1998
ASLANIDIS Odissias Antoniou	* 7 VII 1932	+ 11 V 2003
ASLANIDIS Vasilios A. *agent of a Swiss company*	* Karpathos 5 I 1889	+ 9 II 1966
ASLANIDOU Theodora	* 31 I 2006	+ 23 VI 2006 *died of TBC*

AUTIS Loukas		+ aged 62
AVANTAZIATHOS Elefterios	* 1908 ?	+ 16 IX 1959
AVKOUDI Evagelia E.		+ 22 VII 1969
AVKOUDI Evagelos		+ 20 V 1974
AVKOUDIS Charalambos	* 1912	+ 1982
BAIRAMIS Petros		
BAIRAMIS		
BAROUTSOS Georgios P	* 1868	+ 6 X 1938
BASILIOU Androniki	* 1899	+ 11 XII 1968
BASILIOU Themistokles	* 1888	+ 11 XII 1945
BEGEOT-KISKAS Maria-Tereza	* 1930	+ 22 VII 2002
BELIHOU-KATSAROUAster	* 10 V 1928	+ 18 II 2005
BELISSARIOU Belissarios	* 1893	+ 1954
BELONIAS Epiridion John	* 12 XII 1920	+ 4 VII 1957
BINIARI Zoi	* Korinth 1884	+ 1949
BISOU Eleni	* 1898	+ 31 V 1971
BOSNAKIS Christos		+ 25 X 1923
BOUGADIOTI		
BOUGADIOTI Maria K	* 1867 (75)	+ 22 IV 1942
BROFA Kalliopi	* 1911	+ 2006
BROFA Haralambos G.	* 1902	+ 1959
CHARMANIS Alekos P.	* 11 XI 1947	+ 28 XI 1995
CHARMANIS Jossif	* 1986	+ 2006
CHARMANIS Michael	* 1912	+ 29 VI 2006
CHARMANIS Panagiotis A.		
CHRISANTHOU Eutihia Markella H.	* 1925	+ 1955
CHRISANTHOU Michael	* 1908	+ 1967
CHRISTODOULARIS Konstantinos		+ child
CHRISTODOULOU Michael Anesti	* 8 VI 1919	+ 29 I 1974
DABACOS Menandros J	* Khartoum 26 X 1911	+ 2 XI 1982
DALENTZA Anna E.	* 1919	+ 16 IX 1973

DALENTZAS Emmanuel Th.	* 1942	+ 1999
DALENTZAS Evangelos M.	* 1909	+ 16 IX 1973
DALENTZAS Markos	* 1890	+ 8 II 1968
DALENTZAS Trasimboulos Z.	* 1902	+ 1967
DAMBIASIDOU Afroditi		
DAMIANEA Athina	* 1889	+ 1951
DAMIANEA Irini	* 1909	+ 14 II 1962
DAMIANEAS Kostas	* 1906	+ 1968
DAMIANEAS Suzan	* 2 XI 1989	+ 6 XI 1992 child
DELAPORTAS Spiridion	* 10 V 1928	+ 6 III 2006
DERAKJIAN Tsehai-Sisay	* 22. III 1971	+ 19 IX 2006
DERIDES Emmanuel D.	* 1883	+ 1941
DEROZERIS Polivios	* Constantinople 2 IV 1904	+ Asmara 2 VIII 1957
DIACOMANOLIS Stavros	* Karpathos 1874	+ 1947
DIAMANDAS Stavros	* Kastellorizo 25 XI 1871	+ 15 II 1959
DILAVERIS Alexandros	* 25 III 1916	+ 17 X 2006
DIVANAKAS Markos	* 24 I 1953	+ 24 I 1953
DOMNAKIS Stefanos	* 17 I 1890	+ 30 I 1956
DRITSONAS Ioannis		
DRITSONAS Panagotis		
DRITSONAS Sophia		
DRITSONAS Spiros		
ECONOMIDES Georgios	* 1 XII 1980	+ 14 VII 1942
EFSTRATOS Karagtorgt	* 1888	+ 1976
EFTIMIADOU Eleni	* 1937	+ 21 I 1969
ELEFTHERION Michael	* 1881	+ 1944
ELEFTERIOU Michael	* 1881	+ 1944
EVDAIMON Antonios	* 1876	+ 1953
FASULIS Grigorios	* 18 IX 1932	+ 7 VII 2004
FILI Dimitra	* 1885 (63)	+ 26 IV 1948
FILIPPOU Alexandra		+ 1923 child

FILIS Constantinos S.	* 2 V 1915	+ 30 XI 1974
FILIS Apostolos N.	* 1885	+ 1966
FILIS Basileos N.	* 1888v+ 1979	
FILIS Kosmas G.	+ 4 VIII 1946	+ 20 IX 1946
FILLI Evagelia B.	* 1893	+ 1980
FOKION Maria	* 24 III 1945	+ 1 XI 1968
FOVOS Yoannis G.	* 1886	+ 1965
FRANTZESKAKI Maria	* 10 XII 1922	+ 25 IX 2004
FRANTZESKAKI Alexandra	* 1924	+ 10 IV 1948
FRANTZESKAKIS Georgios P.		
FRANTZESKAKIS Panayotis G.	* 15 V 1864	+ 28 VIII 1954
GALANOS Elipas		+ 3 II 1998
GANOTAKI Fotini Anastasiadi	1924	+ 20 I 2000
GANOTAKIS Achileas	* 1930	+ 1995

Tomb of Alexander Ganotakis

GANOTAKIS Alexandros	* 1911	+ 1977

Businessman, importer of "Omega"-watches, President of the Greek Community

GANOTAKIS Dimitrios G.	* 1920	1980
GANOTAKIS George	* 26 XII 1900	+ 7 VIII 1922
GANOTAKIS Stamatios		
GEORGA Evgenia S.	* Aegina	+ 26 VI 1948
GEORGALIS Yoannis *coffee merchant*	* 20 VII 1940	+ 22 I 2008
GEORGIEV Askale Mariam Mersa	* 9 IX 1907	+ 6 III 1990
GEORGIEV Georgia S.	* 11 I 1926	+ 3 XII 1943
GEORGIEV Georgios S.	* 9 XI 1927	+ 17 IX 1993
GEORGIEV Joanna	* 22 II 1930	+ 21 IV 2008
GEORGIEV Maria	* 29 IX 1929	+ 3 V 1993
GEORGIEV Stefanos G	* 10 X 1878	+ 28 X 1950
GEORGIOS A.	* 26 XII 1900	+ 7 VIII 1922
GEORGIOS Joannas	* 1948	+ 2006
GERASIMIDIS Christos Th.	* 5 XI 1902	+ 25 II 1956
GERMENI Triantafillia G.	* 1874 (75)	+ 23 XII 1949
GERMENI Eleni	* 4 XI 1961	+ 19 X 1969
GERMENI Dionisios Eleni	* 1905	+ 1917
GEROLIMATOU Angelika	* 1902	+ 1959
GIANNOPOULO Sofia G.	* 1929	+ 1936
GIANNOPOULOS Georgios H.	* 1896	+ 1976
GIANOUPAKAS Georgios N	* 1931	+ 1962
GIORGIOU Dimitrios N.		+ 11 XII 1964
GLIPTIS Constantinos	* 1922	+ 2003
GLYPTI Grigori	* 12 I 1929	+ 20 VII 2002
GOPSIS Andreas Zacharias	* 1897	+ 1982
GOUMER John	* 1916	+ III 1967
GOUZOUASIS Elena	* 1909	+ 23 III 1971
GOUZOUVASIS Dimitrios	* 1888	+ 1974
HARAKOPOULOS Constantinos	* 11 IV 1910	+ 1948
HARAKOPOULOS Kostantinos	* 11 IV 1910	+ 1948
HARMANIS Markos Michael	* 1951	+ 13 VII 1991
HARMANIS Michael	* 1912	+ 29 VI 2006

HATZANDREAS Georgis V.	* 1888	+ 17 I 1956
HATZIANDREOU Foto S.	* 5 I 1926	+ 22 IX 1938
HATZIANDREOU Athena G.	* 1890 (63)	+ 9 VIII 1953
HATZIANDREOU Maria Al.	* 1936	+ 1963
HATZINIKITA Emanuel	* 1889	+ 1958
HATZOGLOU Maria	* 26 II 1909	+ 27 II 2001
HATZOGLOU Theodoros	* 1896	+ 1956
HOULES Antonio	* 1912	+ 1948
HRISANTHOS Iraklio Nikolaon	* 7 IX 1923	+ 6 I 2001
HRISTOU Michael	* 1907 (58)	+ 25 V 1965
HRISTOU Emmanuel P.	* 1935 (45)	+ 22 IV 1970
HRYSANTHAKIS Michael	* 1897	+ 1967
HRYSANTHOU Despina	* 1897	+ 1987
ILIENAKI Vassiliou		
IOANNOU Maria B.	* 1874 (78)	+ 21 VI 1952
IOANNOU Vasilios	* 1877	+ 29 III 1942
IOANNOU Zacharias B.	* 20 VI 1905	+ 26 IX 1946
JOANNAS Elleousa		
JUBIN Christine	* 29 IX 1916	+ 22 X 1972
KABADIA Anna G.		+ 1920
KALAFATA Fotini Costa	* 1892	+ 1974
KALAVRIAS Gerasimos L.	* 10 VIII 1910	+ 29 I 1961
KALLAKOS Nicolaos	* 1900	+ 1973
KALLOU Xenia		+ 27 X 1972
KALLINIKOS Evangelos *Major, Greek Army*	* 1917	+ 1960
KALOGEROPOULOS Panajiotis D.	* 25 XII 1900	+ 3 I 1965
KANELLI Ligeri	* Sparta 1900	+ 22 IX 1971
KANELLIS Lykourgos	* Sparta 1897	+ 14 III 1972

KANELLIS Michael	* 1934	+ 1998
KAPAYIANOPOULOS Constantinos	* 1904	+ 1973
KAPAYIANOPOULOS Ioannis	* 10 VI 1957	+ 1 VIII 1996
KARAGEORGIOV Joannis	* 25 III 1925	+ 12 IV 2008
KARAJANNAS Argiria K.	* 1941	+ 1947
KARAKASA Zafiris	*1944	+ 1999
KARAMBA Kaldis	* 1905	+ 10 IV 1986
KARATHANASIS Basileios	* 1897	+ 1955
KARAYANNIS Kostantinos	* 1877 (68)	+ 25 IV 1945
KARAYIDAS Dimitrios	* 30 XI 1885	+ 3 X 1968
KARDASSIS Emmanuel J.	* 1890	+ 1930
KARDOVILI Foteni	* 1876	+ 1960
KARDOVILIS Christos	* 1860	+ 1944
KATSARGIRIS Athanasios	* 1904	+ 1971
KATSAROS Emmanuel	* 1905	+ 1975
KATSAROU Aster Belihou	* 10 V 1928	+ 18 II 2005
KATSIKOANNIS Constantinos G.	* 1884 (78)	+ 14 I 1962
KATSIYVA Achille	* 1904	+ 1 IX 1978
KATSOURIS N.		+ 9 VI 1960
KAVADIA Anna	* 1901 (19)	+ V 1920
KAVADIA Dimitri G.	* 18 III 1942	+13 VIII 1996
KAVADIAS Andreas E. *journalist*	* 1873	+ 1964
KAVADIAS Andreas E.	* 1887	+ 1960
KAVADIAS Georgios G.	* 1944	+ 28 V 1959
KAVADIAS Odisseus A.	* 28 XI 1928	+ 21 IV 1943
KAVADIAS Gerasimos S.	* 15 VI 1881	+ 7 XI 1972
KAVADIAS Katerina	* 15 VIII 1934	+ 3 VI 1995
KAVATAS George	* 21 VIII 1925	+ 22 IX 1986
KAZAKOS Nicolas	* 1900	+ 19 VII 1978
KHOUFALIS Salomon Alemu	* 1930	+ 1981

KIOPRES Athanasios	* 1901 (42)	+ 5 X 1943
KIOUSIS Ioannis		+ I VIII 1979
KIOUSSI Pagona N.	* 1882	+ 1955
KIOUSSIS Nicolas G.	* Macedonia 1876	+ 1951
KIOUSSIS Kostas Nikolaos		
KIPRIOTIS Ioannis		+ 20 XI 1932
KIPRIOTIS Mary	* 8 XI 1914	+ 25 IX 1979
KIRIAS Emmanuel	* 1904	+ 1977
KISKAS Chrisostomos	* 9 VI 1925	+ 17 II 1968
KISKAS Georgios		+ aged 52
KLAVDIANOS Thomas	* 9 VII 1956	+ 12 XI 1959
KOKINATOU Athena P.	* 1860 (77)	+ 26 X 1937
KOLLAROS Dionisios	* 3 III 1905	+ 5 VI 1951
KOLLAROS Nikolaos Dimitrios	* 1949	+ 6 IX 1962
KOLLAROS Stefanos	* 1845	+ 1919
KONITAKITS Georgios K.	* 1928	+ 19 IX 1964
KONSTANTINOU Anton H.	* 1885	+ 1960
KONTOPOULO Marianthy	* 1890	+ 1957
KORDOBILLI Fotini	* 1876	+ 1960
KORDOBILLIS Christos	* 1860	+ 1944
KOSTADIMA Alexandra		+ 32 years old
KOSTI Nicolaos M.	* Karpathos 1889 (43)	+ 21 XI 1932
KOTSIFI Hrisanthi George	* 1909	+ 2003
KOTSIFIS Athanasios G.	* 1930	+ 1981
KOTSIFIS Elena Georgiou	* VI 1921	+ 22 XI 1987
KOTSIFIS Emmanuel G.	* 1931	+ 2000
KOTSIFIS Theodoros E.	* 30 XI 1971	+ 8 XI 1997
KOTSIFIS Violeta G.	* 1902	+ 1956
KOUFALIS Ioannis	* 1918 (76)	+ 23 IV 1994
KOUKOUTSIS Joannis G.	* 1951	+ 1995
Panayotas G.	* 1871	+ 1951

KOUMA A.	* 1927	+ 11 IX 1999
KOUMARIANOS Aristodemos L.		+ 7 XI 1955
KOUMBIS Panagioti	* 1877 (43)	+ 1920
KOUROS Nicolaos	* 1945	+ 2005
KOUROS Nikolaos	* 13 I 1976	+ 12 VIII 1980
KOUROU Nikolaos	* 8 IX 1909	+ 31 VII 1939
KOUTSOUBESIS Andreas	* 1880 (70)	+ 1950
KOUSOUMBESSI Evdokia	* 1880 (100)	+ 15 VI 1980
KREMASTIOTI Andonia B.	* 1883	+ 1960
KREMASTIOTI Andoria K.	* 23 VII 1950	+ 20 I 1959
KREMASTIOTHAS Kostas B.	* 1907	+ 8 IV 1971
KYRIAZIS Evangelos		+ 5 II 1959
LAMBRINIDIS Emilios	* 31 III 1888	+ IX 1947
LAMBRINIDIS Kostandinos	* 1889 (76)	+ 28 VII 1965
LAMBRINIDIS Michael	* 1922	+ 2001
LAMBRINDOU Maria	* 19 VI 1918	+ 11 IX 1983
LEGIEH Agielech		+19 IV 2002
LENTAKI Evangelia	* 1899 (39)	+ 10 III 1938
LEVAKIS Elias	* 1888 (49)	+ 25 XII 1937
LIGOPOS Ekgor H.	* 17 XI 1917	+ 2 XII 1972
LINARDATOS Dionysios	* 1889	+ 1958
LITIS Joannis Louca	* 1919	+ 1 II 1976
LITIS Lukas		+ aged 62
LIVERATOS Charalambos	* Kephallinia 22 XII 1876	+ 2 XI 1944
LIVERATOS Spiros P.	* 1895	+ 14 V 1947
MAGDALINOU Gabriella H.	* 7 VII 1971	+ 26 IV 1974
MAGDALINOU Olga N.	* 21 VI 1936	+ 10 VI 1966
MAKARATZI Alexandra G.	* 1892	+ 1971
MAKAS M.D. Eva		+14.01.1934

MAKRAS Michael	* 10 XII 1906	+ 15 X 1938
MAKRI Loulas Antonio	* Asia Minor	+ 39 years
MAKRIDIS Kostantinos	* 15 XII 1914	+ 9 VIII 1974
MAKRIDIS Michael	* 1928	+ 1975
MAKRIS Constantin N.	* Patras	+ 7 III 1959
MALAGARDO Marigo V.	* Karpathos 5 VIII 1887	+ 5 VIII 1969
MALIARAS Georgios	* 30 V 1914	+ 28 IV 1965
MALLIARA Eugenia H.	* X 1920	+ 26 XII 1947
MALLIARAS Christos	* 1880	+ 1934
MALLIARA Alexandra	* 2 II 1922	+ 15 IV 1997
MALLIARAS Evangelos	* 1880	+ 1953
MALLIARAS George	* 30 V 1914	+ 28 IV 1965
MALLIARAS Vaios Stephanos	* 1930	+ 1995
MALTAS Ekaterini	* 1905	+ 1972
MALTAS Michael	* 1931	+ 1992
MAMALINGA Afroditi	* 22 VII 1933	+ 28 VIII 1977
MAMALINGAS Antonios	* 1922 (79)	+ 24 III 1992
MANOLAKIS Pavlos	* 1871 (68)	+ 17 X 1939
MANOLES Georgios	* 1892	+ 1935
MANOLIS Dimitrios	* 1891	+ 1969
MANOUKAKI Eleni	* Thrakia 1887	+ 1961
MANOUKAKIS Dimitrios K.	*Constantinople 1899	+ 20 XI 1962
MANOUSOS Antonios M.	* 25 V 1953	+ 1 III 1956
MARIAKI Fofo Georg	* 17 XII 1931	+ 9 IX 1949
MARTIRAMONNA Saberio	* 1907	+ 1997
MASTROGIANNIS Hristos	* 1890 (69)	+ 6 II 1959
MATKOVITS Argyro	* 28 II 1882	+ 29 VII 1957
MAVRANTONI Evdokia	* 1889 (85)	+30 VIII 1974
MAVRIKIOS Charalambos	* 1890	+ 1949
MAVRIKIOS Ekaterini	* 1893	+ 1963
MAVROGIANNIS Nikolaos B.	* 1897	+ 1982

MBIZOU Eleni	* 1898	+ 31 V 1971
MELENIOS Odisseas	* 1945	+ 2003
MESTOUSSIS Constantinos	* 1904	+ 1959
METAKOS Lefteris *Pilot, Greek Air Force*	* 1912	+ 1977
METAXAS Georgios	* Chios 1883	+ 1967
MICHAEL Anastias George	* 8 XI 1927	+ 27 X 2004
MICHAELIDIS Maria	* 30 III 1991	+ 30 VI 2001
MICHALAKOU Poulou	* 15 V 1934	+ 28 I 1938
MICHANAMAKRIS Constantinos	* 1921	+ 1997
MIRIALLI Sophia	* 1908 (47)	+ 1947
MISSAILIDIS Aregash Tarekegn		+ 4 IX 1998
MISSAILIDIS Dimitrios	* 1896	+ 9 IX 1974
MISSAILIDIS Tito	* 21 II 1951	+ 10 X 1994
MISAILIDOU Eleni	* 27 I 1939	+ 21 IV 1984
MITSOPOULOS Joannis	* Debre Tabor 15 XI 1932	+ 29 XII 2006
MITSOPOULOU Maria	* Asmara 20 VI 1939	+ 23 V 1999
MITSOU Demetrios Georgiou	* 17 X 1917	+11 VIII 1957
MOLDOVANOS Petros	* 3 X 1950	+ 22 X 1952
MOLDOVANOU Elvira	* 6 VII 1944	+ 2 VIII 1948
MORAITIS Nikolaos	* 1856 (65)	+ 1921
NAKAS Nicolaos Th	* 1909	+ 1981
NAVRIKO G. Iztos	* 1881	+ 1949
NAZIROGLOU Dimitrios	* 1876 (64)	+ 14 VI 1940
NAZIROGLOU Smaragda	* 1882 (55)	+ 26 XII 1937
NAZIROGLOU Stefanos D.	* 23 I 1924	+ 15 XI 1962
NEGOULESCU OLT Dimitrios Ing	* 1909	+ 1975
NICOLAIDES Nicolas	* 3 I 1929	+ 10 XII 1963
NICOLAIDIS Nicola	* 31 I 1929	+ 10 XII 1963
NICOLAOU Athanasios K.	* Levidin 1908	+ 1960

NIKITAS Odysseus		+ 26 VIII 1936
NIKOLAOS Vitleem	* 13 I 1976	+12 VIII 1980
NITTIS Kyriako s		+ 1971
NOUMAIR Georges S.	* 1879 (67)	+ 12 X 1946
NOUMAIR Yvonne	* 16 VII 1966	+ 13 XI 1969
ODOMBIASIDOU Afroditi		
OIKONOMOU Panyiotis	* 1905	+ 1984
ORIOTIS Evtihia	* 1926	+ 2007
ORKOU Angelos	* 1891	+ 1971
ORTENJOGLOU Sofia	* 1908	+ 25 X 1973
PAGONI Ralu	* 1909	+ 1932
PAGOULATOS Georgios	* 1910	+ 14 I 1970
PAHOULIS Maria Paulos	* 13 IX 1981	+ 19 VI 2003
PALLOUIANIDOU Fanoula	* 1957	+ 1973
PANAGIOTIS Tsadikou		
PANAGIOTATOS Dionisis	* 29 I 1930	+ 12 XI 1983
PANAGIOTATOU Anastasias Spr.	* 1927 (35)	+ 6 III 1962
PANAGYIOTATOU Margarita	* 1853 (87)	+ 4 III 1940
PANGALO Demothenes	* 6 VI 1910	+ 22 III 1974
PANNAS Vassilios	* 22 IX 1918	+ 20 II 1978
PANOGIANIDOU Fanoula	* 1957	+ 1973
PAPACONSTANTINOU Eleni	* 10 IV 1922	+ 9 III 1988
PAPACONSTANTINOU Sambicos	* Lindos 18 XII 1912	+ 14 II 1972
PAPADAKIS Stefanos	* 1906 (69)	+ 15 VI 1975
PAPADATOS Athanios	* 1874 (98)	+ 7 X 1972
PAPADILOU Antonios	* 12 VII 1899	+ 8 I 1937
PAPADOPOULOS A.	* 1 V 1935	+ 12 VII 1946
PAPADOPOULOS Evangelos *teacher*	* Chalki 30 V 1893	+ 11 VII 1961

PAPAEMANUEL Dimitrios	* 1873 (65)	+ 28 X 1938
PAPAGEORGIOU Basilios		+ 20 IX 1943
PAPAGEORGIOU Dimitrios A.		
PAPAGEORGIOU Kiriaki A.	* 1850 (96)	+ 14 IX 1946
PAPAGEORGIOU Sophia D.	* 1900	+ 25 V 1957
PAPAGEORGIOU Stavroula	* 1905	+ 1970
PAPAGEORGIOU Venetia G.	* 1894 (48)	+ 26 XI 1942
PAPAHARALAMBOS Christos	* 1883	+ 1962
PAPAHARALAMBOS Taitou	* 15 X 1896	+ 21 I 1950
PAPAKONSTANTINOU Eleni	* 10 IV 1922	+ 9 III 1988
PAPAPOULOU Antonios	* 1 VII 1889	+ 8 I 1937
PAPASINOU Paul	* 12 IV 1941	+ 5 V 1942
PAPATZIMA Stamatia N.	* 12 I 1892	+ 13 I 1970
PAPATZIMAS Haralambos	* 1874	+ 19 XI 1960
PAPATZIMAS Nikolaos J.	* 15 X 1882	+ 2 VIII 1948
PAPAVASILIADES Costas	* 17 XI 1872	+ 20 VIII 1948
PAPAVASILIADOU Andromache	* Aitninioti 2 III 1822	+ 18 I 1916
PAPAVASILIADOU Irini	* 1888 (50)	+ 12 V 1932
PAPPATAKI Oletamanea	* 1897	+ 1952
PAPPATAKIS Sergios	* 1872	+ 1948
PARRI Euterpi K.	* Mekelle 27 XI 1930	+ 12 II 1998
PARRI Karillo		
PARRI Panayioti		
PARRIS Aristidis	* 8 VIII 1925	+ 24 X 1982
PAULEMIKOS Antonios	* VII 1932	+ 28 X 1991
PERDIKIS Stephanos *Advocate, Mexico Square*	* 1897	+ 1968
PETRATOS Gabriel	* Kefallinia 1896	+ 1970
PETRATOS Georgios N.	* 1931	+ 1962
PETRATOS Joannas N.	* 25. V 1919	* 26 III 1985
PETRATOS Nikolaos S.	* 1880 (68)	+ 1948

PETRATOS Spiridion Stratoy	* 1898	+ 1974
PETRATOS Stavros N.	* 23 VII 1923	+ 4 VII 1952
PETRATOU Alemitou Hounde	* 1921 (72)	+ 18 V 1993
PETRATOU Chrysianthi	* Sparta 1897	+ 26 IV 1972
PETRATOU Ekaterini	* 28 VIII 1895	+ 28 VIII 1955
PETRIDIS Pierre	* 29 VI 1907	+ 23 IV 1993
PIRPIRI Klio	* 1910	+ 3 IX 1938
PIRPIRIS Nikolas	* 16 X 1936	+ 12 XI 1937 child
PIRSOS Alkibiades G.	* Pirsojanni 1879	+ 19 II 1942
PISSACA Yoannou	* 8 X 1900	+ 28 IX 1958
PIZANI Maria	* 1 V 1944	+ 9 II 2005
PLAKIOTI Ekaterini	* 1883 (75)	+ 14 IV 1958
PLIODIS Theodoros	* 1909	+ 1984
POEDOROU Christina	* 25 XII 1940	+ 28 IV 1941
POLEMIKOS Michael	* 1891	+ 8 X 1946
PORTOKALAS Michael	* 18 IV 1974	+ 7 XII 1999
PRANTI Chrisanthi P.	* 20 III 1925	+ 13 II 1950
PRESVIANSKAYA Anna	* 1924 (75)	+ 1999
PTROMIAS Spiros		
PURPURI Klio	* 1910	+ 3 IX 1938
PURPURIS Nicolaos P.	* 16 X 1936	+ 12 XI 1937
PYRPYRIS Panayotis P.	* 15 III 1897	+ 3 XII 1970
PYTHARAS Agamemnon	* 22 IX 1915	+30 VIII 1975
PYTHARAS Hector	* 17 II 1917	+ 2 XII 1972
RAPTI Eufrosini H.	* 17 VIII 1887	+ 7 VIII 1957
RAPTIS Haralambos J.	* 25 XII 1875	+ 8 VIII 1952
ROUSOU Maria Nicolaou	* 1940	+ 1940 child 6 mo.
ROUSOU Maria Nicolaou		+ 1933 child 9 mo.
ROUSSOS Evangelos	* *Santorini 1880*	+ *Mojo* 17 III 1960
Mechanic and train-driver, Compagnie du Chemin de Fer Franco-Ethiopien		
ROUSSOS Ioanna Nik.	* 24 IV 1914	+ 10 VII 2000

ROUSSOS Nikolaos Haralambos	* *Cyprus* 10 III 1892	+ 3 IX 1970
ROUSSOU Maria E.	* 20 VI 1883	+ 27 III 1927
SAKELARIDOU Elefteria	* 2 XII 1917	+ 9 V 1975
SANGES Anthi	* Gore 18 X 1923	+ 27 II 1979
SANTAS Eustathios D.	* 1894	+ 1963
SARAGAS Stylianos S.	* Rhodos 1883	+ 24 VI 1955
SASSI Anna	* 1912 (42)	+ 20 X 1954
SAVOUNIERIS Georgiou	* 1941	+ 2004
SEITOU DEGIF Michael Yohannes Mulugeta	* 19 XI 1935	+ 9 III 2001
SGOLOPH Ourania Alexandra	* 1944	+ 1945
SHEWANESH Simatos	* 1891	+ 18 X 1959
SIDERIDIS Emanuel	* 1883	+ 1941
SIDERIDOU Eleni G.	* 3 X 1942	+ 4 IX 1950
SIMONOS Charalambos I.	* 1933	+ 1934
SIMONOS Charalambos S.	* 1956	+ 1969
SINODINOS Dimitrios P.	* Stemnitza 1886 (72)	+ 2 I 1958
SINODINOS Inda Ch.	* 1866	+ 1927
SKALEZI Georgia Georgiev	* 10 I 1926	+ 3 XII 1943
SKALEZIS Georgios	* 1943	+ 2001
SKEVOFILAKAS Konstantinos		+ aged 87
SKOUFOS Filippa	* 1873	+ 1961
SKOUFOS Sambika	* 29 I 1919	+ 26 VII 2006
SKOURIALIS Panayotis J.	* 1897	+ 1965
SKUFOS Philipa	* 1873	+ 1961
SOMBORAC Svetozar In.	* 1 VIII 1909	+ 3 V 1985
SOMBORAC Svetozar	* 1 VIII 1909	+ 3 V 1985
SOUNIOS Anastasios	* 1875 (65)	+ 17 VI 1940
SOULIOTOU Maria	* 1897	+ 1960
SOUNIOTES Yoannis	* 1889	+ 1961
SPANOS Christos T.	* 1914 (34)	+ 12 V 1948
SPERLING Nicolaos	* 1880	+ 1947
SPETSERIS Kostas		

STATIRAS Constantinos	* 1 IX 1900	+ 12 XI 1962
STAVROU Christos G.	* 18 VIII 1975	+ 8 V 2003
STAVROU Christos	* 24 XII 1914	+ 21 IX 1962
STAYRIANOS Anastasia S.		+ 25 V 1958
SYNODINOU Xh. S.	* 1866	+ 1927
TATOS Epich.	* 20 III 1924	+ 29 III 2002
TEFERI Froumentios	* 23 VII 1947	+ 21 IV 1984
THEODOROU Christina	* 25 XII 1940	+ 28 IV 1941 child
THEOFILATOS Nikolaos	* 15 VI 1901	+ 26 VIII 1970
THOMAS Kiriakoula G.	* 1913	+ 25 XII 1950
THOMAS Theodora		+ 2003
THOMAIDOU Paraskevi	* 1900	+ 28 XII 1971
TILIAKOS Georgios	* 1886	+ 1960
TOLIOS Johannis S.	* 1905	+ 1970
TRITAKIS Konstantinos	* Sokion 1893	+ 9 IX 1944
TRITOS Antonios		+ 17 III 1975
TROKALLIS P.P.	* 1891	+ 1953
TROMPETTA Flora	* 1923 (42)	+ 13 XI 1965
TROMPETTA Gerasimos	* 1900 (75)	+ 26 III 1975
TSALIKIS Antonios	* 1892 (47)	+ 1939
TSATSARONIS Nikolaos	* 30 I 1894	+ 8 IX 1957
TSILIDIS Anastasios	* 1922	+ 1987
TZANATOS Dimitrios	* 1909	+ 1991
TZOGIA Eleni B.	* 1890	+ 1967
VAJIA Joanna K.	* 1898	+ 1969
VAJIAS Kostantinos	* 1898	+ 1972
VALENDI Agapite Kouma	* 1927	+ 11 IX 1999
VALENTIS Dimitrios P.	* 26 VIII 1893	+ 19 I 1976
VALENTIS Dionisios Pol.	* Kephalonia 1891	+ 30 IX 1920
VALENTIS Evangelos Pol.	* Kephalonia 10 V 1903	+ 18 XI 1970
VALIANATOS Apollon	* 1936	+ 1988

VAPORIDIS Stavros	*1909	+ 20 XII 1972
VAPORIDOU Anastasia	* 1877	+ 1950
VARBATIS Emmanuel H.	* 1913 (29)	+ 15 III 1942
VASSALOU Ekaterini	* 1913	+ 1996
VAYIANAKI Maria	* 21 V 1925	+ 17 I 1956
VERVERIS Panayotis M.	* 1888	+ 1967
VIOLETTIS Irene	* Mekelle I IX 1922	+ 9 III 2007
VLAHOPOULOS Michael		+ 27 XII 1927
VLAHOS Georgis	*1881	+ 1953
WOLDE-GIORGIS Atseda-Mariam	* Tagoulet 1916	+ 1968
ZAFIRIDES Georgios J.	* Epirus 1905 (38)	+ 3 XI 1943
ZAFIRIOU Elias		+ aged 73
ZAMBOS Athanasios N.	* 25 IX 1929	+ 9 V 2003
ZANNOS Apostolos	* Santorini 1890	+ 30 V 1961
ZEKOS George	* 1857	+ 1917
ZERBOS Solon M.	* 1894 (38)	+ 21 X 1932
ZEREMETIS Apostolos		+ 1956
ZEROZERIS Polyvios	* Constantinople 3 IV 1904	+ Asmara 2 VIII 1957
ZERVOS Christoforos	* 1893 (50)	+ 2 X 1943
ZERVOS Jacob G.	* 1883	+ 1956
ZGOLOMPIS Georgios P.	* 1881	+ 1946
ZISSOS Sotiris	* 6 VIII 1917	+ 12 XI 1992
ZOGRAFIDIS Dimitrios Th.	* Athens 1888	+ 7 III 1948
ZOGRAFOU Euterpi	* 24 X 1939	+ 15 V 1940
ZORBA Efrosini	* 1874	+ 1961
ZORBAS Michael	* 1900	+ 1966
ZOUVELOS Anastasia	* 25 I 1900	+ 7 IV 1955
ZOUVELOS Athanasios	* 1896	+ 30 IX 1967

? Maria	* 1881	+ 1945

In St. George Chapel:

VELISSARIOU Velissarios I.	* Volos 1893	+ 1954

Velissariou Ethiopia Ltd. Building Materials, Sanitary Equipment, Paint; Agents for Mister Lock (USA), Milners Safe (UK), E.&F.Richardson (UK), Simon Redtenbacher (Austria), Garvenswerke (Austria) Office and Shop: Cunningham Street
import – export

In Mausoleum:

ZERVOS Dr. Jacob	* Cephalonia 1893	+ AA 10 VI 1956

3.3. OLD ARMENIAN CEMETERY

Location: N 09° 03.299' E 038° 42.869'
Altitude: 2537 m
Administered by Vartkes Nalbandian, Archdiacon of the Armenian Community in Ethiopia (Bale PLC, Bale House, P.O. Box 1862, Addis Ababa, Tel. 00 251 1 15 53 94, Fax. 00 251 1 15 53 65, Mail: bale.plc@ethionet.et).

The oldest part of the cemetery is the old Armenian cemetery, donated in 1903/04 Ethiopian Calendar by Hagop Bagdasarian (* Van 1873 + Addis Ababa 1952), goldsmith and director of the Imperial Mint established by Emperor Menelik II in the Gebbi in 1903, to the Armenian community. He owned extensive property in the area. Until then, the Armenian community – it was the only one allowed to do so – buried its dead in the cemetery of St. George Church on Menelik II Square. The Armenian community was as old as the town of Addis Ababa itself, and came from the towns in the Armenian-inhabited area in Turkey: Arapkir, Aintab (today Ghaziantep) and Bekesni near Aintab as well as Constantinople (Istanbul) and Smyrna (Izmir), Sebastia (Sivas), Caesarea (Kayersi), Van, Erzerum, but also other provinces of the Ottoman Empire as Cyprus, Alexandria/Egypt or Syria.

The old Armenian cemetery located to the left when entering through the old gate of 1912, is located uphill to the left and covers an area of roughly 1800 m2; additional tombs are found intertwined with Ethiopian Catholic and graves of Euopeans in the adjacent area of the International Cemetery. The Old Armenian Cemetery offers a rather romantic, but nevertheless depressing sight. Weed and grass allow cows to graze there, so visitors should be prepared for the unexpected.

View of the Old Armenian Cemetery

The oldest tomb numbered 1 is of Edward Seferian, who had come to Addis Ababa in 1890 with his brother Krikor[39] from Istanbul as partners of Muradian trading company. In 1929 the Seferians set up their own company.

Until 1923 the Greek Orthodox priest officiated at burials. Many tombs bear the year of death 1917 or 1918, indicating that many Armenians is Addis Ababa became victims to an influenza epidemic. The total number of graves according to the Armenian Community of Ethiopia Old Cemetery List is 308.

An impressive tomb in the Old Armenian Cemetery

[39] Krikor Seferian died in Italy, where they also had business, around 1950.

No.	Grave	Name	
1	191	ABADJIAN Dikran	*confectioner, died of bronchitis*
2	160	ABUSEFIAN Puzant	*photographer, died of pneumonia*
3	184	ADANALIAN Hovhannes	*carpet repairer*
4	40	ADANALIAN Eghisapet	*housewife*
		ADANALIAN Armenak	*1917–1926, child, died of diphteria*
5	182	ADANALIAN Yeranig	*housewife*
6	183	ADANALIAN Yervant	*student, suicide*
		ADANALIAN Haroutioun	*trader*
		ADANALIAN Hagop	*employee, died of heart attack*
		ADANALIAN Hagop	*retired*
7	164	AFARIAN Marie	infant
		AFARIAN Tzaghaganoush	*infant, died of pneumonia*
8	76	AGHLAGHANIAN Jeffrey/Yervant	** 10 IX 1952 + 1 I 1953, businessman, died of typhoid*
9	41	AHAKINIAN Bedros	*tailor, died of heart failure*
		AIVADIAN Diran	*child, died at birth*
		ARABIAN Hilda	*infant, died of pneumonia*
10	118	AKTERIAN Fotina	*housewife*
11	220	anoymous	
12	246	anoymous	
13	243	anonymous	
14	201	anonymous	
15	6	anonymous	
16	251	anonymous	
17	107	anonymous	
18	19	anonymous	
19	256	anonymous	
20	159	anonymous	
21	259	anonymous	
22	44	anonymous	
23	214	anonymous	

24	74	ANTRNIKIAN Haroutioun	*watchmaker*
25	149	ARSHAVIR Dr. Terzian	*owner of medical loboratory*
26	270	ASLANIAN Dilbar	*housewife, *Sebastia(Sivas) 1895,+ AA 1953*
		ASLANIAN Garbis	*driver, died in car accident*
27	11	ASSADOURIAN Hovhannes	*soap-manufacturer*
28	23	ASSADOURIAN Payloun	*Housewife*
29	10	ASSADOURIAN Takouhi	*Housewife*
		ATSEDE Wossenyelesh	*Housewife*
30	255	AVAKIAN Dudu	*Housewife*
		AVAKIAN Haroutioun	*Businessman*
31	230	AVAKIAN Lia	*Housewife*
32	254	AVAKIAN Setig	*Carpenter*
33	196	AVEDISSIAN Mihran	*Carpenter*
		AVEDISSIAN Santoukht	*Housewife*
34	264	AZNAVORIAN Vahan	*Goldsmith*
35	247	AZNAVORIAN Mamas	*retailer, died of pneumonia*
36	249	AZNAVORIAN Mardiros	*Businessman*
37	264	AZNAVORIAN Mardiros	*businessman, died of tuberculosis*
38	264	AZNAVORIAN Markarid	*Housewife*
		AZNAVOURIAN Masis	*1897 – 1960 trader*
		AZNAVORIAN Sarkis	*cafe owner*
39	263	AZNAVORIAN Vartouhi	*Housewife*
40	174	BABADJANIAN Boghos	*Watchmaker*
41	150	BABADJANIAN Markar	
42	151	BABADJANIAN Panos	*Goldsmith*
43	207	BAGHDASSARIAN Hrant	*owner of printing press, goldsmith*
44	111	BAGHDASSARIAN Hripsime	*housewife*
		BAGHDASSARIAN Isgouhi	** 1875 + 1960 housewife*
		BAGHDASSARIAN Hagop	*goldsmith*
		BAGHDASSARIAN Ardashes	*businessman, died of pneumonia*
		BAGHDASSARIAN Armenak	*proprietor*
45	158	BALOUNTZIAN Armig	*housewife*

46	27	BARSIGIAN Maritza	*1896 – 1973 dressmaker, died of pneumonia*
47	27	BARSIGIUAN Toros	*1883 – 1918 carpenter*
48	27	BARSIGIUAN Vartouhi	*1912-1929, student, died of typhoid*
49	83	BASSMADJIAN Dikranouhi	*housewife*
50	38	BEHESNILIAN Antranig	*5 VI 1911 – 6 VIII 1957 businessman*
51	32	BEHESNILIAN Alice	*housewife*
52	13	BEHESNILIAN Haig	*businessman*
53	36	BEHESNILIAN Kathleen	1891 – 1943 *housewife*
		BEHESNILIAN Haratioun	*pensioner*
		BEHESNILIAN Ardashes	*child*
		BEHESNILIAN Arax	*infant*
		BEHESNILIAN Sprouhi	*housewife, died at childbirth*
		BEHESNILIAN Yeghia	*trader*
		BEHESNILIAN Siranoush	*businessman*
		BEJEAU Valentine	*secretary, died in car accident*
		BEKIARIAN Makrouhi	*housewife*
		BILEMDJIAN Feride	*housewife*
54	211	BILEMDJIAN Nerses	1904 – 1959 Gojjam, *shoemaker*
55	257	BOGHOSSIAN Charlotte Daka	1880 – 1948 *housewife*
56	257	BOGHOSSIAN[40] Krikorios	1861 – 1940 *businessman*
57	224	BOGHOSSIAN Mihrtad	*trader*
58	114	BOYADJIAN Azniv	** Tikranakert (Diyarbekir) 18 II 1883 + Addis Ababa 3 IV 1948, housewife*
59	114	BOYADJIAN[41] Bedros	** Tikranakert (Diyarbekir) 18 V 1868*

+ Addis Ababa 14 V 1928came to Addis Ababa in 1905, working as a court photographer for Emperor Menelik and later Empress Zawditu and Ras Tafari Makonnen

60	139	BOYADJIAN Dikranouhi (Dicky)	** 1916 – 1977*
61	114	BOYADJIAN Haigaz	** Alexandria 24 IV 1901 + AA 5 VI 1941*

arrived in Ethiopia at the age of 5 Court photographer in 1929; opened a cinema in Piazza, near today's restaurant 'Castelli', destroyed in May 1936.

---

[40] See EAE, vol. 2, entry Boghossian, Eskender.

[41] Les Boyadjian – Photographes arméniens à la cour du Négus, exposition presentée à l'Hôtel de Sully, 19 June to 2 September 2007; the author thanks Mr. Vartkes Nalbandian for a copy of this publication.

		BOYADJIAN Haigaz	
		BOYADJIAN Hripsime	
62	114	BOYADJIAN Koharig	* *Addis Ababa 10 II 1909 + AA 20 II 1936*
63	141	BOYADJIAN Loussentak	*1910 – 1984*
64	140	BOYADJIAN Torkom (Tony)	* 1920 - 1987, *court Photographer in 1941*
65	63	BROUSALIAN Mihran	1892 – 1951, *pharmacist*
66	27	BROUSSALIAN Noemi	1910 – 1942, *housewife*
67	61	BROUSSALIAN Parounag	1897 – 1955, *pharmacist*
		BROUSSALIAN Sirpouhi	housewife
68	62	BROUSSALIAN Varoujan	*pharmacist, * 18 X 1926 + 27 IX 1982*
69	170	BUDUSHIAN Dikran	*merchant*
		BZDIGIAN Dikran	*farmer*
70	268	CHAGHATSBANIAN Hripsime	*housewife*
71	218	CHAGHATSBANIAN Mardiros	*carpenter retailer*
		CHAGATSBANIAN Baydzar	*housewife*
72	9	CHILINGIRIAN Mariam	*housewife*
73	9	CHILINGIRIAN Hagop	*brick manufacturer*
74	283	CHILINGIRIAN Vahan	*gunsmith*
75	9	CHILINGIRIAN Vartanoush	*housewife*
76	203	DARAKDJIAN Serpouhi	*housewife*
77	204	DARAKDJIAN Hagop	*truck driver*
78	144	DARAKDJIAN Krikor	*tanner & shoe manufacturer*
79	205	DARAKDJIAN Serpouhi	*child*
80	195	DARAKDJIAN Koharig	
		DARAKDJIAN Kohar	*housewife*
		DEMIRDJIAN Sarkis	*teacher*
81	39	DEOVLETIAN Dr H.	
82	52	DERDERIAN Barnabas	*accountant, church servant*
83	21	DERDERIAN Haiganoush	*housewife*
84	53	DERDERIAN Nartouhi	*housewife*
85	277	DERENTZ Alice	*housewife*
86	7	DERGHAZARIAN Anitsa	
		DERGHAZARIAN Mardiros	

		DERGHAZARIAN Sarkis	*shoemaker*
87	102	DERHOVHANESSIANArdemis	*housewife*
		DER PARTOGH Kevork	*teacher*
88	206	DERSTEPANIAN Mardiros	
89	229	DERSTEPANIAN Marie	
		DERVAHANIAN Pilibbos	*accountant, died of typhus*
		DEUKMEDJIAN Elise	*housewife*
		DEVEDJIAN Prapion	*housewife*
90	120	DJERRAHIAN Armenouhi	*housewife*
91	265	DJERRAHIAN Bob	* 20 V 1959 + 5 VII 1961
92	33	DJERRAHIAN Haroutioun	* 25 III 1875 + 12 II 1945 *confectioner*
93	17	DJERRAHIAN Ovsanna	*housewife*
94	171	DJIDEDJIAN Prlantouhi	*housewife*
95	18	DJIYERDJIAN Mamas	
96	4	DONIKIAN Garabed	
97	123	DONIKIAN Roupen	*tailor*
98	24	DONIKIAN Veronica	*housewife*
		DONIKIAN Haygouhi	*housewife*
99	80	DOWELL Amy Marie	* 7 II 1964 + 11 III 1964
		DOWELL Marie née KHATCHADOURIAN	* 18 I 1937 + Egypt 3 VII 1965
100	210	EBEYAN Boghos	1859 – 1933 *merchant*
101	95	EBEYAN Dikran	*goldsmith*
		EBEYAN Serpouhi	*housewife*
102	243	EKNEYAN Jirayr	*businessman*
103	29	ERZINGATZIAN Angel	*housewife*
104	130	ERZINGATZIAN Hagop	*grocery owner*
105	29	ERZINGATZIAN Haig	*artist printer, painter*
106	127	ERZINGATZIAN Krikor	*shoemaker*
107	29	ERZINGATZIAN Vahan	
108	128	ERZINGATZIAN Zabel	*housewife*
		ERZINGATZIAN Yervant	*employee*

109	106	FELEKECH Beshale	
110	240	FERMANIAN Ara	*shoemaker, importer of shoes*
111	261	FERMANIAN Dirouhi	*housewife*
112	180	GARABBEDIAN Kegham	* 29 IX 1950 + 9 I 1951, *died of pneumonia*
113	227	GARABEDIAN Armenouhi	*housewife*
114	157	GARABEDIAN Edward	1910 – 1981, *distributor of spirits & textiles,*

importer exporter, Cunningham Street

115	176	GARABEDIAN Roza *née ISRAELIAN*	* Smyrna 1884 + 25 VI 1945 *housewife*
		GARABEDIAN Rosa	*child*
116	177	GARABEDIAN Sarkis	*ironsmith*
117	227	GARABEDIAN Vartouhi	*housewife*
118	227	GARABEDIAN Zarouhi	*housewife*
119	138	GARIGIAN Garabed	*businessman, orchard owner*
		GEOVDELERIAN Garabed	*agronomist, died of typhoid*
120	55	GEOVDERELIAN Levon	
121	161	GEUVDJELIAN Panos	*carpenter*
122	226	GERBEDENIAN Mariam	*housewife*
123	225	GERBEDENIAN Mgrditch	*retailer*
		GERBEDENIAN Loussarpi	*housewife*
124	216	GHAZARIAN Hovhannes	*ivory carver*
125	241	GHAZARIAN Mardiros	*shoemaker*
126	241	GHAZARIAN Vartouhi	*housewife*
127	165	GHOURLIAN Hapet	*building construction*
128	166	GHOURLIAN Krikor	*student*
129	16	GHOURLIAN Zarouhi	*housewife*
		GHOURLIAN Zarouhi	*seamstress*
130	50	GUEVHERIAN Hovhannes	*priest*
131	51	GUEVHERIAN Haiganoush	*housewife*
132	190	GULESSERIAN Hovsep	*café owner, sweets & pastry shop*
133	189	GULESSERIAN Yeghia	*sweets & pastry shop*

134	188	GULESSERIAN Zarouhi	*housewife*
135	280	HAGOPIAN Avak	*goldsmith one of the "Arba Lijoch"*
(The 40 orphans)			
		HAGOPIAN Dikran	*employee*
		HAGOPIAN Yervant	*mechanic*
		HAIGAZIAN Sofia	*housewife*
		HAIGAZIAN Garbis	*businessman, developer*
		HAILEGIORGIS	infant
136	167	HAKESSIAN Sarkis	*firearms repairer*
		HALADJIAN Mihran	*businessman*
		HALADJIAN Haiganoush	*teacher*
		HANEJIAN Epime	*housewife*
		HAROUTIOUN Zapanelian	*employee*
		HATSAKORDZIAN Yervant	*baker*
		HAZARIAN Dikran	*mechanic*
137	215	HAZARIAN Jirayr	*child*
138	258	HEKIMIAN Khoren	*mechanic*
139	59	HINODOIAN Yeranouhi	* 31 X 1919 + 10 VII 1923
140	276	HOVHANESSIAN Sarkis	*caravan leader*
		HOVHANESSIAN Melidos	
141	65	HOVIAN Krikor	** Constantinople 1849 + Addis Ababa 1925*

astronomer, architect emigrated to France in 1880, where he studied at the Ecole Nationale des Ponts et Chaussées, graduating in 1885; arrived in Djibouti in 1904 and in Addis Ababa in 1905 appointed chief engineer of the Ethiopian Government; involved in numerous construction projects, built together with Minas Kherbekian Hotel Taytu 1907, observatory in the Gebbi, Armenian School, Bullet Factory, old Ministry of Trade, Tafari Makonnen (today: Yekatit 12) – Hospital, house of Lidj Yeassu in Fiche, as well as i.a. Russian Embassy Bridge, French Embassy Bridge, German Embassy Bridge and Aqaqi Bridge and Kirkos, St. Emanuel, Debre Berhan Selassie and Entotto Mariam Churches.

		HURMUZIAN Angel	*pianist, painter*
		HURMUZIAN Koharig	*housewife*
142	14	HURMUZIAN Nishan	*businessman*
		INEKDJIAN Avedis	*ironsmith*
144	178	ISRAELIAN David	* Smyrna 1895 + 11 XI 1940, *importer of shoes*
145	177	ISRAELIAN Dirouhi	* Smyrna 1858

			+ 1941, *housewife*
146	155	ISRAELIAN Hagop	* Smyrna 1885 + IX 1932, *merchant in coffee beans*
147	179	ISRAELIAN Kasbar	*merchant in coffee beans*
?		*ISRAELIAN Kegham*	* *Smyrna 1898 + 6 VI 1971*
148	156	ISRAELIAN Ohan	* *Smyrna 1890 + AA 1935, merchant in coffee beans*
		JERMAKIAN Avedis	*shoemaker*
		KAIPAKIAN Hagop	*employee*
		KALFAIAN Edward	*child*
		KALFAIAN Haig	*mechanic*
		KALFAIAN Sarkis	*child*
		KALOUSTIAN Kaloust	*secretary*
149	238	KALOUSTIAN Vahan	*1892 – 1938 carpenter*
150	238	KALOUSTIAN Yeranig	*1907 – 1973 housewife*
		KALYDJIAN Marie	*infant*
		KAMBOURIAN Serpouhi	*wife of a priest*
		KARAGEUZIAN Grapos	*employee*
		KARAMANIAN Mariam	*housewife*
		KARAMANIAN Hovhannes	*businessman*
		KARAMANIAN Mateos	*agronomist*
		KARASEFERIAN Ardashes	*goldsmith*
151	68	KARASEFERIAN Elise	*housewife*
152	110	KARASEFERIAN Elise	*housewife*
153	20	KARIBIAN Alex	1924 – 1979 *businessman*
154	20	KARIBIAN Vergine	1917 – 1998 *housewife*
155	132	KASSABIAN Garabed	*businessman*
156	228	KASSABIAN Ghazar	*businessman*
157	47	KASSABIAN Nouriday	*housewife*
158	66	KASSABIAN Vartouhi	*housewife*
159	67	KASSABIAN Zakar	*driver*
160	82	KAYMAKIAN Annig	*housewife*

161	126	KAYPAKIAN Antranig	*shoemaker*
162	104	KAYPAKIAN Boghos	*merchant*
		KAYPAKIAN Maria	*1922 – 1945, student, died of menenghitis*
		KAYPAKIAN Shushan	*1932 - 1933*
163	223	KAYSERLIAN Maksoud	*shoemaker*
164	173	KAZANDJIAN Eugenie	*housewife*
		KAZANDJIAN Sarkis	*shoemaker*
165	73	KAZANDJIAN Simon	*photographer*
		KEHEIAN Kevork	*tanner*
		KEHEYAN Sirvart	*housewife*
166	43	KENADJIAN Alice	*child, died of menenghitis*
		KENADJIAN Avedis	*businessman*
167	92	KENADJIAN Garabed	*businessman*
168	12	KENADJIAN Hagop	*government employee*
169	42	KENADJIAN Hagop	
170	244	KENADJIAN Haroutioun	*hoemaker*
171	245	KENADJIAN Levon	*bar owner*
		KENADJIAN Meriye	*housewife*
172	262	KENADJIAN Meroum	1895 – 1942 *housewife*
		KENADJIAN Nazareth	*café owner*
		KENADJIAN Nerses	*restaurant owner*
173	25	KENADJIAN Ovsanna	*housewife*
174	146	KEORHADJIAN Apraham	*Caesarea/Kayseri + 1955* in 1908 or 1910

entered the service of Matig Kevorkoff's tobacco monopoly later served Emperor Haile Selassie for more than 30 years in various capacities, i.a. as treasurer of the palace

175	147	KEORHADJIAN Elise	*dress maker*
176	146	KEORHADJIAN Haigouhi	*housewife*
		KEVORKIAN Dikran	*died of hepatitis*
177	77	KEVORKIAN Edward	* AA 1924 + 14 X 1995, *manager of Seferian Co.*
178	77	KEVORKIAN Shemavon	* Sevas 1894 + 17 II 1939, *businessman*
179	169	KEVORKIAN Vahan	*businessman*
?		KEVORKOFF Noemie	** Alexandria 1 III 1874 + AA 1 XII 1937, housewife*

		KEZELIAN Hovhannes	*mechanic*
		KHACHADOURIAN Dirouhi	*seamstress*
180	279	KHACHADOURIAN Gron	*pharmacist*
181	79	KHACHADOURIAN Lucia	1912 – 1961 *housewife*
		KHACHADOURIAN Magdaghine	*housewife*
182	54	KHATCHADORIAN Marie	*housewife*
183	81	KHATCHADOURIAN Sarkis	*1910 – 1964 construction foreman*
184	46	KHERBEKIAN Hripsime	*housewife*
185	252	KHERBEKIAN Isgouhi	*housewife*
186	28	KHERBEKIAN Karekin	*truck driver*
187	26	KHERBEKIAN Mariam	*housewife*
188	45	KHERBEKIAN Minas	** ca. 1874 + 1968/69 civil engineer,*

early road-builder in AA, built with Krikor Hovian Hotel Taytu 1907, Bullet Factory, old Ministry of Trade, Tafari Makonnen (today: Yekatit 12) – Hospital, house of Lidj Yeassu in Fiche, as well as i.a. Russian Embassy Bridge, French Embassy Bridge, German Embassy Bridge and Aqaqi Bridge and Kirkos, St. Emanuel, Debre Berhan Selassie and Entotto Mariam Churches.

189	129	KHERBEKIAN Yeghisapet	*housewife*
190	222	KHOUDANIAN Dikran	*carpenter*
191	222	KHOUDANIAN Payloun	*housewife*
192	109	KIZIRIAN Hovhannes	
		KORAGHIAN Abraham	** 15 VII 1881 + 7 XII 1955*
		KORAGHIAN Eliza	*1952 - 1996*
193	163	KOUYOUMDJIAN Maritza	*housewife*
194	86	KOUYOUMDJIAN Meline	*teacher*
		KRALIAN Dikranouhi	*housewife*
195	8	KRIKORIAN Hagop	*railway station-master*
196	101	KRIKORIAN Hrant	*1895 – 1952 carpenter*
		KRIKORIAN Vahan	*photographer*
197	5	KRIKORIAN Zabel	** Smyrna 1879 + AA 1923, sister of Haig Patapian, housewife*
		KURKDJIAN Marie	*infant*
198	112	LATIFIAN Sahag/Isaac	*pharmacist*
199	58	LUCCHIN Gabriele	* 5 V 1968 + 9 V 1968

200	202	MALKHASSIAN Armenouhi	*housewife*
201	275	MALKHASSIAN Badaskhan	*housewife*
202	70	MANUELIAN Bedros	*employee*
203	69	MANUELIAN Hagop	*businessman*
204	71	MANUELIAN Nouritsa	*housewife*
		MANUELIAN Nouritza	*housewife*
205	185	MARDIROSSIAN Karekin	*driver*
206	237	MARGOSSIAN Boghos	*firearms repairer*
		MAVULIAN Hagop	*mechanic*
208	208	MAVULIAN Sarkis	*baker*
		MELIKIAN Christine	*housewife*
		MELIKIAN Kevork	*mechanic*
209	281	MELIKIAN Missak	*tailor*
		MELIKIAN Sarkis	*businessman*
		MELIKIAN Setrag	*businessman*
		MELIKIAN Soghome	*housewife*
210	108	MENESHIAN Samuel	*textile dyer*
		MERDINIAN Haroutioun	*employee*
211	125	MESSROBIAN Antreas	*charcoal trader*
212	56	MESSROBIAN Garabed	*employee*
213	135	MESSROBIAN Hagop	1880 – 1949
214	31	MESSROBIAN Mardiros	*charcoal dealer*
		MESSROBIAN Messrob	*charcoal producer*
215	135	MESSROBIAN Mariam	1920 – 1992 *housewife*
		MESSROBIAN Nazli	*housewife*
		MESSROBIAN Nishan	
216	134	MESSROBIAN Sirarpi	*housewife*
		MINASSIAN Hratchhouhi	*housewife*
		MINOIAN Perouz	*housewife*
217	278	NALBANDIAN Haroutioun	*ivory carver*
218	113	NEDOURIAN Nerses B.	* 1882 + 14 V 1928, *businessman*

219	187	NERSESSIAN Elamsd	*housewife*
220	209	NERSESSIAN Hripsime	*housewife*
		OHANJANIAN Haroutioun	*medical doctor*
		OHNIGIAN Marie	*infant*
		OHNIGIAN Sirarpi	*housewife*
221	186	PAKHTIKIAN Arsen	*employee*
222	154	PAKHTIKIAN Hrant	*businessman*
223	53	PAKHTIKIAN Meroujan	*child, died of menenghitis*
224	181	PAKHTIKIAN Nazeni	*housewife*
207	253	PAMBOUKIAN Mariam	*housewife*
225	121	PAMBOUKIAN Ovsanna	*housewife*
226	219	PAMBOUKIAN Haig	*businessman*
227	232	PAMBOUKIAN Isaac	*shoemaker, leather décor*
		PANOSSIAN Ardashes	*driver*
228	4	PAPAZIAN Aghavni	1904 – 1974 *housewife*
		PAPAZIAN Antranig	*employee*
229	2	PAPAZIAN Baghdig	1888 – 1916 *architect, civil engineer*
		PAPAZIAN Bedros	*businessman*
230	3	PAPAZIAN Boghosig	1922 – 1933
		PAPAZIAN Vahe	*coffee merchant*
231	263	PAROUNAKIAN Arpen	*housewife*
232	172	PARSEGHIAN Haroutioun	*radio technician*
233	168	PATAPANIAN Haig	*Smyrna/Izmir 1882, employee, author, author of the history of the Armenian community*
234	168	PATAPAN Makrouhi	*housewife*
235	136	PATAPANIAN Karnig	*photographer/ farmer*
236	273	PESHDIMALDJIANArdashes	1888 – 1953 *translator*
?	N	PESHDIMALDJIA Michel	* 17 X 1926 + 3 III 1983
237	271	PESHDIMALDJIAN Pergrouhi	1902 – 1980 *housewife*
238	272	PESHIDIMALDJIAN Sybil	*housewife*

239	89	POGHARIAN Garo	
240	88	POGHARIAN Kourken	*bakery owner*
241	269	POGHARIAN Nevart	*housewife*
242	152	POGHARIAN Sonig	*housewife*
243	145	POGHARIAN Vahan	*businessman*
244	175	POGHARIAN Yacoub	
		PURZETIAN Ardashes	*trader*
245	238	PURZETIAN Diran	*secretary, died of drowning*
		PURZETIAN Onnig	*shopkeeper*
246	239	PURZETIAN Peruz	*housewife*
247	119	REISSIAN Alice	*housewife*
		RISOU Maria	*student*
		SAKADJIAN Khachig	*tinsmith*
248	22	SAKAIAN Krikor	*ironsmith, lock-maker*
249	32	SARAFIAN Armenak	*mechanical engineer*
250	274	SARIAN Araxi	*housewife*
251	274	SARIAN Terenig	*grocery owner*
252	15	SARKISSIAN Marie	*housewife*
		SARLIAN Araxi	*housewife*
		SARLIAN Terenig	*trader*
253	1	SEFERIAN[42] Edward	*businessman; came to Addis Ababa from*

Istanbul with his brother Krikor (+ Italy 1950), partners of Muradian trading company, established Seferian Company in 1929.

254	84	SEMERDJIBASHIAN	
255	233	SEMERDJIBASHIAN Atsede	18 I 1901 + 10 II 1957 *housewife*
256	266	SEMERDJIBASHIAN Garabed	
257	234	SEMERDJIBASHIAN Hovhannes	12 VIII 1893 + 9 X 1947, *employee of*

British Legation; messenger between British minister Thesiger and Ras Tafari Makonnen in the preparation of the coup against Lidj Iyasu later drogman and interpretor of the German Legation in the 1930s; assassinated

		SEMERDJIBASHIAN Prianti	*housewife*

[42] See EAE, vol. 4, entry Seferian & Co.

		SEMERDJIBASHIAN Sarkis	*trader*
		SEMERDJIBASHIAN Satenig	*housewife*
258	34	SEVADJIAN Avedis	*Aintab 1886 + Harar XI 1946, *tanner & shoe manufacturer*
259	35	SEVADJIAN Menoush	* Aintab 10 III 1855 + AA 1 XII 1918 *housewife*
260	60	SEVADJIAN Vigen	
261	37	SEVAFJIAN Hovsep	* Aintab 5 XII 1889 + AA 25 XI 1918 *photographer*
262	194	SHAMASSIAN Christine	*housewife*
		SHAMASSIAN Dikran	*gunsmith*
		SHAMASSIAN Simon	*gunsmith*
		SHAMSSIAN Markrid	*student, died of typhus*
		SHEBETDJIAN Hagop	*ironsmith*
		SHEFTAIAN Anna	*housewife*
263	116	SHIRIGDJIAN Elise	*housewife*
264	212	SHISHMANIAN Sarkis	*teacher*
		SHISHMANIAN Fotinis	
265	260	SIMONIAN Haroutioun	*carpenter*
?		SIMONIAN Artin	1889 – 1946
266	267	SIRAGANIAN Yevnige	1898 – 1920, B. & F. Bible Society
267	249	SISSIAN Hagop	*deacon*
268	250	SISSIAN Zemroukht	*housewife*
269	199	SOUKIASSIAN Amassia	*civil engineer*
270	200	SOUKIASSIAN George	*mechanic, died in motorcycle accident*
271	137	STAMBOULIAN Jeanette	* Djibouti 18 IX 1940 + 7 XII 1940
272	90	STAMBOULIANVartkes/Joseph shoemaker	
273	91	STEPANIAN Haig	
274	242	STEPANIAN Teshkhouhi	*housewife*
275	99	SURMEYAN Barkevouhi	Istanbul 1890 + AA 1966, *housewife*
276	100	SURMEYAN Vahan	* Agen 1894 + Vienna 1956 *printing press & stationery*
277	213	TANIELIAN Zarouhi	*housewife*
278	87	TARPINIAN Dzaghig	*housewife*

279	64	TARPINIAN Vahe (father)	*grocery owner*
280	30	TARPINIAN Vahe (son)	* Halep (Aleppo) 1918 + AA 1962 *shoemaker*
281	83	TAVITIAN Araxi	*housewife*
		TAVITIAN Joseph	*dentist*
282	103	TERZIAN	
283	148	TERZIAN Araxi	*housewife*
284	192	TERZIAN Arshavir	1924 – 2002
		TERZIAN Azadouhi	*infant*
285	148	TERZIAN Emanuel	*dentist*
286	115	TERZIAN George O.	* 25 XII 1907 + 29 IX 1945, *carpenter*
287	142	TERZIAN Hnazant	*housewife*
288	142	TERZIAN Hovhannes	
		TERZIAN Kevork	*mechanic, died of pneumonia*
289	117	TERZIAN Mamas	*broker*
		TERZIAN Maritsa	*housewife*
290	142	TERZIAN Nartouhi	*housewife*
		TERZIAN Negdar	*housewife*
291	142	TERZIAN[43] Sarkis	*Arapkir + AA 1915 (shot)*

lived in Erzerum, Kars, Smyrna,left Turkey in 1882, arrived in Harar 1883; instrumental in capturing arar for Emperor Menelik in 1887; Governor of Harar, Nole and Kombolcha area in 1887; 1889-1895 purchasing Gras rifles forEmperor Menelik in Belgium[44]; 1905 importer of first "Aveling & Porter" traction engine 1907 established Filawoha Baths.

292	198	TERZIAN Setrag	*soft drink production*
293	217	TERZIAN Siran	*housewife*
		TERZIAN Sona	*child, died of pneumonia*
294	142	TERZIAN Takouhi	*housewife*
		TERZIAN Terfanda	*housewife*
295	142	TERZIAN Vartouhi	*housewife*
296	197	TERZIAN Yevnige	*housewife*
297	124	TERZONTZ Mihrtad	*businessman*
		TERZONTZ Siranig	

---

43 See EAE, vol. 1, entry Armenians.
44 For details see Jonathan A. Grant, Rulers, Guns and Money – The Global Arms Trade in the Age of Imperialism (2007).

298	133	TILBIAN Anna	* Marash + AA V 1957, *housewife*
299	131	TILBIAN Nishan	* Marash + AA 8 XI 1952, *shoemaker*
300	193	TOPALIAN Dirouhi	*housewife*
301	231	TOPDJIAN Hripsime	*housewife*
		TOROIAN Satenig	*teacher, died of pneumonia*
		TOULOUMBADJIAN Haig	*employee, died of malaria*
		TOVMASSIAN Kevork	*employee*
302	282	VARARANIAN Hagop	*photographer*
303	98	VARJABEDIAN Haiganoush	*housewife*
		VARTANIAN Garo	*goldsmith*
		VARTANIAN Markar	*tailor*
		VORPERIAN Haroutioun	*coffee trader*
304	85	VORPERIAN Kevork	*businessman, tailor*
		VOSGIAN Takouhi	*housewife*
305	54	YAZEDJIAN Aghavni	*housewife*
		YAZEDJIAN Araxi	*1875 – 1955, carpet maker*
		YAZEDJIAN Levon	*1869 – 1927, artist, photographer*
		YAZEDJIAN Levon	*proprietor, suicide*
306	162	YAZEDJIAN Hagop	*miller, died by homicide*
		YAZEDJIAN Robert	*carpet maker*
307	148	YEGHIAIAN Boghos	* Sparta 1906 + 17 VI 1962, *company manager*
		ZAMANIAN Vartanoush	
308	221	ZIREKIAN Hetoum	*employee*

3.4. NEW ARMENIAN CEMETERY

Location: N 09° 03.488' E 038° 42.880'
Altitude: 2552 m in NW corner
Administered by Vartkes Nalbandian, Archdiacon of the Armenian Community in Ethiopia (Bale PLC, Bale House, P.O. Box 1862, Addis Ababa, Tel. 00 251 1 15 53 94, Fax. 00 251 1 15 53 65, Mail: bale.plc@ethionet.et).

The Armenian community is also the owner of the New Armenian cemetery, which is walled in - in contrast to the old; it is the highest part of the Gulele cemetery, located at an altitude of 2530 m. The area was bought by the Armenian community in 1961/62 from the son of Baghdassarian when it became clear that no more burials were possible in the Old Armenian cemetery.[45] The first tomb on the left side is of musician and composer Nerses Nalbandian (* Aintab III 1915 + London XI 1977), the father of Vartkes Nalbandian, who in 1963 had composed the hymn of the Organisation of African Unity "Let us all unite and celebrate together", since 2002 African Union.

The oldest grave is No.3 in Row 1 - Missikian Hovhannes (* Arapgir 1906 + Addis Ababa 21 VII 1962), the most recent the tomb of Victor Tchaghabatzbanian (* 1 X 1935 + 9 XII 2008). Here we find the grave of Khosrof K. Boghossian (* 1904 + 1970), Colonel of Ethiopian Army, veterinarian in charge of the Imperial Cavalry and Chief Equerry.

It is interesting to note the places of birth on the graves, indicating that at the end of the 19th century n Armenian community existed in Harar and a smaller one in Addis Ababa. Unlike in the Old Armenian Cemetery, many tombstones in the New Armenian have inscriptions in English or French; the wrought-iron cross of Garabed Atamian seems somewhat out of place and reminds of the grave of Koloman von Mattanovich in the Catholic part.

The total number of graves according to the "Liste du Nouveau cimetière arménien d'Addis Ababa – Gulélé" is 231, although when visiting the cemetery the author could count only 220 graves. Total number of burials of Armenians according to the Armenian register would amount to 549. It is interesting to note that the number of burials in the 1990s or after 2000 is considerably lower than those of the period 1962 to 1990, falling to only two in the third millennium - a telltale sign that the Armenian community of Addis Ababa is diminishing.

---

[45] The Armenian community also owned a cemetery in Dire Dawa, which no longer exists. Its register is presently kept by Mr. Vartkes Nalbandian.

The place of death in the following list, unless otherwise indicated, is Addis Ababa

Left row:

1	ADANALIAN Hagop	* Ayntab 1901	+ 17 IV 1973	*employee*
2	KHASRDJIAN Kévork	* Garin	6 III 1983	*photo framer*
3	MISSAKIAN Hovhannes	*Arapgir 1906	+ 21 VII 1962	*carpenter*
4	anonymous			
	BOGHOSSIAN Vahram			
	DER BOGHOSSIAN Anna Terziani			
	Rebecca			
	SEMERDJIBASHIAN Philipos			*employee*
5	ADANALIAN Haroutioun	* Ayntab 1876	+ 1963	*carpet repair*
6	PARSEGHIAN Azniv	* Ayntab 1897	+ 1971	*housewife*
7	PARSEGHIAN Norayr	* 17 VIII 1932	+ 5 IX 1999	*goldsmith*
8	PAPAZIAN Antranig	* 1909	+ 1963	*bank employee*
	OHNIGIAN Arsham			*school teacher*
9	OHANESSIAN Melidos	* 1881	+ 1969	*merchant*
10	HIRMIZIAN Anjel	* Rodosto 1897	+ 1965 (Tekirdag)	*housewife*
11	TCHAGHTSBANIAN Baydzar	* 1909	+ 1964	*housewife*
12	anonymous			
	KHACHADOURIAN Sarkis			*merchant*
	KHACHADOURIAN Yeprem			*mechanic*
13	MEKHDJIAN Hripsim é	* Ayntab 1892	+ 1970	*housewife*
14	DÉMIRDJIAN Sarkis	* 1894	+ 1964	*pruner of fruit trees*
15	VORPÉRIAN Arägash Danno	* 1923	+ 1998	*housewife*
16	HAZARIAN Mannig	* Addis Ababa 1920	+ 1966	*housewife*
17	AYVAZOULIAN Josef	* 12 XII 1907	+ 5 I 1967	
18	PARSEGHIAN Hovhannes	* 1886	+ 1967	*goldsmith*
19	NORAREVIAN Dr. Yervant	* 1880	+ 1967	*dentist*
20	ANTABLIAN Lucia	* 1895	+ 1967	*housewife*

21	MARGOSSIAN Margos Bogos	* Harar V 1915	+ London XII 1975	*mechanic*
22	MARGOSSIAN Dikran	* 1912	+ 1968	*mechanic*
23	PETERSON George Patrick *killed by an employee*	* 1908	+ 1968	*manager*
24	CHORBADJIAN Krikor	* 1892	+ 1968	*embroidery work*
25	ASLANIAN Tavit	* Sébastia (Sivas) 1888	+ 1969	*carpet maker, mended the carpets in the imperial palaces, died of heart failure*
26	AVAKIAN Artin	* 1885	+ 1968	*cinema owner*
27	KAZANDJIAN Apraham	* Djebel Mousa 20 IV 1893	+ 22 III 1969	*businessman*
28	VARJABEDIAN Serovpe	* Beledjig (Bilecik) (1901)	+ 1969	*accountant*
29	ADANALIAN Hagop Haroutim	* 1911	+ 1970	*employee*
30	POGHARIAN Hérminé	* 1895	+ 1970	*housewife*
31	SARAFIAN Loucine	* Bolis (Bolu) 1897	+ 1970	*housewife*
32	KOUYOUMDJIAN Varaskad	* Bolis (Bolu) XII 1890	+ X 1973	*shoemaker*
33	KOUYOUMDJIAN Takouhi née HAGOPIAN	* Gévé 1892	+ 1970	*housewife*
34	KNADJIAN Aznive	* 1901	+ 1971	*housewife*
35	AZNAVORIAN Haygaz	* 1909	+ 1972	*goldsmith*
36	anonymous			
37	POGHARIAN Vartiter	* 1926	+ 1972	*secretary*
38	KOUYOUMDJIAN Hovhannes	* Marash (Maras) 1896	+ 1972	*carpenter*
39	HAZARIAN Aroussiag	* Ayntab 1898	+ 1972	*housewife*
40	KNADJIAN Nazareth	* 1892	+ 1973	*bar owner*
41	HAYGAZIAN Arfia	* 1900	+ 1973	*housewife*
42	HAYGAZIAN Avedis	* 1876	+ 1931	
43	VALANTIN Béj	* Addis Ababa 1920	+ 20 VII 1973	*secretary*
44	MÉLIKIAN Djordj	* 1926	+ 1973	*mechanic*
45	KERMENIAN John	* 10 VII 1901	+ 13 II 1974	*employee*
46	ASSADOURIAN Khatchig	* Constantinople 1896	+ 26 X 1974	*trader*
47	BÉHÉSNILIAN Siranoush	* 1893	+ 1975	*housewife*
48	SARKISSIAN Kévork	* Van 1912	+ 1975	*truck driver; one of the "Arba Lijoch" (The 40 orphans)*

49	MESROBIAN Antranig	* 1935	+ 1987	*bar owner*
50	MESROBIAN Nichan	* 1924	+ 1977	*employee*
51	POGHARIAN Noubar V.	* AA 1 III 1915	+ 30 III 1971	*businessman, suicide*

Tomb of composer Nerses Nalbandian

Second Row

52 NALBANDIAN Nerses * Aintab III 1915 + London XI 1977

musician and composer, father of Vartkes Nalbandian; in 1963 composed the hymn of the Organisation of African Unity "Let us all unite and celebrate together", since 2002 African Union.

53 BEHESNILIAN Samuel * Behesni 1878 + 1971

businessman; agent and importer of major type writer manufacturers for Ethiopia and Djibouti

54 Anonymous

55 Anonymous

56	NALBANDIAN Hagop	* Aintab 1901	+ 1962	*musician*
57	AVAKIAN Setrag	* Aintab 1914	+ 1962	

soft drinks producer "Sinalco"factory owner

58	BABAYAN Berdj	* Izmir ? 1886	+ 1964	*spinningfactoryowner*
59	AZNAVORIAN Hagop	* 1904	+ 1963	*lawyer*
60	NALBANDIAN[46] Kévork	* Aintab 1897	+ 1963	*captain*

composed Haile Selassie's National Anthem "Ethiopia hoy dess ibalish" (1926), Tafari March and the opera "Gonderewan Gebre Mariam" (Gebre-Mariam from Gondar, 1929/30)

61	JIDEDJIAN Vergine	* 15 XII 1896	+ 31 V 1963	*housewife*
62	DJIDEDJIAN Nigoghos	* 18 II 1884	+ 25 X 1968	*goldsmith*
63	BEHESNILIAN Hagop	* Addis Ababa 14 VIII 1914	+ 31 VII 1965	*businessman*
64	NALBANDIAN Nartouhi	* Halép(Aleppo)1890	+ 1964	*housewife*
65	BOGHOSSIAN Aghassi	* Aintab 1886	+ Beirut 1964	*businessman suicide*
66	MEKHDJIAN Kévork	* Aintab 1886	+ Beirut 1966	*gunsmith*
67	HAZARIAN Mihran	* Gésaria(Kayseri)1880	+ 1964	*Carpet weaver*
68	TERZIAN Mouchegh O.	* Harar 19 II 1905	+ 20 XI 1965	*businessman*
69	SAKADJIAN Pavlos	* Darson 1909	+ 1966	*tinsmith*
70	EBEYAN Garbis	* Constantinople1885	+ 1967	*employee*
71	VORPÉRIAN Haroutiun	* 1898	+ 1966	
72	AINTABLIANProf. Sarki	* Marash15VIII1885	+ 3 VII 1966	*teacher,diedofmalaria*
	AINTABLIAN Lucia	* 1893	+ 1967	*housewife*
73	KHERBEGUIAN Yervant	* 1909	+ 1966	*mechanic*
74	BOGHOSSIAN Khosrof K.	* 1904	+ 1970	*colonel*

Ethiopian Army, Veterinarian in charge of Imperial Cavalry

75	PAROUNAGUIAN Prapion	* Arapgir 1888	+ 1967	*housewife*
76	CHAKERIAN Zarouhi	* Bolis 1894	+ 1967	*housewife*
77	YERZINGATSIANYervant	* Harar 1912	+ 1967	*employee*
78	SEVADJIAN Yeranouhi	* Aintab 8 V 1893	+ 15 III 1969	*housewife*
79	KAZANDJIANSarkisLevon	* Svedia/Sweden1909	+ 1967	*employee*
80	SHISHMANIAN Sarkis	* Adiaman 1913	+ Ethiopia 1967	*shoemaker*
81	SAKADJIAN Hripsimé	* 15 XII 1921	+ 4 IX 1976	*employee*

[46] See EAE, vol. 1, entry Armenians.

	née AVAKIAN			
82	BABLANIAN Hmayag	* Nakhitchevan 1897	+ 1964	*businessman*
83	BABLANIAN Sirvart H.	* Cairo ? 1914	+ 1956	*school teacher*
84	DÉOKMEDJIAN Elisa K.	* Broussa 1888	+ ?	*housewife*
85	MANASSERIAN Aghavni	* Broussa 1896	+ 1971	*housewife*
86	STEPANIAN Michel Z.	* Harar 19 XII 1922	+ 19 IX 2000	*businessman*
87	STEPANIAN Kegham Z.	* Harar 6 IX 1920	+ 2 VII 1989	*businessman*
88	STEPANIAN Araxi	* 26 IX 1926	+ 28 III 1969	*housewife*
89	GHAZAROSSIAN Etouart	* Arapgir 1903	+ 1969	*shirt maker*
90	BEHESNILIAN Joseph	* 21 X 1920	+ 5 II 1970	*flour mill*
91	ATAMIAN Garabed	* 5 V 1912	+ 19 IX 1969	*coffee merchant*
92	KNADJIAN Mérié	* Ayntab 1892	+ 19701925	*housewife*
93	MESROBIAN Nazli	* Kharpert 1895	+ 1970	*housewife*
94	HAKALMAZIAN Garabed	* Aslanbeg 1907	+ 15 XI 1970	*music teacher*
95	DONIGUIAN Haygouhi	* Adana 1895	+ 1971	*housewife*
96	AVAKIAN Artin	* 1925	+ 1971	*cinema owner*
97	KIZIRIAN Nerses	* Ayntab 5 XI 1907	+ 6 V 1971	*photographer*
98	MAVOULIAN Hagop	* Ayntab 1910	+ 1971	*mechanic*
99	Anonymous			
100	ZAMANIAN Menagae Armenag	* Harar 1894	+ 1971	*accountant*
101	DJERMAGUIAN Avedis	* Hasia 1915	+ 1972	*tinsmith*
102	GERNEDENIAN Loussarpie	* Larnaca 1925	+ 1973	*housewife*
103	AZNAVORIAN Satenig	* 1903	+ 1973	*housewife*
104	KATCHADOURIAN Dirouhi	* 29 VIII 1910	+ 27 IX 1973	*housewife*
105	KHERBEKIAN Aznive	* 1893	+ 1974	*housewife*
106	YEREVANIAN Ardemis	* Bardizag 1890	+ 1974	*housewife*
107	YEREVANIAN Garabed	* Bardizag 1882	+ 1937	*shoemaker*
108	ZANAZANIAN Eise	* Ayntab 1889	+ 7 VI 1974	*housewife*
109	ZANAZANIAN Soghomon	* Ayntab 1880	+ Athens 23 XI 1947	
110	SEMERDJIBASHIAN Vartouhi	* Harar 1916	+ 1975	*housewife*
111	DARAKDJIAN Yesayi	* Boro Hounas dan 1925	+ 1975	*mechanic*
112	EBEYAN Aroussiag	* AA 22 IX 1890	+ 9 XI 1975	*housewife*

Central Row

113	YAZEDJIAN ZinashPaylak	* IX 1929	+ V 1998	*housewife*
114	YAZEDJIAN Leon P.	* 1933	+ 1970	*employee*

Third Row

115	KARASÉFERIAN Ardaches	*1905	+ 1975	*goldsmith*
116	SATÉNIG Ardaches (Wzo)	* 1968	+ 1985	*housewife*
117	LAPPINE Youra D.	* Orel 16 XI 1910	+ 22 X 1997	

Russian Orthodox, representative of General Motors in Ethiopia, importer of Chevrolet cars. co-owner of MOENCO

118	KÉCHICHIAN Yeprem	* AA 1915	+ 1981	*goldsmith*
119	KHATCHADOURIAN Khatchig	* 1908	+ 1978	*mechanic*
120	VOSGUIAN Ardaches	* Adapazar 1889	+ 1979	*schoolteacher*
121	MESSROBIAN Dzaghig	* 1888	+ 1977	*housewife*
122	HAYGAZIAN Garbis	* AA 17 V 1931	+ 20 IX 1975	*employee*
123	SARKISSIAN Vahan	* Sis (Kaz) 1908	+ 19 VI 1976	

businessman; one of the "Arba Lijoch" (The 40 orphans)[47]

124	BALIAN Lousaper	* Martzvan(Merzifan)	+ 1976 1890	*teacher*
125	PURZETIAN Nubar	* 1907	+ 1976	*mechanic*
126	AVAKIAN Setrag	* Ayntab 1890	+ 5 I 1948	*glass fitter*
127	AVAKIAN Makrouhi née BILEMDJIAN	* Ayntab 1897	+ 26 X 1976	*housewife*
128	AVAKIAN Setrag S.	* Aleppo 1919	+ 23 XII 1976	
129	ERZNGATSIAN Hripsimé	* Bolis 1908	+ 1979	*housewife*
130	KALFAYAN Hayg	* Constantinople 1875	+ 18 III 1945	
131	KALFAYAN Agilliné	* Bolis 1879	+ III 1939	*housewife*
132	AZNAVORIAN Giorgio	* Addis Ababa 1909	+ 1977	*employee*
133	PARSEGHIAN Armenak	* Syria 1899	+ IV 1978	

Qualified Optician, Haile Selassie I Avenue

134	SÉMERDJIAN Armen	* AddisAbaba 1903	+ 1978	*employee*

[47] Jean ECKIAN, Le Roi des Rois et les 40 orphelins, in: Nouvelles d'Armebnie, No. 150, Mars 2009, Paris 2009, pp. 54-56.

135	ADJEMIAN Arsén	* Sepasdia 1896	+ 1979	*schoolteacher*
136	POGHARIAN Anna			*sales woman*
137	POGHARIAN Filip	* 1909	+ 1979	*tailor*
138	KÉORHADJIAN Torkom	* 1918	+ 1994	*flourmill*
	MESROBIAN Markrid	* 1904	+ 1979	*housewife*
139	KÉORHADJIAN Nerses	* Addis Ababa 1916	+ 1979	*agriculture*
140	DARAKDJIAN Mihran	* Hounasdan 1926	+ XII 1979	*mechanic*
141	DARAKDJIAN Hovsép	* 19 IV 1955	+ 26 VI 1981	*mechanic*
142	DER NERSESSIAN Mesrob	* Van 1910	+ 1980	*repairer of firearms*
143	TERZIAN Anna	* 1900	+ 1983	*housewife*
144	TERZIAN Vahra	* 1894	+ 1980	*linguist*
145	ASLANIAN Mariné	* AA 4 I 1926	+ 28 II 1980	*housewife*
146	MESROBIAN Vartan	* 1 IX 1975	+ 23 VI 1980	(child)
147	KEVORKIAN Armenouhie	* 1895	+ 5 XI 1980	*housewife*
148	KAYSERLIAN Nevart	* 1907	+ 1980	*housewife*
149	KAYSERLIAN Maksoud	* 1891	+ 1951	*restaurant*
150	SISSIAN Sdepan	* 1908	+ 1981	*truck driver*
151	TCHÉKIDJ Andon	* Bolis 1918	+ 1981	*employee*
152	GHARIBIAN Baghdasar	* Van 1910	+ 1981	
dealer in coffee bean; sone of the "Arba Lijoch" (The 40 orphans)				
153	BAGHDASSARIAN Ghevont	* Van 1885	+ 1934	*goldsmith*
154	BAGHDASSARIAN Mari	* Arapgir 1989	+ 1981	*housewife*
155	PAMOUKIAN Hayg	* 1888	+ 1954	*businessman*
156	PAMOUKIAN Arkhén	* 1906	+ 1981	*housewife*
157	MAVLIAN Dudu (Mrs.)	* Aintab 1891	+ 10 XII 1981	*housewife*
158	GARABEDIAN Sirarpi	* 1930	+ 1936	*housewife*
159	GRABEDIAN Zarouhi	* Van 18?8	+ 1940	*housewife*
160	GARABEDIAN Armenouhi	* 1916	+ 1936	*housewife*
161	Anonymous			
162	KARIBIAN Asdghig	* 1903	+ 1984	*housewife*
163	MALKHASSIAN Hovhannes	* Van 1910	+ 1984	*mechanic*
164	PARSEGHIAN Sona	* 1938	+ 2 XII 1984	*housewife*
165	KALAYDJIAN Haroutiun	* Ayntab 1902	+ 1986	*truck transport*

166 POGHARIAN Asdghig * 1923 + 1986 *housewife*

167 ANTRANIKIAN Varoujan * Nazareth 1917 + 8 IX 1986

restaurant owner, Varuj-Restaurant in Nazareth/Adama

168 TERZIAN Avedis * Harar 1904 + 25 VII 2000 *translator*

169 TERZIAN Verjin * Arapgir 1909 + 1987 *dress maker*

170 BOGHOSSIAN Khatchig * Addis Ababa 1900 + 1987 *gvt. employee*

171 SHAMASSIAN Hrant *mechanic*

172 BEHESNILIAN Aroussiag * 1908 + 1988 *housewife*

173 GÉVHÉRIAN Noubar * 1916 + 1991 *salesman*

174 TCHAGHATZBANIAN Nevart * 1930 + 1988 *housewife*

175 TAVITIAN Marta * Déorteol 1893 + 1989 *housewife*

176 DJERRAHIAN Robert * 8 XII 1916 + 8 V 1989 *cinema owner*

177 KASSABIAN Antranig * Arapgir 4 IX 1917 + 26 IV 1990 *tailor*

178 PAROUNAGUIAN Jirayr * 21 I 1930 + 26 V 1991 *truck transport*

179 TOROSSIAN Sahag * 1907 + 1992

truck transport; one of the "Arba Lijoch" (The 40 orphans)

180 GIULÉSSÉRIAN Panos + 1994 *mechanic*

181 DARAKDJIAN Marta + 1994 *dress maker*

182 HAZARIAN Parsegh + 1994 *employee*

183 KNADJIAN Avedis * 1914 + 19?? *employee*

184 KANADJIAN Anahid * 14 V 1930 + 23 XII 1995 *cashier*

Fourth Row

185 TCHALGDJIAN Azniv * 1912 + 1994 *school teacher*

186 TCHALGDJIAN Tatéos * Erzerum 1909 + 1984 *employee*

187 GIULÉSÉRIAN Manichag * Antab 1882 + 3 V 1980 *housewife*

188 GIULÉSÉRIAN Mari * Egypt 1912 + 1992 *businessman*

189 GIULÉSÉRIAN Haroutiun * Ayntab 1901 + 1980 *employee*

190 ZAMANIAN Zarouhi * 1901 + 1981 *housewife*

191 POGHARIAN Azniv * Ayntab 1907 + 1988 *housewife*

192 ERZNGATSIAN Levon * Harar 1905 + 1979

193 KEUZEULIAN Anna * 1900 + 1981 *housewife*

194 PARSEGHIAN Archalouys * 1905 + 1994 *housewife*

195 KÉORHADJIAN Yervant * 1 VI 1913 + 23 IV 2002 *flourmiller*

196 KÉORHADJIAN Haygaz * 1920 + 1985 *flourmiller*

197 KÉORHADJIAN Toros * 1922 + 1985 *flourmiller*

198 WÄRNINÄSH Maryo Woizero * 1898 + 1976 *housewife*

199 DER NERSESSIAN Victoria * Arapgir 1916 + 16 VII 1986 *housewife*

200 TCHÉOPDJIAN Taniel * Asba Tafari 17 VII 1935 + 12 X 1995 *businessman*

201 KÉVORKIAN Arménouhi * 1912 + 1983 *housewife*

202 KÉVORKIAN Vahan * 1898 + 1960 *businessman*

203 ASLANIAN Kegham * *Alexandria/Eg.* 25 I 1915 + 9 VIII 1984
owner of Shoa Shoe-Factory, Piazza, Addis Ababa

204 NERSESSIAN Elmast

205 NERSESSIAN Melkon * 1908 + 1986 *shoemaker*

206 MESROBIAN Hagop * 1928 + 1998 *shoemaker*

207 KAYSERLIAN Yervant * Addis Ababa 1927 + 1987
manager of Singer Company

208 SISSIAN Vazkén * 1913 + 1996 *Wood-work industry*

209 APIKIAN Levon * Bolis 1906 + 1987 *businessman*

210 APIKIAN Roza née ARVANITOPOULOS * 22 IX 1938 + 12 III 1997 *secretary*

211 BAGHDASSARIAN Archag * 1921 + 1988 *businessman*

212 GÉVHÉRIAN Hamesd * 1925 + 1992 *housewife*

213 MARKARIAN Jirayr * 1906 + 17 X 1999
employee; one of the "Arba Lijoch" (The 40 orphans)

214 PARSEGHIAN Berg * Addis Ababa 1926 + 27 XII 1987 *salesman*

215 BAGHDASSARIAN Hrant * 1890 + 1935 *goldsmith*

216 POGHARIAN Achod née VARJABEDIAN ? * 1919 + 1988 *tailor*

217 BAGHDASSARIAN Vahak * 1919 + 1996 *goldsmith*

218 PIURZÉTIAN Takouhi * 1925 + 1999 *housewife*

219 BOGHOSSIAN Jeanne K. * Addis Ababa 21 I 1909 + 12 XII 1994 *housewife*

220 BOGHOSSIAN Louise * Addis Ababa + 5 II 1999 *housewife*

12 V 1910

221	SHAMASSIAN Markos			*employee*
222	BOGHOSSIAN Suzanne	* AddisAbaba1914	+ X 1999	*housewife*
223	BOGHOSSIAN Elise	* AddisAbaba1907	+ XI 1999	*housewife*
224	Anonymous			
225	DER NERSESSIAN Isgouhi	* 10 XI 1935	+ 24 II 2000	*dress maker*
226	KÉVORKIAN Varouj	* 1930	+ 1998	*employee*
227	DAVIDIAN Hamesd	* 1909	+ 1998	*sales woman*
228	POGHARIAN Hovhannes	* 7 I 1911	+ 9 VI 1997	*employee*
229	GIULÉSÉRIN Kévork	* 1924	+ 1995	*employee*
230	ESKIDJIAN Nishan B.	* 1943	+ 1995	*employee*
231	VAGHARCHAGUIAN Sirvart	* 1919	+ 2001	*housewife*

not numbered

AZNAVOURIAN Satenig	* *Arapkir* 1903	+ 1973	
BOGHASSIAN Charlotte Dakie	* 1880	+ 1948	
BOGHOSSIAN Aghassi	* AddisAbaba1905	+ 1964	
EBEYAN Lousig/Lucie	* 1884	+ 1962	
KASSABIAN Mardiros	* Arapkir 1916	+ 1988	
KENADJIAN Aznive	* Aintab 1901	+ 1971	*housewife*

KERMANIAN Hovhannes/John	*10 VII 1901	+ 13 II 1974
MARGOSSIAN Dikran	* 1912	+ 1968
MARGOSSIAN Margos Dikran	* Harar V 1915	+ London 23 XII 1975

father was purchaser of the court of Emperor Menelik II, married to an Ethiopian

PARSEGHIAN Noray	* 17 VIII 1932	+ 5 IX 1999

silversmith, Piazza, Addis Ababa

Nubar	* 1907	+ 1976
Kerghan Z.	* 1920	+ 1989
Michael Z.	* 1922	* 2000
TCHAGHABATZBANIAN Victor	* 1 X 1935	+ 9 XII 2008

3.5. CATHOLIC CEMETERY "SAN PIETRO E PAOLO"

Location: N 09° 03.371' E 038° 42.936'
Altitude: 2537 m
Administered by:
Father Angelo, Tel. 00251 911 201482 and Father Roberto, Holy Saviour Catholic Church (San Salvatore), *Churchill Road, La Gare, Addis Ababa, P.O.Box 633, Tel. 00 251 11 5516442, depending from: Ethiopian Catholic Archbishop, represented by Abba Gebre Mariam Amente Abeya, Catholic Cathedral Church of the Holy Nativity (Santa Nativita della Beata Maria Virgine), Arada Kifle Ketema, Kebele 14, House 371 (office and residence; opposite Café Tomoka), Tel. 00251 11 112457*

Comitato Cimitero Italiano:
Mr. Guido Checchin, Ethiopian General Industry Installation Supply Pvt. Ltd. Co., P.O.Box 3358, Addis Ababa, Tel. 00 251 11 1570506, Mobile 00 251 911 638789.

This cemetery is believed to have been established around 1929 on an area of 3500 m2, which after the Italian occupation of Ethiopia in 1936 was expanded to 48.000 m2; it would seem that Italian authorities were not allowing Ethiopian and Eritrean Catholics to be buried in the Catholic Cemetery of Gulele. In 1960 Emperor Haile Selassie donated the whole area as well as additional land to the Ethiopian Catholic Church, which took over administration of the Catholic Cemetery, which now covers an area of 62.130 m2. Although officially one Catholic cemetery, it is divided for administrative reasons into a Catholic cemetery, administered by the "Comitato Cimitero Italiano", and an Ethiopian Catholic Cemetery; the Catholic cemetery is not walled in and its is sometimes difficult to locate its exact borders with the adjoining International and Old Armenian cemeteries.

During the years of the Derg – regime of Colonel Mengistu Haile Mariam (1974 – 1991), the cemetery gradually fell into disrepair. Marble covers of tombs were stolen, as well as stones and metal decorations and used as building materials[48]. Photos commemorating the dead had been destroyed. Cattle, sheep and goats were grazing among the dilapidated tombs. When a new "Comitato Cimitero Italiano" was established in 2001, it set out to restore the cemetery and its graves, a task that took one year to complete. The committee, originally comprising 3 Catholic priests and 12 members of the Italian community of Addis Ababa has by 2009 dwindled to three members. In 2006, water was introduced to the cemetery making gardening much easier; the cemetery also has electricity.

Today, the so-called "Italian" cemetery offers a welcome sight, which comes at a price, however. Annual maintenance costs are 75.000 to 80.000 ETB[49], including salaries of gardeners, workers and guards. According to the head of the cemetery's committee, a businessman born in Asmara, but whose family originates from Gorizia, Friuli, it would be fine if every member of the Italian community of Addis Ababa would pay 1 ETB per day for the upkeep of the cemetery. Some Italian con-

[48] A story familiar to the author from the Jewish Cemetery in Bassateen, Cairo; see Rudolf AGSTNER, Kein Wiedersehen mit Bassateen?, Aufbau, 17 July 1996, p. 24, New York 1996.

[49] At the time of writing in January 2009, 1 EURO corresponded to 14.40 ETB.

tractors in Addis Ababa, like Varnero, Elmi or Guardano assist in repair work to be carried out or by making contributions. Donations from the Italian community amount to 40.000 or 45.000 ETB annually. Roughly 80 % of annual maintenance costs are covered by donations, additional contributions are very much welcome.

The "Italian" Catholic Cemetery comprises an area of roughly 28.000 m2, which until 2009 used to be divided into 19 "campi" (in the old numbering, which will be changed soon) with a total of 1508 tombs – of which all in Camp I have been removed between 2007 and 2009 - and 110 "colombaia." This part of the cemetery is well kept and it is here that tombs can be most easily located, as in 2003/2004 the Comitato Cimitero Italiano, having finished restoration of the cemetery, undertook the task to draw a list of all graves whose inscriptions could still be read. Many entries, in particular of the older "campi", are marked "ignoto", "insicura presenza" or "erboso" and are not listed below. The term "Itlaian" is however misleading: while originally an exclusively Italian cemetery, in the course of time also Catholic citizens of many other nationalities were buried here.

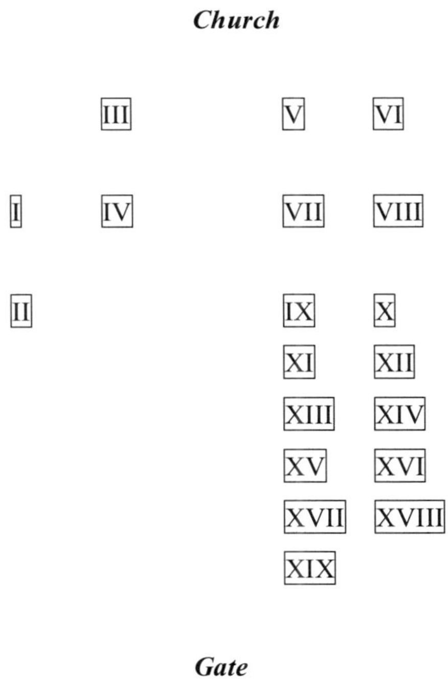

Distribution of the 19 "campi" (old numbering) of the "European" Catholic Cemetery

The Ethiopian Catholic Cemetery is rapidly expanding at the expense of the older parts of the Catholic cemetery. Graves in this part have inscriptions in Amharic and thus practically impossible to read for foreigners; as all those buried in this part are Ethiopian nationals, they are not included in this article. As "campo I" has already been vacated of existing tombs and been handed over to the Ethiopian Catholic Church, and as "campo VI" is soon sharing the same fate, the need to construct an "ossario" will arise soon. Construction costs are estimated at 400.000 ETB. Mr Checchin would happily accept contributions.

"European" Catholic Cemetery (Italian Sector)

View of the Catholic Cemetery

Campo N. I

tombs: 417, all removed in 2007-2009, names that can be read: 151

No. 11 PILOTTO Antonia	* 22 VI 1940	+ 13 VII 1940	child
No. 12 POLITI Maria Grazia	* 23 VII 1940	+ 25 VII 1940	child
No. 16 MIGLIO Margherita	* 11 II 1940	+ 22 IX 1940	child
No. 22 PUGI Roberto	* 24 VI 1939	+ 29 VIII 1940	child
No. 25 FINELLI Carmine	* 26 VIII 1940	+ 27 VIII 1940	child
No. 27 MONTAGNI Silvio	* 7 IV 1940	+ 12 VIII 1940	child
No. 35 MACHIN Franzi	* 31 X 1940	+ 1 XI 1940	child
No. 40 CINQUE Eva	* 3 VI 1940	+ 27 XI 1940	child
No. 42 Angioletta	* 16 VIII 1940	+ 13 XII 1940	child
No. 46 LIBERTINO Gianfranco Maria	* 31 VII 1940	+ 12 II 1941	child
No. 48 STELLA Roberta	* 5 X 1940	+ 2 II 1941	child
No. 50 ROVITO Annamaria	* 17 IV 1940	+ 5 II 1941	child
No. 67 ZAFAME Silvia Mercedes			
No. 68 RODA Lidia Elena	* 12 VI 1939	+ 22 III 1941	child
No. 72 DE MEGISTRIS Annamaria	* 11 XI 1938	+ 16 II 1941	child
No. 73 ZAMBOLO Giuseppe	* 15 V 1925 Gottolegno	+ 11 IV 1940 Ficce AOI	
No. 76 SARTORI Giulio	* 16 I 1912	+ 17 V 1940 Blue Nile	
No. 80 TRUSSADRI Andrea	* 5 IX 1890	+ 8 IX 1940	
No. 84 BACICHETTI Mario	* 13 IX 1913	+ 4 VII 1940	
No. 86 CHIOSTERGI Aldo	* 10 X 1895	+ 14 X 1940	
No.111 CAPANNOLI Natale	* 24XII1889 MassaM.	+ 4 II 1941 Addis Ababa	
No.117 TRAPLETTI Bepi	* 11 X 1920 Casazza	+ 3 III 1941 Addis Ababa	
No.134 MALNATI Bruno			
No.143 CONTI Maria in Politi	* 10 X 19104 Firenze	+ 14 VI 1941 Addis Ababa	
No.147 PAFETTI Aristodemo	* 1873 Orbetello	+ 28 II 1941 Addis Ababa	
No.149 FOCACCIA Teresa	* 4 XII 1961	+ 8 XII 1961	child
No. 150 LEGGIA Adriana	* 22 VII 1960	+ 19 VII 1961	child

No.151 DIANO Rita	* 22 V 1961	+ 30 VI 1961	child
No.152 STAENDER Bernhard	* 6 IV 1961	+ 8 IV 1961	child
No.155 ESPOSITO Giorgio	* 25 I 1960	+ 3 II 1961	child
No.156 D'ALESSANDRO Rossana	* 25 I 1961	+ 9 IX 1961	child
No.157 DE LUIGI Ulvia	* 28 III 1962	+ 24 II 1963	child
No.161 D'AMICO Giancarlo	* 16VII1954DireDawa	+ 3 III 1960 Addis Ababa	
No.162 PORRO Vittorio	* 20 XI 1960	+ 10 II 1961	child
No.163 PORRO Antonetta	* 15 XII 1959	+ 21 II 1960	child
No.164 SGARBI Dorina Maria	* 22 X 1959	+ 9 XI 1959	child
No.165 LA MANTIA Patrizia Elvira	* 4 IV 1963	+ 26 X 1963	child
No.166 ORSINI Paola	* 25 VIII 1963	+ 25 VIII 1963	child
No.167 OLIVIERO Graziella		+ 4 IV 1962	
No.168 BENVENUTI Paola		+ 30 X 1959	
No.170 DI FABIO Gabriele	* 28 XII 1957	+ 27 VII 1959	child
No.171 VIEL Roberto		+ 31 V 1959	
No.172 FRATTA Ima	* 2 IV 1957	+ 27 III 1959	child
No.173 ROSAZZA Maria	* 9 IX 1957	+ 27 III 1959	child
No.178 ZANUSSI Bernardo Rienzo	* 14 III 1959	+ 29 IV 1959	child
No.179 RICCI Rita	* 22 VIII 1958	+ 25 VIII 1958	child
No.180 ZAMPOGNA Franco	* 18 VI 1958	+ 21 VI 1958	child
No.182 GRASSI Giulio	* 30 XII 1957	+ 30 XII 1957	child
No.183 FRANZONI Vittorio	* 13 X 1963	+ 29 X 1963	child
No.184 COMMIJS Anna Dorien	* 6 VIII 1963	+ 21 VIII 1963	child
No.188 PADUA Andrea	* 23 XII 1939	+ 18 III 1941	child
No.189 LARENZA Aldo	* 30 VII 1941	+ 23 V 1942	child
No.190 LOVATI Vittoria	* 23 III 1940	+ 18 V 1941	child
No.193 RASTRELLO Viviana	* 4 X 1940	+ 6 IX 1941	child
No.196 GOTTI Pietro	* 16 II 1947	+ 22 VIII 1955	
No.199 IACOVELLI Domenico	* 22 IV 1962	+ 25 IV 1962	child
No.200 BELLISTRI Caterina	* 29 VIII 1963	+ 1 III 1964	child
No.203 ROSINI Riccardo	* 27 I 1964	+ 14 IV 1964	child

No.205 BRICHIERI-COLOMBI Roberta		+ 10 V 1965	
No.206 RECH Marina Antonia	* 28 III 1965	+ 12 IV 1965	child
No.209 BELLISTRI Pietro Paolo	* 29 VI 1965 Addis Ababa	+ 8 I 1966 Addis A.	child
No.210 REYNOSO Leonardo	* 4 X 1965	+ 6 X 1965	child
No.212 AMARA Luciana		+ 21 II 1967	
No.213 PISANO Rosanna	* 1 X 1964	+ 18 II 1966	child
No.214 ALBA Leggio	* 21 X 1967	+ 19 XI 1967	child
No.216 SACCONI Fausta	* 5 VIII 1968	+ 10 VIII 1968	child
No.221 KAY Suttora		+ 3 IV 1941	
No.228 RICERGATO Anna Maria			
No.229 FAVA Liliana	* 13 VII 1940	+ 21 IV 1941	child
No.230 FAVA Franca	* 24 V 1941	+ 24 V 1941	child
No.231 FAVA Luciana	* 6 XI 1943	+ 7 XI 1943	child
No.236 VALSECCHI Giuliana	* 13 V 1941	+ 13 V 1941	child
No.241 SCIORILLI Lugio Romano	* 26 XII 1940	+ 19 V 1941	child
No.248 QUARTO Erminia			
No.250 VITELLI Mariella	* 2 VI 1941	+ 2 VI 1941	child
No.251 CALCAGNI Paolo	* 16 VI 1941	+ 16 VI 1941	child
No.252 CAFAGNA Raffaele	* 11 II 1941	+ 28 VIII 1941	child
No.258 FURNARI Silvia	* 12 VII 1941	+ 16 VII 1941	child
No.261 FORNERO Teresa	* 24 VIII 1941	+ 24 VII 1941	child
No.262 FERRARI Gianluca	* 1 III 1941	+ 28 VIII 1941	child
No.271BISESTI Francesco			
No.277 VENTURELLU Giovanni	* 22 VIII 1941	+ 3 IX 1941	child
No.288 VIANELLO Lucera	* 28 VI 1940	+ 6 II 1942	child
No.289 STRAPAZZON Renata	* 9 I 1941	+ 2 II 1942	child
No.290 MANNI Silvana	*28 XII 1941	+ 16 I 1942	child
No.293 Giulia	* 21 II 1941	+ 14 I 1942	child
No.295 LANZIELLO Pia Consolata	* 23 XII 1941 Addis Ababa	+9 I 1942 Addis Ababa	child
No.296 LANZIELLO Oreste Giuis	* 4 VI 1938 Viareggio	+ 24 I 1942 Addis Ababa	
No.298 ROSSAMA Moschino			

No.299 CASERTA Amadeo	* 23 VII 1943	+ 30 XII 1943	child
No.305 GIUGLIOTTI Maria Luisa	* 3 VI 1942	+ 3 VI 1942	child
No.306 NEGRO Francesca	* 17 IX 1940	+ 28 IV 1942	child
No.309 CONTE Mamo Paolo	*16 XII 1943	+ 1 VI 1944	child
No.311 BARBIERI Giovanni	* 29 X 1945	+ 29 III 1946	child
No.313 FINNI Viola	* 29 III 1945	+ 6 XII 1945	child
No.314 FURLANE Luciana	* 15 X 1943 Massawa	+ 29 IX 1945 Addis Ababa	
No.325 ANFOSSO Nino	* 3 X 1947	+ 22 XII 1948	child
No.327 MONALDI Gigi	* 14 VII 1948	+ 1 VIII 1948	child
No.329 PATANE Sarina	* 29 VIII 1945	+ I 1947	child
No.330 BRASACCHIO Vittorio	* 30 VII 1943	+ 7 VII 1945	child
No.331 TESTA Gianfranco	* 20 XI 1946	+ 2 XII 1946	child
No.334 LACATENA Tonino	* 28 IV 1959	+ 5 V 1959	child
No.335 LACATENA Tonino	* 12 XI 1956	+ 12 XII 1956	child
No.336 MARTINELLI Rosa	* 1 IX 1956	+ 29 VIII 1958	child
No.337 MINIACI Carmelo	* 2 1 1954	+ 12 VII 1955	child
No.339 DABBOUS Alexander	* 23 VII 1950	+ 2 III 1951	child
No.340 CIASOTTO Luisa	* 21 IX 1950	+ 22 XI 1950	child
No.343 MAIOLI Livia	* 23 XI 1948	+ 27 III 1948 ?	child
No.344 PISCOPO Maria	*12 XI 1948	+ 20 XI 1948	child
No.345 DUTTO Anna Maria	* 4 IX 1948	+ 4 IX 1948	child
No.346 MONTI Giovannina	* 1 IV 1947	+ 16 VI 1948	child
No.347 MONTI Liliana	* 2 XI 1949	+ 4 VII 1950	child
No.348 TOSATO Carlo Antonio	* 7 IX 1946	+ 4 V 1958	child
No. 350 DI LEONE Mammo	* 4 VI 1947	+ 8 VIII 1947	child
No.351 MARGAGLIO Enrichetta	* 14 IX 1948	+ 28 IX 1948	child
No.352 MARGAGLIO Rosina	* 22 IX 1947	+ 4 XI 1947	child
No.353 DI MATTEO Valeria	* 18 IV 1955	+ 9 IX 1957	child
No.356 GALLILINI Renato	* 10 VI 1961	+ 1 I 1962	child
No.357 LUCOTTI Felice	* 28 X 1945	+ 16 II 1952	
No.358 STRAIOTTO Pietro			

No.361 MIGLIETTA Carlo	* 21 X 1947	+ 24 XI 1949	child
No.362 DE FRANCO Giuseppe		+ 5 IV 1949	
No.363 VENEZIANI Maria	* 1 I 1947	+ 1 IV 1949	child
No.364 SALVO Vincenzo	* 25 II 1947	+ 25 XI 1948	child
No.365 AMENDOLAGINE Rossana	* 25 VII 1948	+ 28 VIII 1948	child
No.366 BELLI Renza	* 21 III 1948	+ 18 V 1948	child
No.368 BETTONI Maria Agostina			
No.369 VIGLIOTTA Iolanda	* 2 VII 1947	+ 15 XII 1947	child
No.370 MEDICI Ferdinando			
No.371 MASTROPASQUA Rina	* 1902 Corato	+ 1940 Addis Ababa	
No.373 ANDORLINI Anna	* 1933	+ 10 VI 1940	
No.374 PULVIRENTI Salvatore	* 1 I 1 1881 Fiume Freddo Sic.	+ 2 VIII 1940 Addis Ababa	
No.381 PAURI Ettore	* 8 VIII 1880 Ancona	+ 27 XII 1940 Addis Ababa	
No.385 SABADINI Nadia	* 1 X 1957	+ 2 X 1957	child
No.386 LOMBARDO Serafina	* 1 IV 1956	+ 15 VIII 1956	child
No.388 RICCI Domenico	* 23 IV 1955	+ 25 IV 1955	child
No.394 CRESCIMBENI Carolina	* 11 XI 1953	+ 11 XI 1953	child
No.399 VENEZIANI Rosa		+ 1954	
No.400 PORRO Antonio	* 31 X 1952	+ 11 II 1953	child
No.402 GALLO Nini Franco	* 1940	+ 20 X 1941	child
No.403 CONTINI Giancarlo	* 23 IV 1940	+ 1941	
No.404 PICCHIN Gabriel	* 3 VI 1941		
No.406 DE BERNARDI Pierluigi			
No.408 LAPORTA Francesco	* 6 II 1942	+ 6 II 1942	
No.410 MATTIELLO Albertina	* 4 III 1937	+ 4 XI 1937	child
No.411 MATTIELLO Luigi	* 2 III 1940	+ 5 III 1941	child
No.412 MATTIELLO Raffaella	* 31 VII 1941	+ 14 II 1942	child
No.413 Dida	* 11 XI 1939	+ 3 III 1942	child
No.414 TAGLIENTE Antonietta	* 19 VII 1940	+ 2 V 1942	child
No.415 TALDERIGI Bianca Maria	* 5 V 1945	+ 28 IV 1946	child
No.417 KOSZEGI Gyula	* 14 VII 1908 Szuletett	+ 29 VIII 1948 Megahalt	

Campo N. II

tombs: 142, many unidentified or overgrown, names that can be read: 79

No. 1 MAUTTINI Elena	* 5 VII 1898 AlbanoLaziale	+24XII 1941 AddisAbaba
No. 2 PUGNO Corrina		+ 21 II 1942
No. 3 PUGNO Danila	* 21 IX 1911 Verona	+ 15 I 1942 Addis Ababa
No. 5 CAPONERI Nello	* 7 X 1911 Citta delle Pieve	+ 4 I 1942
No. 6 BUCALOSSI Adescar	* 25 XII 1912 Certaldo	+ 14 I 1942 Addis Ababa
No. 7 MONTANARI Paolo	* 23 VII1894 Scandiano	+ 24 I 1942 Addis Ababa
No. 8 UGONINO Luigi[50]	* 9 I 1899	+ 27 I 1942
No. 9 BROWN Genevieve Marie		
Emilie née LE PLAY	* 1904	+ 1975
No. 11 SENI Dott. Pietro		
No. 12 DE PERSIS Costanza	* 5 X 1927 TorriceFrosinone	+ 28 II 1942
No. 14 PECCHIARI Bruno	* 1886 Milano	+ 1942 Addis Ababa
No. 15 CERNY Olga	* 27 IV 1919	+ 2 III 1943
No. 16 MAGGI Ing. Ulderico		
No. 17 FRANCHETTI Salvatore	* 25 XII 1906	+ 10 XI 1943
No. 18 FOGHINI Arturo	* 27 III 1909	+ 2 XII 1943
No. 20 TAROZZI Augusto	* 16 I 1913	+ 9 III 1944
No. 21 PAVANELLO Dott. Ugo		+ 4 VIII 1945
No. 22 CANTARELLA Mario	* 1911	+ 1945
No. 25 FOSCHIA Pietro	* 1909 Ragogna, Udine	+ 1949 Addis Ababa
No. 26 MONTALBANO Domenico		
No. 28 ROSSI Pompilio	* 1902 Perugia	+ 1949 Addis Ababa
No. 30 RUSSO Gaetano	* 17 III 1911 Augusta	+ 16VII1950AddisAbaba
No. 31 ADRIANI Vittoria	* 3 III 1941	+ 10 II 1946
No. 32 ROLLE Mario	* 9 VI 1899 Bella	+ 7 VI 1946 AddisAbaba

[50] Worker at the Addis Ababa "Lancia" branch.

No. 33 PELLIN Pietro	* 5 X 1900 Seren del Grappa	+11 X 1946 Addis Ababa
No. 35 GNARGINI Enrico	* 3 VIII 1899 Chianciano	+ 7 V 1947 Addis Ababa
No. 36 NICOLITTI Serafino	* 26 XII 1910	+ 14 V 1947
No. 37 BARAFANI Emilio	* 6 V 1912 Umberti de Perugia	+ 9 VII 1947
No. 38 TESSARI Giovanni		
No. 39 MOCOR Antonio	* 16 II 1911	+ 20 III 1948
No. 40 MAROZZI Nicola	* 16 IV 1906	+ 27 IV 1948
No. 41 LEZUO Fridolino	* 1 IV 1915 Colle Santa Lucia	+ 14 XII 1948
No. 43 LUMINATO Pero	* 7 X 1913 Cagliari	+30VIII1949AddisAbaba
No. 44 ROCCA Antonio	* 21 VIII 1908 Ramponio,Como	+ 22 IX1949AddisAbaba
No. 45 CATTELAN Giuseppe	23 V 1909 Vicenza	+ 1 I 1950 Addis Ababa
No. 48 BETTI Luigi	* 12 XI 1908 Basel, CH	+22XII1947AddisAbaba
No. 49 TRANOUILLI Tommy	* 1907 Italia	+ 23 III 1948AddisAbaba
No. 50 IURIA Vincenzo	* 10 VII 1926	+ 28 V 1980
No. 51 IURIA Giuseppe	* 19 III 1891	+ 1 I 1948
No. 52 IURIA Luisa	* 1929	+ 22 II 1997
No. 53 IURIA Caterina	* 27 IV 1924	+ 28 XII 1988
No. 56 SAN FELICE Angela in Riva	* 11 X 1888	+ 16 VII 1975
No. 57 MANGANO Rosolino	* 1911 Palermo	+ 5 I 1949 Addis Ababa
No. 58 CUGINE Alide	* 1907	+ 14 I 1949 Addis Ababa
No. 59 ALBERTINI Alfredo	* 3 IX 1905 Genova Sestri	+ 16 VI 1949AddisAbaba
No. 60 RIVA Adriana	* 30 V 1941 Asmara	+ 13 VII 1949 Dire Dawa
No. 61 RIVA Cav. Alessio	* 17 VII1874 Cavaglia,Verc.	+ 3 XI 1959 AddisAbaba
No. 63 ALTONGI Emil	* 14 XI 1920 Cairo	+ 14 II 1950AddisAbaba
No. 64 DECIMO Ing. Decimo	* 27 IX 1894	+ 8 III 1950
No. 66 CARMINELLO Pietro	* 24 X 1902 Cheren, Eritrea	+ 21IX1951AddisAbaba
No. 71 ZAPPA Mario	* 22 VIII 1918	+ 28 IV 1945
No. 72 CIPOLETTI Mariano		
No. 78 DI GLERIA Filippo	* 1897	+ 1946

No. 79 GAUDIOS Gerardo	* 7 II 1913 Culliano, Sicily	+27 VII 1946 Addis Ababa
No. 80 ROMANI Fioravante	* 8 VIII 1902	+ 23 I 1947 Addis Ababa
No. 81 LUPIERI Battista	* 15 VI 1910	+ 2 IV 1964
No. 83 RIVA Guglielmo	* 28 IV 1910 Asmara	+ 10 XI 1973 Addis Ababa
No. 84 SCHETTINO Ciro	* 24 III 1899	+ 28 V 1951
No. 87 TANDA Gianni in Olivieri	* 24 VI 1906 Bastia	+ 8 VII 1942 Addis Ababa
No. 88 LICHELLI Pierina	* 28 VI 1914	+ 23 VI 1942
No. 92 BERGA Sebastiano	* 10 IX 1908	+ 3 III 1942
No. 93 KLOKINIS Jeannot	* 14 III 1938 Addis Ababa	+ 25 III 1946
No. 94 CUCCO Michele	* 1901	+ 11 III 1942
No. 97 TOLARDO Giovanni	* 7 XI 1926	+ 18 III 1942
No.101 PEZZOLLA Egidio	* 5 XI 1915	+ 19 VII 1951
No.102 MARCIANO Loris	* 2 II 1909	+ 19 XI 1951
No.103 MOSONI Vittorio	* 15 III 1912 Bognanco Ossola	+ 31 XII 1951
No.106 CHIAESE Enrico	* 23 II 1899	+ 29 IV 1942
No.109 PRONE Michele	* 1906	+ 31 I 1942
No.117 RIVA Natalina		
No.119 GALLINO Giacomo	* 2 XI ?	+ 9 VI 1954
No.120 GALLINO Margherita		
No.121 CAMELI Pietro	* 11 IX 1909 Ascoli Piceno	+ 28 II 1952 Addis Ababa
No. 123 DAL MONTE Angelo		+ 13 IV 1952
No.126 MOGNO Achille		
No.131 MINARDI Mario	* 1904	+ 12 XII 1941
No.133 PICCIANTI Francesco	* 31 VIII 1874 Livorno	+ 12 II 1941 Addis Ababa
No.141 TOSCANO Michele	* 23 I 1911 Stigliano Matera	+ 6 II 1952 Addis Ababa

Campo N. III

tombs: 127, many unidentified or overgrown, names that can be read: 31

No. 1 BERTONE Angela in Curato	* 2 X 1910	+ 18 VIII 1959
No. 2 MARTINI Paolo	* 24 III 1914	+ 7 IX 1939
No. 6 PANZIRONI Mariano		
No. 7 CONSTANTE Raimondi		
No. 8 ONERI Eugenia Ferrari	* 9 V 1910 Cremona	+ 19 IX1939AddisAbaba
No. 10 ELORIMO Vittorio	* 11 XI 1908	+ 26 XI 1939
No. 13 VERONESI Pier Domenico	* 14 II 1940	+ 1 VIII 1941 child
No. 15 ORIGLIA Giovanni	* 1 VII 1916	+ 4 V 1964
No. 17 FABBRI Fernanda Biagini		+ 16 III 1940
No. 25 BONETTI Giusippina	* 3 II 1899	+ 30 IX 1939
No. 29 BONENTI Virginio	* 22 III 1910 Bondo	+ 20 X 1939 Trento
No. 30 FORNI Lino	* 1900 Golese, Parma	+ 28 X 1959AddisAbaba
No. 40 CATTANI Adriano	* 10 VII 1892 Modena	+ 1 IX 1939
No. 45 FARCOMENI Giovanni	* 1902	+ 1939
No. 46 DALLA CHIUSA Tommaso	* 11 VI 1893	+ 30 VIII 1939
No. 57 VANZEN Italo	* 1911	+ 1939
No. 65 CAPRARA Aldo	* 1892	+ 14 XII 1939
No. 84 GRANDI Remolo	* 25 III 1932	+ 8 I 1940
No. 86 LA MOIA Vittoria		+ 3 III 1940
No. 87 MARCHI Walter	* 26 X 1910	+ 3 III 1940
No. 88 CALOCERO Baldacchino	* 1898	+ 1940
No.108 VISCONTI Enza	* 23 I 1922	+ 9 V 1940
No.109 FAGHERAZZI Giovanni	* 23 VII 1906	+ 14 IV 1940
No.112 DI BELLA Renato	* 15 VI 1933	+ 3 V 1940
No. 117 CASADIO MONTANARI	* 1902	+ 20 VIII 1937 Armando
No. 119 GHIDINI Pericle	* 1903	+ 26 VII 1939

No.120 CUZZOLA Maria in Bruno	* 11 VII 1910	+ 9 III 1940
No. 123 DE LIETO Ing. Vollaro		
No.124 GIULIO Com. Tony		+ 2 IV 1940
No.125 BINACCI Pietro Paolo	* 11 XI 1909	+ 22 III 1940
No.127 RIZZATI Rina in Bartolucci	* 23 XI 1908	+ 18 I 1940

Campo N. IV

tombs: 64, names that can be read: 58

No. 2 MONARI Linda in Tedeschi	* 8 III 1906 Mantova	+ 27 V 1941 AddisAbaba
No. 3 CARVILIO Conte Massimo	* 17 II 1882 Roma	+ 4VIII1941AddisAbaba
No. 4 SPALAZZI Mario	* 25 III 1913 Roma	+ 28 II 1997AddisAbaba
No. 5 GALIMBERTI Ottavio	* 11 VI 1906 Urbino	+ 20 I 1997 Addis Ababa
No. 6 VECCHIA Carolina Gabresi	* 14 XI 1914	+ 8 X 1996
No. 7 LUCENTE Vincenzo	* 5 I 1912 Sora	+ 15IX1996AddisAbaba
No. 8 FORD Mignon Lorraine Innis	* 19 XI 1905 Barbados W.I.	+ 15 I 1995 AddisAbaba
No. 9 BRAVO Antonio	* 12 I 1913 SanVito/Tagliam.	+13 IX1941 AddisAbaba
No. 10 SAMBO Domenico	* 22 X 1892 Venezia	+ 3 IX 1941 AddisAbaba
No. 11 OPPENDISAMO Paola	* 23 IX 1887	
No. 14 BARDAZZA Mario	* 1881	+ 1941
No. 15 MALTESE Vincenzo	* 16 VII 1920 Venezia	+ 17VII1997AddisAbaba
No. 16 DEL GAUDIO Milena	* 22 VI 1971 AddisAbaba	+ 2 XII 1999 USA
No. 17 DEL GAUDIO Antonio	* 26 VII 1943AddisAbaba	+ 9 II 2000 Berlin
No. 18 TIRELLA Anna	* 9 III 1922 Keren,Eritrea	+15 III2000AddisAbaba
No. 21 MANTOVANI Romeo	* 4 I 1900	+ 7 V 1941
No. 22 CIPRIANI Giuseppe	* 23 X 1906 Prato	+ 15 VIII 1991
No. 23 CIPRIANI Guido	* 23 XI 1904 Prato	+ 17III1992AddisAbaba
No. 24 GABRESI Ugo	* 17 IV 1942	+ 21 V 1998
No. 25 VENDITTO Ing. Amadeo	* 13 VIII 1910 Cusano Mutri	+ 30 I 1998AddisAbaba
No. 26 SONSOLE Sebastiano	* 7 III 1912 Putignano, Bari	+ 16 II 1996AddisAbaba

No. 27 FABBRI Fulvia in KHATCHADOURIAN	* 6 IV 1964	+ 16VI1995AddisAbaba
No. 28 FABBRI Dino	* 16 III 1913 Italia	+ 8 V 1995 Ethiopia
No. 29 CAMPARA Secondo	* 15 II1910Ventimiglia	+ 27 I 1995 Addis Ababa
No. 30 SOLIGNO Cav, Uff. Michele	* 1 V 1915 Cheren, Eritrea	+ 11 I 1995AddisAbaba
No. 31 CORBEZZOLO Arturo	* 31 I 1914 Ascea	+ 7 XII 1994AddisAbaba
No. 32 MUSSO Giuseppe	* 9 X 1910 Carru	+ 29 XI 1993
No. 33 LONINI Enrico	* 15 V 1913 Spezia	+ 17IX1993AddisAbaba
owner of Café – Paticceria "Enrico" in General Wingate Street		
No. 34 PROTA Giovanni	* 1900	+ 1982
No. 35 PROTA Maria	* 1902	+ 1993
No. 36 BAF in SCOPEL Onelia	* 10 X 1913 Johannesburg	+ 19 VI 1992 Roma
No. 37 TONIOL O Bruno	* 28 II 1911 Bocon, PA	+ 8 III 1992AddisAbaba
No. 38 CUSTURERI Cav. Demetrio	* 20 VIII 1911 Reggio Calabria	+ 22 I 1992AddisAbaba
No. 39 DESIDERI Nino	* 8 VIII 1917	+ 2 I 1992
No. 40 GALLOTTI Carlo	* 24 VII 1882	+ 18 IX 1941
No. 41 FACCO Sergio		+ 5 VIII 1950
No. 42 SETTI Vinicio	* 7 X 1945 Addis Ababa	+ 12 VI 1987 Addis Ababa
No. 43 BERTILLI Sandrina	* 23 VIII 1914 Asmara	+ 8 V 1987 Addis Ababa
No. 44 REGALLI Angiolino	* 5 X 1902 Sillavengo	+ 17 II 1987 Addis Ababa
No. 45 CORRA Giorgio	* 1949	+ 1986
No. 46 FORNASARI Maria Spalazzi	* 21 XI 1912 Bondeno	+ 21XIII 1986AddisAbaba
No. 47 FORNASINI Armando	* 2 VII 1912 Venezia	+ 18 XI 1986 Addis Ababa
No. 48 CARDINI Alfredo	* 9 XII 1907 Carnaioro LU	+ 16 XI 1986 Addis Ababa
No. 49 FIUME Armando	* 25 XII 1914 Napoli	+ 2 IX 1986 Addis Ababa
No. 50 MEREU Cav. Antonio	* 1911	+ 1986
No. 51 BRACCA Francesco	* 7 IX 1904 Villapiana/Cos.	+ 22 X 1941 Addis Ababa
No. 52 AGA Imilda	* 12 II 1938	+ 17 V 1995
No. 53 GALIMBERTI Cav. Zaccaria	* 29 II 1908	+ 17 VI 1986
No. 54 FAVIA Stefania	* AA 31 X 1948	+ AA 27 II 1990

No. 55 PERUCCI Nino	* 21 XI 1927	+ 17 IX 1940
No. 57 PRESCIUTTI Virgilio	* 9 VI 1869	+ 27 XI 1941
No. 58 PRESCIUTTI Martina Bolli	* 11 XI 1872	+ 13 XI 1945
No. 59 CERFEO Nicola	* 1894	+ 1965
No. 60 SALVIATO Lorenzo		
No. 61 ACHILLE Trani Angelo	* 1911	+ 2 VI 1981
No. 62 DESIDERI Attilio	* 23 V 1997 Aquila	+ 11 XI 1941
No. 63 PICCARDO Antonio	* 1904	+ 1986
No. 64 SANGES Luigi	* 11 VI 1944	+ 7 V 1986 Kinshasa

Campo N. V

tombs: 182, names that can be read: 161

No. 1 BONACORSI Anna	* 1875	+ 1939
No. 2 MADRE Maria Balduina	* 1900	+ 12 IX 1940
No. 3 GREMO Carlo	* 7 VII 1909	+ 15 XII 1962
No. 4 BOVA Francesco	* 9 X 1904 Bivongi, Calabria	+ 16 VII 1963
owner of "Coin-Box"; Bar-Alimentaire		
No. 6 RIBONI Andrea	* 1905	+ 1962
No. 7 RAMPI Oddone	* 23 XII 1911	+ 13 VIII 1973
No. 8 ROCCA Cesare	* 1910	+ 1962
No. 9 RUOZI Angelo	* 15 X 1907 S. Lazzaro, Parma	+ 5 I 1964 Addis Ababa
No. 10 TIBERTI Giovanni	* 1907	+ 1964
No. 11 TOSI Cesare	* 1911	+ 1968
No. 12 ALTAVILLA Cav. Luigi	* 16 III 1898	+ 27 III 1963
No. 13 TESSARDI Giuseppe	* 1911 Trento	+ 1963 Bardar
No. 14 BATONI Pacifico	* 10 XI 1897	+ 4 XII 1962
No. 15 GUGLIELMINOTTI Bianco B.	* 1917	+ 1954
No. 16 CHIARANTANO Marcello	* 18 V 1910	+ 6 X 1953
No. 17 ROUCEK Frantisek Univ.Prof.		+ 29 XII 1952

Rektor Vysokeho Uceni Prazskeho Zemrel (Chancellor of Prague Highest Learning Institution) N 09° 03.404' E 038° 42.895'

No. 18 OVIGLIO Tito Cav. Prof. Arch.	* 1897	+ 1953
No. 19 ACHKAR Edouardo	* 10 III 1908	+ 2 I 1956
No. 20 ARCHKAR Marguerite	* 25 IV 1912	+ 29 VI 1999
No. 21 ROZIK Vitezlav J.	* 25 XII 1895 Bzova	+ Addis Ababa 9 V 1955

Tomb of Czechoslovak colonel Vitezslav Rosik

No. 22 ZERBINATI Giuseppe		
No. 23 DI MAIO Angelo in Scarra	* 6 II 1888	+ 1 V 1951 Addis Ababa
No. 24 SCIARRA Carlo Belviso	* 4 11 1898	+ 6 II 1956 Addis Ababa
No. 25 BALDONI Edelnord	* 18VII1909 Pergola, Pesaro	+ 2 II 1953 Addis Ababa
No. 26 TONI Mario	* 12IX1896 Monfestino Mod.	+ 8 IV 1954 Addis Ababa
No. 27 TOSTI Remo	* 29XI 1905 San Terenziano	+ 17 III 1954 Addis Ababa
No. 28 MARINO Mario Latterio	* 1 XII 1899	+ 23 IX 1961
No. 29 VUINOVICH Mario		+ 1961
No. 31 VENEZIANO Giovanni	* 24 III 1908 Scigli Ragusa	+ 24 XII 1961

No. 32 IAMUNDO Salvatore	* 26 VII 1912	+ 18 XI 1976
No. 33 BRUSADIN Valentino	* 28 VI 1908	+ 19 VII 1976
No. 34 FRANCHI Giovanni		
No. 36 ROCCHI Ing. Adolfo	* 1881	+ 1956
No. 37 ROSSI Leonardo	* 1905	+ 1956
No. 38 ZAPPI Adolfo	* 1914	+ 1956
No. 39 ROMAGNOLO Abramo		+ 30 XII 1955
No. 40 CALLINI Giuseppe	* 1903	+ 1955
No. 41 BASSI Augusto	* 25 VIII 1915	+ 13 V 1955
No. 42 RIZZO Francesco	* 1891	+ 155
No. 43 BASSA Ernesto	* 1904	+ 1955
No. 44 DELISI Derardino	* 1903	+ 1904 *no longerexisting*
No. 45 SCIELZO Tomas	* 4 I 1910	+ 30 VII 1976
No. 46 PAROLI Paul	* 11 VII 1892 Brescia	+ 18 VII 1976 Addis Ababa
No. 47 DE PASCALE Armando	* 27 VIII 1910	+ 16 VI 1964
No. 48 PERCARIO Giorgio	* 17 XI 1944	+ 12 XII 1964
No. 49 SINICCO Giuseppe	* 1896	+ 1952
No. 50 SALVO Ignazio		
No. 51 SESSA Erdole		
No. 52 BIANCHI Ettore	* 1892	+ 1953
No. 53 ATLENI Pietro		+ 3 VIII 1953
No. 54 BERNINI Silvio		+ 23 VIII 1953
No. 55 MANSUETO Raffaele		
No. 56 PERSEGHIAN Paul	* 1937	+ 1953
No. 57 BARTALINI Yeshi	* 1928	+ 24 VI 1977
No. 58 OLIVATO Dario	* 3 XI 1910	+ 3 V 1976
No. 59 BARTALINI Mario	* 28 XI 1911	+ 27 IV 1976
No. 60 BONNANO Corrado	* 6 IX 1901	+ 5 VII 1964
No. 61 MOSCA Com. Francesco	* 14 XI 1914	+ 16 VI 1964
No. 62 TEALDI Antonio	* 1904	+ 1955

No. 63 BOGIA Bagio	* 1909	+ 1954
No. 64 ROSATO Giuseppe		+ 9 VIII 1954
No. 65 CILIANI Pietro	* 1913	+ 1954
No. 66 VENEZIA Domenico Mario	* 1898 Torino	+ 1954
No. 67 NASIR Yosep Dott.		+ 6 V 1954
No. 68 MULLONI Piero	* 1909	+ 1954
No. 69 GUALLO Giuseppe	* 1897	+ 1954
No. 70 SANGES Ludovico	* 1 XI 1893	+ 1 VIII 1964
No. 71 BAZELE Luigi	* 1911	+ 1977
No. 72 GARUGLIERI Giuseppe	* 1 I 1906 Greve in Chianti, FI	+ 25 IV 1976 Addis Ababa
No. 73 CRUSTINA Ditto	* 6 XII 1950	+ 13 III 1976
No. 74 VITO Giuseppe	* 15 III 1902 Portici Napoli	+ 11 III 1976 Addis Ababa
No. 75 PECOL Eugenio	* 1910	+ 1976
No. 76 CARIOTTI Balilla	* 14 IV 1914 Offida	+ 5 II 1976 Nazareth/Adama
No. 77 LINARDATOS Elena	* 22 I 1922	+ 22 VIII 1999
No. 78 TAGLIANETTI Mariano	* 14 VIII 1899	+ 26 I 1976
No. 79 PRIMO Giorgi	* 27 V 1909 Bari	+ 6 XII 1975 Addis Ababa
No. 80 TESTORE Caterina	* 10 IV 1923 Cheren/Eritrea	+ 24 XI 1975 Addis Ababa
No. 81 POZZI Aurelio	* 14 I 1906	+ 10 VIII 1975
No. 82 DIANO Francesco	* 16 VI 1909 Siderno, Reg.C.	+ 24 XII 1975 Addis Ababa
No. 83 DI FRANCESCO Pasqualino	* 12 I 1908	+ 20 VII 1975
No. 84 MONTENERO Annibale	* 20 I 1911	+ 25 VIII 1975
No. 86 AGNESSI Giuseppe	* 13 VII 1915	+ 22 V 1976
No. 87 PAPI Mario	* 31 I 1907 Livorno	+ 12 VII 1964 Dire Dawa
No. 88 PATELLI Angelo	* 21 III 1913	+ 16 IX 1977
No. 89 BATTESTINI Augusto	* 13 I 1914	+ 21 IV 1975
No. 90 RICCI Edoardo	* 13 X 1910 Asmara	+ 20 III 1975 Addis Ababa
No. 91 FERRI Basilo	* 5 III 1911 Savigno, Bologna	+ 10 I 1977 Addis Ababa
No. 92 DANGELO Francesco	* 10 XI 1904	+ 1 XI 1974
No. 93 SANTO Conte	* 30 I 1907 Maglie di Lecce	+ 1 VIII 1975 Addis Ababa
No. 94 DE SANTIOS Orlando	* 12 VII 1904	+ 24 XII 1974

No. 95 TOGGIA Stefano	* 10 VI 1910	+ 2 X 1974
No. 96 LONGO Tommaso	* 5 VI 1911	+ 17 IX 1974
No. 97 NAPOLI Diego	* 12 IX 1908 Canicatti	+ 12 IX 1974 Addis Ababa
No. 99 FIORINI Cesare	* 17 VII 1901	+ 26 V 1975

Addis Ababa – not Tyrol: wrought-iron tombstone of Koloman von Mattanovich

No.100MATTANOVICHKolomanv.	* 16V1899Temesvar/Hungary	+ 3 VII 1976 Addis Ababa
No.101 OBIT Giuseppe	* 19 V 1908	+ 28 IV 1975
No.103 FABRIS Albino	* 21 VIII 1913	+ 13 III 1975
No.104 BAIJOT Adolph	* 13 X 1912 Addis Ababa	+ 5 III 1975 Addis Ababa
No.105 SABA Antonio	* 11 I 1910 Postoia	+ 24 II 1975 Addis Ababa
No.106 DI LEO Germelo	* 24 IV 1904 Loganegro	+ 21 II 1975 Addis Ababa
No.107 FERRAMOLA Eugenio	* 3 VII 1899	+ 16 II 1975
No.108 ANTENORE Olivia	* 8 II 1912 Uswil, St.Gallen	+ 18 VIII 1974 Mojo
No.109 DAL CORSO Audino	* 6 II 1912	+ 26 XI 1975

No.110 STELLA Romeo	* 27 IX 1908	+ 25 IV 1974
No.111 CORBI Ernesto	* 7 XI 1934 Asmara	+ 13 III 1974 Addis Ababa
No.113 RICCI Franco	* 16 XI 1947	+ 25 V 1975
No.115 BRUSTENGHI Luigi	* 14 V 1909	+ 7 III 1975
No.117 FARINA Pietro	* 11 I 1941	+ 31 III 1974
No.119 SGROI Vincenzo	* 13 III 1911	+ 27 I 1974
No.120 OTT Romano	* 10 VI 1939 Roma	+ 6 I 1974 Shashamane
No.121 GATTI Libero	* 8 X 1907	+ 2 IX 1975
No.122 FIORENTINI Vittorio	* 1902	+ 1974
No.123 SCHILLER Rudolf M. Baron *advisor to the Ethiopian Ministry of Justice*	* 19 VII 1911	+ 21 XI 1973
No.126 STRAPPAZON Alessandro	* 22 VII 1892 Arsie, Feltre	+ 7 X 1973 Addis Ababa
No.128 DI STEFANO Raffaele	* 7 VI 1902	+ 13 V 1975
No.129 DI GREGORIO Anello	* 9 VIII 1902 Pescara	+ 2 VI 1986 Addis Ababa
No.130 VECCHI Leonello	* 1910	+ 1955
No.132 VOCHTA Josef	* 1898 Lanzhot	+ 1964 Jimma Czechoslovak
No.133 IMPERATI Ferdinando	* 27 IV 1912	+ 12 V 1986
No.134 BOLDRINI Andrea	* 15 VIII 1910	+ 2 VII 1963
No.136 PALMIERI Raffaele	* 3 XII 1901 Roscigno, Salerno	+ 3 I 1973 Addis Ababa
No.138 BONFANTI Antonio	* 11 IV 1926 Dibouti	+ 25 III 1973 Addis Ababa
No.139 MAMITE Sigona	* 24 IV 1905	+ 26 II 1973
No.140 GIANNECHINI Mebrate Deb.	* 17 IX 1930	+ 12 XII 1974
No.141 GIANNECHINI Carmelo	* 24 X 1911 Lucca	+ 5 II 1973
No.142 DE VITA Vincenzo	* 13 XII 1911	+ 31 XII 1972
No.143 HADZO PAULUS Giovannina	* 1906	+ 1972
No.144 VAN BILDEN Anille		+ 3 XI 1964
No.145 VALACHOS Andre	* 5 VIII 1949	+ 21 IV 1973
No.147 ORLANDI Domenico	* 22 VII 1907 Roma	+ 21 VIII 1973
No.148 MICARELLI Giovanni	* 27 XII 1905	+ 13 V 1975
No.149 PERRUCCIO Domenico	* 1907	+ 1978
No.150 MARAVIGLIA Alberto	* 1912	+ 1963

No.152 LUCCHIN Francesco	* 30 X 1904	+ 18 XII 1972
No.153 ZANNINI Rugero	* 1907	+ 1964
No.156 ROUSSOS Anna	* 3 V 1913 Suez	+ 19 VII 1972
No.157 MASENTI Dott. Aldo	* 20 VII 1905	+ 22 V 1972
No.158 NIGOGHOSSSIAN Kerope	* 5 V 1888 Brussa, Turkey	+ 20 IX 1950 Harar
No.159 NIGOSGHOSSIAN Pascalis	* 14 VII 1923	+ 18 II 1951 Harar
No.160 MENEGATI Alfredo	* 17 X 1890	+ 23 VIII 1964
No.161 ABI CHACRA Salim	* 1 VIII 1898 Deriel Kamar	+ 17 IV1972 Addis Ababa
No.162 LIU Mario	* 6 XII 1956	+ 21 VI 1971
No.163 Chinese citizen	* 5 I 1901	+ 20 VI 1984
No.164 AVERSA Giovanni	* 25 VI 1899 Roma	+ 20 IX 1964 Addis Ababa
No.165 LOEB in Sansone Ivonne	* 22 VII 1927	+ 10 IX 1964
No.166 VICCARO Francesco	* 27VII1906MilitelloCatania	+ 11 X 1962 Addis Ababa
No.167MACULANMariucciaAgiola	* 5 VI 1928 Bengasi, Libya	+ 8 XI 1952 Addis Ababa
No.168 MAZZONI Germino	* 16VIII1904CastelArquato	+ 6 VII 1975 Addis Ababa
No.169 LOVERING Donald Stiven		+ 1954
No.170 CAVALIERI Fermo	* 3 X 1905	+ 19 X 1976
No.171 ZUCCA Mario	* 1911	+ 1953
No.172 MACARIO Ing. Carlo	* 1898	+ 1962
No.173 MASCIOLI Alberto	* 18 II 1899	+ 18 V 1953
No.174 DABBOUS Helene	* 1910	+ 1962
No.175 REGGEB Elias	* 1893	+ 1962
No.176 PINTO Raffaele	* 16 VII 1911 Malfi	+ 22 IV 1962 Addis Ababa
No.178 DARETTO Ettore	* 13 VII 1908 Pasiano	+ 10 III 1976 Addis Ababa
No.179 CAPISI Giovanni	* 1 XI 1902 Italia	+ 11 IV 1976 Addis Ababa
No.180 COSTA Aurelio	* 26 V 1915 Mancanicci, Mess.	+ 27 VIII1962Nile Valley
No.181CALABRESEAmendolaElena	* 19 I 1914 Marzi Cosenza	+ 3 X 1962
No.182 LIU SIAO SAN Joseph	* 1 XII 1920	+ 3 XI 1985

Campo N. VI

tombs: 175, names that can be read: 158

No. 1 ANTONIETTI Giulio	* 1907	+ 1961
No. 2 SKOCZEK Dott. Kasimierz		
No. 5 DI PEDE Aldo	* 8 III 1908 Roma	+ 29 VI 1961 Addis Ababa
No. 6 ZAGO Francesco	* 13 IV 1908	+ 19 V 1960
No. 7 TARTARI Livio		+ 1963
No. 8 CONTAMESSA Dario	* 10 II 1911	+ 3 V 1961
No. 9 MILAZZO Mario		+ 1964
No. 10 SOLOMONI Maria v. Gerevini	* 17 V 1906 Castel Goffredo	+ 18 XII 1967 Addis Ababa
No. 11 GEREVINI Guido	* 9 VIII 1899 Castel Goffredo	+ 2 III 1969 Addis Ababa
No. 12 FUMAGALLI Fermo		+ 25 II 1981
No. 13 IORI Sigifredo	* 28 X 1909 Borzano, R.E.	+ 22 V 1981
No. 14 MURONI Mariangela in Iori	* 3 III 1907 Bonorva, Sassari	+ 22 III 1976
No. 15 CARNEVALE Vincenzo	* 7 V 1912 Sora	+ 16 VII 1981
No. 16 MICHELANGELI Giuseppe	* 5 IV 1907 Roma	+ 5 IV 1978 Addis Ababa
No. 17 MINNETI Salvatore	* 15 IX 1897	+ 30 IV 1978
No. 18 PINNA Giuseppe	* 25 IX 1913 Sardegna	+ 5 VII 1981 Awasa
No. 19 PIERINI Luigia Beatrice	* 18 III 1877 Brescia	+ 23 I 1961 Addis Ababa
No. 20 GARNERONE Pietro	* 30 I 1898 Firenze	+ 10 II 1961 Jimma
No. 21 BETTONI Ernesto	* 1904	+ 1977
No. 22 ZUCCHINI Alberto	* 30 IX 1911 Minerbio, Bol.	+ 26 V 1977 Addis Ababa
No. 23 LATINI Armando	* 14 II 1906	+ 10 IX 1977 Addis Ababa
No. 24 GABRINI Andrea	* 30 VIII 1911 Asmara	+ 12 VIII 1977 Addis Ababa
No. 25 RIGOLI Filippo	* 4 VII 1913	+ 6 VIII 1977
No. 26 BONSIGNORI Enrico	* 11 XII 1910 Pietra Santa	+ 16 XI 1977 Addis Ababa
No. 28 BUCK Edwin Solomon	* 12 III 1905	+ 1 VIII 1971
No. 29 RIETJE-DEGENAATS Looijen	* 12 X 1925	+ 22 VII 1969
No. 30 IAMELE Giuseppe	* 22 III 1913 Celenza Valfotore	+ 25 VIII 1969 Addis Ababa

No. 31 CORRADINI Celeste	* 11 X 1905 Dolle, Pr. Verona	+ 4 IX 1981 Addis Ababa
No. 33 ARENA Francesco	* 26 X 1908 Ferville, Tunisia	+ 5 X 1981 Addis Ababa
No. 34 MAFFI Mario	* 13 X 1940	+ 18 I 1982
No. 35 GARABEDIAN Maria	* 12 IX 1920	+ 18 11 1999
No. 36 ITANNI Giovanni		+ 5 II 1982
No. 37 SABADKA Jozef	* 18 II 1908 Slowewsko	+ 9 I 1961
No. 38 GIJSBERS Wilma Wijnanda	* 6 V 1957	+ 2 XII 1960 Wonji
No. 39 FINAZZI Ernesto	* 4 X 1908	+ 19 IV 1978
No. 40 DEL GAUDIO Mario	* 8 XII 1910 Calvano, Napoli	+ 21 I 1961 Addis Ababa
No. 41 SLAVIERO Francesco	* 1912	+ 1960
No. 42 PARODI Pietro	* 1987	+ 1960
No. 43 ANNONI Natale	* 1901	+ 1960
No. 44 PICCA Franco	* 1 I 1910 Palma Campania	+ 21 I 1978 Addis Ababa
No. 45 FORNO Vittorio	* 15 VI 1908 Montalso Scar.	+ 10 VIII 1960 Wongi
No. 46 PORTALUPI Alda in Preda	* 8 VIII 1908 Milano	+ 26 IX 1960 Addis Ababa
No. 47 BINUTTI Italico	* 1905	+ 1960
No. 48 DE GIER Werner	* 9 XII 1918 Gorkum	+ 27 XII 1967 Wongi[51]
No. 50 BERNARDONI Erminio	* 23 IV 1909 Stender, Illinois	+ 26 IV1982 Addis Ababa
No. 51 TEDESCHI Vittorio		+ 14 IV 1982
No. 52 GARIBALDI Aldo Aloatti	* 26 XII 1924	+ 8 III 1982
No. 53 LOMBARDO Giuseppe	* 6 IX 1915	+ 26 II 1982 Addis Ababa
No. 54 LANGIANO Ernesto	* 8 XI 1923	+ 26 II 1982 Addis Ababa
No. 55 TRUCCO Filippo	* 14 V 1910 Savigliano	+ 18 VI 1961 Addis Ababa
No. 56 HOMBERGEN Wim	* 7 X 1951	+ 4 IX 1960 Wonji
No. 57 RIGHETTI Supremo	* 11 V 1896	+ 25 VIII 1960
No. 58 MARCHI Vittorio	* 1925	+ 1960
No. 59 MASONI Emilio	* 1911	+ 1960

[51] De Gier, Hombergen and Lentjes Sabel most probably worked for the Wonji Sugar Estate, established in 1951 – after the loss of its plantations in Indonesia - by the Handelsvereeniging Amsterdam (HVA) on 5000 hectares near Wonji; see: Bahru ZEWDE, Environment and Capital: Notes for a History of the Wonji-Shoa Sugar Estate (1951-1974) in: Bahru ZEWDE, Society, State and History – Selected Essays, pp. 120-146, Addis Ababa 2008. Wilma Gijsbers was probably the daughter of a Dutch employee of HVA.

No. 60 VIDALE Ernesto	* 25 II 1897 Vicenza	+ 27 VI 1960 Addis Ababa
No. 61 DI STEFANO Giuliano	* 28 II 1911 S.Giuliano di Pug.	+ 24 VI 1960
No. 62 FARINA Umberto	* 14 III 1912	+ 28 IV 1960
No. 63 SANTI Angeli	* 24 III 1913	+ 16 IV 1960
No. 64 ARMELLIN Umberto	* 1906	+ 1960
No. 65 LENTJES SABEL M.H.P.	* 5 III 1927	+ 12 II 1967 Wonji
No. 66 FEDELE Lomatel	* 19 VII 1906 Sospirolo	+ 3 II 1983 Addis Ababa
No. 67 MEGGI Lodovico		+ 13 XI 1982
No. 68 ZIROTTI Oreste	+ 28 IX 1982 Addis Ababa	
No. 69 BARITE Carlo	* 27 VIII 1908	+ 6 IX 1982 Addis Ababa
No. 72 SZEMBERG Ludwig	* 22 XII 1895	+ 24 XI 1959
No. 73 DE FRANCO Salvatore	* 30 IV 1904 Pignano, Cosenza	+ 12 XII 1959 Addis Ababa
No. 74 BOTTI Aderito	* 1887	+ 1960
No. 75 BRICHIERO Giancarlo Colom.	* 28 III 1932	+ 17 XI 1959
No. 76 GAZZOTI Antero	* 1908	+ 1960
No. 77 ROSSETTI Luigi	* 1897 Ferrara	+ 1960 Addis Ababa
No. 78 HOFER Ettore	* 1892	+ 1960
No. 79 GERRATANA Antonio	* 1905	+ 1959
No. 80 OPPEDISANO Giulia	* 1909	+ 1959
No. 81 SOLIGNO Lorenzo	* 11 VIII 1951 Keren, Eritrea	+ 15 XI 1959 Addis Ababa
No. 82 GAVAZZA Giovanni	* 23 VIII 1897	+ 21 II 1965
No. 83 MORELLO Romano	* 14 VII 1912 Padova	+ 22 IX 1983 Addis Ababa
No. 84 SILVESTRI Ippolito	* 6 II 1905 Asmara	+ 6 IX 1983 Addis Ababa
No. 85 SERAVALLE Giovanni		+ 1 VIII 1983
No. 86 BOGLINO Dott. Giacomo	* 1899	+ 1983
No. 87 FERRERINI Bruno		+ 26 II 1983
No. 90 VALERI Giovanni	* 1905	+ 1959
No. 91 D'AVENIA Carmine	* 1900	+ 1959
No. 92 CARLUCCI Chiara	* 12 I 1904 Clemente	+ 3 VII 1959
No. 93 RINALDO Silva	* 1907	+ 1959
No. 94 BRACCONI Luigi	* 1902	+ 1959 Addis Ababa

No. 95 SETTI Giulio	* 27VII1897 FornovoTara, PA	+ 18 IV 1959 Addis Ababa
No. 96 ZURZOLO Agostino	* 1905	+ 1961
No. 98 SANTI Marino	* 5 VII 1910 Poggio Renat. FE	+ 20 III 1959AddisAbaba
No. 99 CLIFFORD van der STAAY Nancy	* 3 II 1935	+ 13 I 1965
No.101 DESIDERTO Gliorio	* 2 XII 1914	+ 2 II 1984
No.102 BACCHIELLI Dario	* 8 I 1917 Italia	+ 1 II 1984 Addis Ababa
No.103 IACCARINO Guglielmo	* 25 XI 1905 Sorrento	+ 9 VI 1975 Addis Ababa
No.104 IACCARINO Filomena	* 3 XI 1909 Sorrento	+ 19 XII 1983AddisAbaba

Tomb of South-Tyrolean Siegfried Molling

No.106 MOLLING Siegfried	* 13XI1913 *BressanoneBZ*	+ 1959 *Addis Ababa*
No. 107 SORDINA Vittorio	* 1911	+ 1959
No.108 BIANCONI Gino	* 1904	+ 1964
No.109 POLI Panteri Rina	* 21V1906 Corna d'Arfo Bres.	+ 4 XI 1959 Addis Ababa
No.110 SAITTA Giuseppe	* 1913	+ 1958
No.111 MASCIOLI Gaudenzio	* 1909	+ 1958
No.112 ZANNI Attilio	* 10VII1912 FortWilliam,Can.	+ 30 VI 1958
No.113 DE RONCHIS Zeno	* 12 XII 1904 Roma	+ 3 XII 1987 Addis Ababa
No.114 DE RONCHIS Giulia	* 1886 Roma	+ 1958

No.115 CAMIELLI Mariano		+ 21 IV 1958
No.116 RIZZOTI Amieto	* 1900	+ 1959
No.117 DI CANDIO Aronne	* 2 VIII 1910 Treviso	+ 2 I 1965 Addis Ababa
No.118 PROTA Giuseppina in KAYPAGHIAN	* 4 IX 1922 Asmara	+ 25 VIII 1984 Addis Ababa
No.119 MAZERY Jeanne	* 26 X 1906	+ 13 VIII 1984
No.120 GALETTI Meikle	* 1951 Asmara	+ X 1984
No.122 TAFFARA Vito	* 1903 Catania	+ 1984 Addis Ababa
No.124 DI STEFANO Roberto	* 26 III 1947	+ 25 II 1958
No.125 FRIZATTI Primo	* 1902	+ 1958
No.126 CALDERONE Giuseppe	* 24 III 1908 Leonforte Enna	+ 2 II 1958 Addis Ababa
No.127 FIASCHI Walter	* 1902	+ 1958
No.128 SIA?TRI Anna	* 1938	+ 1958
No.129 BLASI Mario	* 18 III 1904	+ 5 I 1958
No.130 RACZIEWICZ Ryta	* 9 XII 1891	+ 8 XII 1957
No.131 ROMBOLI Carlo	* 1893	+ 1957
No.132 BONFANTI Gino	* 1897	+ 1957
No.133 ISINGRINI Rodolfo	* 19 III 1905 Verbania	+ 16 VIII 1957 Addis Ababa
No.134 BELLINGERI Leonzio	* 18 III 1902	+ 31 XII 1964
No.136 DELPOZZO Giovanni	* 15 X 1906 Forino	+ 22 VII 1985 Addis Ababa
No.137 LEDDA Antonio	* 5 VII 1915	+ 15 V 1985
No.138 DE VITA Francesca	* 11 VI 1951	+ 25 III 1985
No.139 MARAZZI Geom. Carlo	* 1902	+ 1985
No.140 GUERRA Elio	* 2 IX 1910	+ 15 X 1984
No.141 PERUZZI Turiddo	* 1900 Siena	+ 1957 Addis Ababa
No.142 BIONDO Giuseppe	* 21 X 1911 Marsalla	+ 27 VII 1957 Addis Ababa
No.143 GAZZOTTI Secondo	* 1908	+ 1957
No.144 CANTONI Luigi	* 1884	+ 1957
No.145 GAIMANTONI Francesco	* 1909	+ 1957
No.146 SELLERI Adelmo	* 22 XI 1909 Caste Guelfo	+ 28 III 1957 Addis Ababa
No.147 BRICCOLI Arcangelo	* 1908	+ 1957
No.148 SKOCIR Antonio	* 21 XII 1910	+ 19 III 1957
No.149 DIMARIA Giuseppe	* 1904	+ 1957

No.150 MARANO Eduardo	* 1906	+ 1956
No.151 TAGLIAVIA Piero	* 15 III 1946	+ 31 XII 1964
No.152 GILARDI Pietro	* 18 V 1904 Alzano Lombardo	+ 9 VIII 1978 Addis Ababa
No.154 NARDELLI Mariano	* 28 V 1906 Methelhill, Scotl.	+ 26 X 1985 Addis Ababa
No.155 COMIGNANI Antonio	* 17 V 1913	+ 22 X 1985
No. 156 MASSO Ruggiero	* 1903	+ 1985
No. 157 MACCHINI Pietro	* 4 X 1909 Brome Lomellina	+ 19 VIII 1965
No.158 ERDEY Janos vitez		
No.159 CASTELLANO Antonio Felice	* 27 VII 1895 Torino	+ 9 XI 1956 Addis Ababa
No.160 GIORDANO Fironi	* 24 V 1914	+ 22 IX 1956
No.161 MARGAGLIO Vittorio	* 13 VIII 1893	+ 21 IX 1956
No.162 RANFIERI Edgardo	* 1901	+ 1956
No.163 GUALTIERI Barattieri	* 1910	+ 1956
No.164 FORGIONE Rocco	* 19 VII 1900	+ 21 VI 1956
No.165 SGARBI Enrico	* 22 XI 1911	+ 17 VI 1990 Addis Ababa
No.166 DORA Larenza in SGARBI	* 31 VIII 1906 Roliano	+ 20 VI 1956 Addis Ababa
No.167 TREVISAN Olivier	* 6 XIII 1897 Noventa Vicent.	+ 10 VI 1956 Addis Ababa
No.168 FERRERI Giuseppe	* 1904	+ 1956
No.169 ARENA Francesco	* 15 III 1912 Mattinata	+ 2 IX 1973 Addis Ababa
No.171 CHIAPPINI Ernesto	* 18 III 1892	+ 19 II 1965
No.172 MIOTTO Roberto	* 2 IX 1913	+ 2 VII 1978
No.173 GARGIANI Raffaelo	* 29 V 1915	+ 6 IX 1970
No.174 GRAZIOSI Enrico	* 1913	+ 1981
No.175 RIZZELLO Salvatore	* 28 V 1913 Spongano, Lecce	+ 19 XII 1985 Addis Ababa

Campo N. VII

tombs: 119, names that can be read: 112

No. 1 BUZZELLI Amico	* 1905	+ 1965
No. 2 MUSSI Mario	* 1911	+ 1965
No. 3 VECCHIA Agostino	* 24 VIII 1911	+ 12 XI 1989
No. 4 GABRESI Aurelio	* 8 II 1930	+ 23 III 1965
No. 5 GIACOMINI Umberto	* 1904	+ 1965

No. 6 BONIFATI Vincenzo	* 4 VI 1917 Castrovillari	+ 5XI1977Nazareth/Adama
No. 7 VALENTINI Luciano	* 27 VII 1945	+ 14 V 1965
No. 8 TESTA Rag. Corrado	* 19 XII 1898	+ 1 V 1965
No. 9 CONCATO Angelo		+ 1965
No. 10 MAZZARELLI Aldo	* 17 III 1917	+ 28 VI 1965 Addis Ababa
No. 11 QUADRI Umberto	* 4 III 1912 Bergamo	+ 3 VIII 1965 Addis Ababa
No. 12 GATTABIANI Gino	* 1899	+ 1965
No. 13 AVERSA Francesco	* 20 X 1901 Napoli	+ 10 IX 1966 Addis Ababa
No. 14 FANTINI Riccardo		+ 26 III 1967
No. 15 FUSCO Luigia	* 31 VII 1903 Roma	+ 21 II 1968 Addis Ababa
No. 16 FUSCO Alberto	* 28 XI 1903 Roma	+ 29 III 1974 Addis Ababa
No. 17 GIANNANTONI Enrico	* 23 X 1904	+ 29 XII 1968
No. 18 TASCA Francesco	* 29 V 1913	+ 25 IV 1971
No. 19 NARDIN Mario	* 23 II 1906	+ 1 XI 1965
No. 20 LOCHE Giuseppe		+ 11 IX 1966
No. 21 SARTINI Valentino	* 9 V 1896	+ 2 V 1967
No. 23 GROSSI Amadeo	* 19 III 1911	+ 1 I 1969
No. 24 BOTALLA Angelo	* 8 IX 1905	+ 5 IX 1969
No. 25 HOUDEK Vita J.	* 27 IX 1920	+ 20 XI 1965
No. 27 TROVATO Silvestro	* 31 VIII 1908 Troina, Catania	+ 19 V 1967 Addis Ababa
No. 28 STRINA SACCHI Giovanni		
No. 29 GIACINTI Emilia	* 23 I 1902	+ 5 I 1969
No. 30 CICORIA Paolo	* 8 III 1934 Asmara	+ 13 IX 1969 Addis Ababa
No. 33 MALAVASI Giulio	* 15 IX 1917	+ 1 VII 1980
No. 34 LA MONACA Galogero	* 3 V 1907	+ 13 IV 1968
No. 35 BALATTI Dante	* 15 X 1909	+ 30 I 1969
No. 36 FERRO Giuseppe	* 23 II 1912 Giarratana, Sirac.	+ 3 X 1969 Shashemene
No. 37 MASSA Alessandro	* 11 IV 1908	+ 31 XII 1965
No. 38 BACCHELLI Albano	* 2 V 1917 Mirandola	+ 28 X 1966 Addis Ababa
No. 39 DE FRANCO Antonio	* 28 II 1911 Dipignano	+ 2 VII 1967 Addis Ababa
No. 40 FRANCESCONE Facondo	* 23 VIII 1902	+ 29 XII 1967
No. 42 BARBIERI Siro	* 10 VI 1899	+ 14 X 1969
No. 43 PERANI Francesco	* 1908	+ 1966

No. 44 SCHIERANO Giovanni	* 15 I 1915 Moldes, Argentina	+ 27 IX 1966 Addis Ababa
No. 45 VENTURA Luigi	* 1912 Vada	+ 1967 Addis Ababa
No. 46 BIANCHI Dott.Ing.edile Arturo	* 27 I 1893 Padova	+ 12 V 1968 Addis Ababa
No. 47 CARDOSI Marino	* 8 VI 1913	+ 14 II 1969
No. 48 POLITI Luigi	* 5 III 1899	+ 26 X 1969
No. 49 TAZZIOLI Mario	* 1 V 1935	+ 17 I 1966
No. 50 PISANI Avv. Giovanni	* 3 I 1899	+ 6 V 1930
No. 51 TURCO Antonio	* 23 VII 1907 Paludi Cosenza	+ 1967 Addis Ababa
No. 52 BORNER Mario Paolo	* 13 XII 1918 Berman D	+ 19 V 1968 Addis Ababa
No. 53 IZZO Luigi	* 5 IV 1905 San Potito Sannitico, Caserta	+ 19 II 1969 Addis Ababa
No. 54 VITALI Rag. Plinio	* 19 VIII 1891 Lugano CH	+ 6 XI 1969 Addis Ababa
No. 55 LIU WAN TSENG John	* 1904	+ 3 I 1969
No. 56 MARONGIU Angelo	* 28 III 1907 Flunimaggiore Caliari	+ 9 XI 1966 Addis Ababa
No. 57 RAIMONDI Giovanni	* 26 IV 1904 Bondeno Ferrara	+ 22 II 1968 Addis Ababa
No. 58 PORTA Paolo	* 17 V 1894 Montmagno, Asti	+ 24 V 1968 Addis Ababa
No. 59 SCIARRA Mauro	* 21 VI 1929	+ 3 III 1969
No. 60 LUVANO Salvatore	* 14 VIII 1912 Mussomeli Caltanissetta	+ 7 XI 1969 Addis Ababa
No. 61 BALESTRI Silvio	* 2 V 1904 Rimini	+ 22 II 1966 Butajira road
No. 62 TOSCANO Maria in LA MONACA	* 12 X 1911 Castel Vetrano	+ 18 XI 1966 Addis Ababa
No. 63 DE RUGGIERO March. Ant.	* 14 I 1902 Napoli	+ 23 XI 1967 Addis Ababa
No. 64 D'ALESSANDRO Domenico	* 15 IV 1902 Pratola Peligna L'Aquila	+ 1 VII 1968 Dancalia
No. 65 TORRONI Amadeo	* 14 IV 1910 Paciano Perugia	+ 10 III 1969 Addis Ababa
No. 66 CONVENTINI Vincenzo	* 9 VIII 1912 Martina Franca Taranto	+ 27 XI 1969 Addis Ababa
No. 67 XOMPERO Antonio		+ 21 III 1966
No. 68 CASPARI Mammarella		+ 26 XI 1966
No. 69 SALVETTI Lino	* 5 II 1920 Malonno (Brescia)	+ 1 XII 1967 Addis Ababa
No. 70 MARINI Marco	* 11 IV 1898 Care Vicenza	+ 13 VIII 1968 Neghelli Bor.

No. 71 ZUCCATO Attilio	* 11 IV 1915	+ 23 III 1969
No. 72 PASQUA Gaetano	* 6 VIII 1894 Austa, Siracusa	+ 30 XI 1969 Addis Ababa
No. 73 POGGIO Giovanni		+ 19 IV 1966
No. 74 BERTI Augusto	* 19 I 1906	+ 12 I 1967
No. 75 MARTIGNETTI Alfredo	* 9 IV 1914 Serino, Avellino	+ 8 XII 1967 Addis Ababa
No. 76 NAZEL Ghaleb	* 10 III 1897	+ 4 IX 1968
No. 77 CARELLI Giacomo	* 14 IV 1910 Villa D'Alme	+ 4 IV 1969 Addis Ababa
No. 78 PORRO Cav. Cesare	* 23 X 1912 Rogliano, Cosen.	+ 16 XII 1969 Addis Ababa
No. 79 LOTITO Egisto		+ 19 VI 1966
No. 80 SEGALLA Bartolo	* 9 V 1905 Vicenza	+ XII 1967 Addis Ababa
No. 81 DE ANGELI Romeo	* 7 I 1908 Sanguineto, Verona	+ 24 XII 1967 Addis Ababa
No. 82 GHALEB Khalil	* 20 V 1884	+ 11 VI 1962
No. 83 CARLUCCI Francesco	* 12 X 1905 Bari	+ 16 VI 1969 Awora Melcha
No. 84 FALESIEDI Fabio	* 14 IX 1906	+ 13 XII 1969
No. 85 SORAVIA Maria	* 2 IX 1911 Sappada	+ 7 VII 1966 Addis Ababa
No. 86 VENEZIA Concetto	* 8 XII 1904	+ 26 I 1967
No. 87 DIVICINO Umberto	* 3 II 1903 Napoli	+ 29 XII 1967 Addis Ababa
No. 88 MILANO Giuseppina	* 2 III 1904	+ 6 IX 1968
No. 89 MARCONI Giovanni	* 11 IX 1933	+ 17 VI 1969
No. 90 OTTONELLO Vincenzo	* 19 VII 1900	+ 24 XII 1969 Addis Ababa
No. 91 MELILLO Angelo Antonio	* 18 V 1910 Moliterno	+ 27 VII 1966 Addis Ababa
No. 92 GALLONI Guglielmo	* 1909 Milano	+ 1967 Addis Ababa
No. 93 CATALDO Gaetano	* 7 V 1904	+ 30 XII 1967
No. 94 MUNTUORI Nicola	* 2 VIII 1904	+ 5 X 1968
No. 95 TARISTANO Michelangelo	* 13 V 1906	+ 12 VII 1969
No. 96 BARRA Alfonso	* 7 X 1896	+ 29 XII 1969
No. 98 SPASIANANO Silvio	* 7 III 1908 Castellamare Di Stabia	+ 28 II 1967
No. 99 GIGLI Tito	* 11 III 1895 Celano, L'Aquila	+ 6 I 1968 Ambo
No.100 CANERO Pietro	* 7 XI 1908	+ 7 X 1968
No.101 PIETRANGIOLI Armando	* 9 X 1906 Deruta, Perugia	+ 21 VII 1969 Addis Ababa
No.102 DIONISIO Ernesto	* 26 VIII 1891 Enemonzo, Ud.	+ 11 I 1970 Addis Ababa
No.103 CONTI Ferdinando	* 1910	+ 1966

No.104 ROSSI Giuseppe	* 22 IV 1899	+ 18 III 1967
No.105 GRANDE Gaetano	* 1 I 1910	+ 11 I 1968
No.106 GROTTO Giovanni	* 30 VII 1897	+ 26 XI 1968
No.107 PIOVESAN Ugo	* 13 I 1895	+ 8 VIII 1969
No.108 DONDERI Giuseppe	* 25 V 1912 Ghevio Novara	+ 27 I 1970
No.109 DAL BO' Anna	* 1907	+ 1966
No.110 SOLITO Michele		+ 20 III 1967
No.111 RICCI Cesare	* 1909	+ 1970
No.112 BIANCHI Federico	* 19 IV 1910 Maiolo, Pesaro	+ 2 IV 1968 Asba Tafari
No.113 PECORA Luigi	* 30 VI 1898 Grumentonova Potenza	+ 6 XII 1969 AddisAbaba
No.114 PAVAN Umberto	* 11 VIII 1907	+ 8 XII 1968
No.115 SERPETRI Ottavio	* 8 VI 1914	+ 9 III 1971
No.116 SERPETRI Fabio	* 4 XI 1962	+ 8 III 1964
No.117 GERFEDA Giacomo	* 21 VIII 1903 Polsamo,Taran.	+ 31 I 1970 Addis Ababa
No.119 DA RUGNA Rachele	* 29 XIII 1902 L'Amon,Bell.	+ 17 II 1970 Addis Ababa

Campo N. VIII

tombs: 89, names that can be read: 59

No. 2 Stefano		
No. 4 POMPOSI Ubaldo	* 21 X 1911 Pistoia	+ 1 IV 1970 Addis Ababa
No. 5 PEPE Saveria	* 23 VII 1955 Addis Ababa	+ 5 VI 1970
No. 6 CONSTANTINI Alessandro	* 16 VI 1911 CivitaVecchia	+ 16 VII 1970 Addis Ababa
No. 7 FRANCIONI Ottavio		
No. 8 LOSI Ciro	* 9 VI 1904	+ 23 VIII 1970
No. 9 LOTTI Pietro	* 28 I 1911 Trofarello, Torino	+ 10 VIII 1970AddisAbaba
No. 10 ZERBINI Gilberto	* 7 IX 1890	+ 3 IX 1970
No. 14 CARLET Giovanni	* 9 VI 1964	+ 11 I 1971
No. 15 MASSA Paolo	* 13 IV 1967	+ 2 IV 1971
No. 17 SINGARELLA Claudio	* 26 VIII 1965 Addis Ababa	+ 11 VI 1971 Addis Ababa
No. 22 PENAZKOVA Klaudia	* 16 IV 1972	+ 12 XI 1972 Rhodisia
No. 24 PETRO Angelo Giovanni	* 4 VI 1970	+ 24 II 1982

No. 25 PIETRO Angelo	* 1921	+ 18 VI 2005
No. 28 ABLAH Atinyo	* 14 I 1975	+ 12 IV 1975 child
No. 29 ZANCHI Pasqaule	* 6 IV 1990	+ 6 IV 1990 child
No. 30 WAHU NJOROGE Elizabeth	* 26 I 1975	+ 29 X 1975 child
No. 32 HONORATI Alessandro	* 25 VIII 1969	+ 2 III 1979
No. 34 MANDRELLI Costantino	* 27 XI 1984	+ 17 XII 1984 child
No. 35 BIRUK Abiy	* 13 VIII 1986	+ 23 IX 1988
No. 36 SCUDERI Betelem Metasebia	* 12 V 1972	+ 13 I 2000
No. 42 STANISLAO Esposito	* 23 III 1908 Portici	+ 4 IX 1970 Addis Ababa
No. 43 GUELI Rocco	* 22 IV 1903	+ 14 IX 1970
No. 44 GUZZINI Aldo	* 14 VII 1913 Arezzo	+ 8 X 1970 Addis Ababa
No. 45 GRECO Rita	* 14 VII 1950 Asmara	+ 12 X 1970 Addis Ababa
No. 46 DONDI Alessandro	* 13 III 1898	+ 11 X 1970
No. 47 LAMBRUSCHI Mario	* 1 IX 1900	+ 22 X 1970
No. 48 COMMFERRARI Alfredo	* 9 I 1898 Roma	+ 28 XII 1970 Addis Ababa
No. 49 COMPARINI Ilario	* 10 IV 1909	+ 25 X 1970
No. 50 CAMAGGI Giuseppe	* 9 III 1910 Monghidoro, Bol.	+ 23 II 1971 Addis Ababa
No. 51 Ilio		+ 25 III 1979
No. 54 BASCHIERI Aldo	* 29 IX 1910	+ 3 VIII 1970
No. 55 DEIANO Daniele	* 1911 Sardegna	+ 1971 Addis Ababa
No. 56 DUTTO Bartolomoeo	* 1892	+ 1970
No. 57 GRAFFI Michele	* 18 V 1905	+ 11 VI 1971
No. 59 MANDRELLI Amilcare	* 3 IX 1903	+ 24 V 1971
No. 60 PANELLI Giovanni	* 28 IV 1912 Lucca	+ 18 VII 1971 Addis Ababa
No. 61 PAULICELLI Dott. Savino	* 23 IX 1884 Canosa di Puglie	+ 9 VI 1971 Addis Ababa
No. 62 GRECO Alfonso	* 9 VIII 1908 Altalilla Irpina Avellino	+ 29 XI 1971 Addis Ababa
No. 63 RIZZO Maria	* 5 X 1905 Asmara	+ 22 X 1973 Addis Ababa
No. 66 PEVERATTI Attos	* 10 VII 1903 Ferrara	+ 1 VII 1971 Addis Ababa
No. 67 ALBIZZAI Agatino	* 28 VII 1909	+ 2 II 1972
No. 68 HASARIAN in CHINAIA Maria Lvnig	* 12 IX 1927 Addis Ababa	+ 29 X 1971 Addis Ababa
No. 69 MIELE Luigi	* 9 XI 1919	+ 22 XII 1972

No. 70 BERGAMINO Anna		
No. 71 FRANZETTI Camillo	* 6 XI 1913 Varese	+ 24 I 1972 Addis Ababa
No. 72 FURGONE Antonio	* 10 VI 1911	+ 16 III 1972
No. 73 MARSELLI Alvaro	* 20 III 1915	+ 3 XI 1972
No. 74 CASTRINI Mario	* 20 VI 1914	+ 30 VIII 1972
No. 75 VINCENZO Maria	* 25 I 1909	+ 28 XI 1978
No. 78 MACOGGI Francesco	* 1895	+ 1972
No. 79 MORFIA Michele	* 13 VI 1906 Monreale	+ 16 III 1972 Addis Ababa
No. 80 BELLISTRI Francesco	* 24 VIII 1907	+ 5 XI 1972
No. 81 SATTA Marcello		+ 20 XI 1976
No. 82 GHERMANDI Mansueto*	3 IX 1913	+ 25 XI 1978
No. 83 ANTONETTI Alfredo	* 1909	+ 18 I 1979
No. 84 MARCIANO Matilde	* 12 II 1886	+ 27 I 1979
No. 86 DEFARVI Domenico	* 1919 Torino	+ 14 III 1979 Addis Ababa
No. 87 COMMERATA Angelo	* 25 XII 1937 Asmara	+ 23 III 1979 Addis Ababa

Campo N. IX

tombs: 22, names that can be read: 19

No. 3 HAMRUSCH Rodolfo	* 29 X 1911 Pola (Austria)	+ 27 VIII1979AddisAbaba
No. 4 LODI Ernesto	* 4 III 1913	+ 26 IX 1979
No. 5 SANGES Luigi	* 3 I 1923 Napoli	+ 13 IX 1979 Addis Ababa
No. 6 BIANCHI Lucrezia	* 4 V 1894 Poggiferro	+ 31 X 1979 Addis Ababa
No. 7 HARDY Arthur		+ 29 I 1932
No. 8 HARDY Yvonne		+ 30 IX 1954

owner of "Yvonne Hardy" shop in Ras Makonnen-street, importer of Parfums de Luxe, Chocolate, Silk, shoes, lingerie and other luxury items

No. 9 HARDY Jean Paul	* 14 V 1928	+ 19 XI 1979
No.10 HARDY Pierre	* 16 I 1920	+ 15 IX 1988
No.12 SPADONI Coraldino	* 27 XI 1912	+ 10 I 1980
No.13 BIANCHI Rosa	* 28 XI 1956	+ 20 I 1980
No.14 MANCINI Margherita in DIOTALLEVI	* 17 XII 1899 Gubbio	+ 8 II 1980 Addis Ababa

No.15 BARELLA Luciano		+ 6 III 1980
No.16 TETI Iolanda	* 14 VII 1943 Asmara	+ 4 IV 1980 Addis Ababa
No.17 RIVA Luigi	* 1 VII 1908 Asmara	+ 17 IV 1980 Addis Ababa
No.18 MIOTTO Armando	* 15 IX 1951	+ 19 IV 1980
No.19 PRASCA Giovanni Battista	* 13 VII 1924 Rivanolo Cav.	+ 18 IV 1980 Addis Ababa
No.20 COSENTINI Domenico	* 2 II 1896 Falerna	+ 19 V 1980 Addis Ababa
No.21 CASTELLARI Luigi	* 5 XII 1909 P. Recanati	+ 2 VI 1980 Addis Ababa
No.22 LA PIERRE Hector	* 14 II 1913	+ 10 VI 1980

Campo N.X

tombs: 15, names that can be read: 15

No. 1 GANDINI Giuseppina in FERRARESI	* 23 III 1940 Asmara	+ 14 VIII 1980Addis Ababa
No. 2 PANARELLO Filippo	* 30 V 1914 Vittoria	+ 28 VIII 1980Addis Ababa
No. 3 HADGO Magdalena Maria	* 10 VI 1925	+ 7 IX 1980
No. 4 ERMINATI Giuseppe	* 18 V 1906 Cheren, Eritrea	+ 11 IX 1980 Addis Ababa
No. 5 LAURINDO Serrano	* 29 VIII 1898	+ 15 IX 1980
No. 6 CANUTI Giovanni	* 8 X 1898	+ 27 IX 1980
No. 7 RAPISARDI Giuseppe	* 6 X 1933	+ 6 X 1980
No. 8 ZORZAN Luigi	* 13 VII 1913 Adria (Rovigo)	+ 31 X 1980 Addis Ababa
No. 9 BORSATTI Adolfo	* 23 X 1909 Bodeno Ferrara	+ 2 XI 1980 Addis Ababa
No.10 SERNESI Sergio	* 26 VII 1912 Zocca (MO)	+ 13 XII 1980 Addis Ababa
No.11 CARICATI Mario	* 1903	+ 22 XII 1980
No.12 FANTINI Giuseppe	* 1910	+ 1981
No.13 PAYR Franz	* 4 IV 1908 *Poitschachgraben*	+ 8 II 1981 Debre Zeit

Austrian from Carinthia; farmer in Harar and later in Bishoftu/Debre Zeyt; producer of strawberry champagne and purveyor to the court of Emperor Haile Selassie

No.14 COCONARI Aldo	* 1 XI 1911	+ 23 I 1986 Nazareth
No.15 WOLDETENSAY Wogayehu	* 1910	+ 1986

Campo N. XI

tombs: 19, names that can be read: 19

No. 1 VENTURINI Valeri	* 25 XI 1907 Vittorito	+ 23 XI 1987 Addis Ababa
No. 2 CARLINI Silvio	4 IV 1911 Citta di Castello Perugia	+ 6 V 1989 Addis Ababa
No. 3 PAGANI Oreste	* 9 XI 1912 Legnano	+ 19 IV 1989 Addis Ababa
No. 4 PAGLIARELLA Antonio	* 13 I 1914 Veroli	+ 5 II 1989
No. 5 RESCINITI Rocco	* 15 II 1914 Roscigno (Saler.)	+ 6 IV 1989 Addis Ababa
No. 6 ROSSI Tamara	* 18 VIII 1905 Russia	+ 2 IX 1988
No. 7 MARAZZANI Conte Giovanni	* 30 IV 1907	+ 16 VIII 1988
No. 8 BENAZZI Oliviero	* 28 VIII 1912	+ 29 VII 1988
No. 9 VALENTINI Geise	* 4 V 1903 Bevagna (Perugia)	+ 9 VIII 1988 Addis Ababa
No.10 WESTFALL Franca-Maria	* 2 IX 1938	+ 10 VII 1988
No.11 PALMOS Emilio		+ 4 VII 1988
No.12 CARGNELUTTI Guglielmo	* 12 III 1907	+ 4 VII 1988 Addis Ababa
No.13 VASSALLO Raffaele	* 10 XII 1913 Avellino	+ 29 IV 1988 Addis Ababa
No.14 MICHELA Lorenzo	* 14 XI 1954	+ 13 IV 1988
No.15 GIUFFRE Renato		+ 1988
No.16 OTTAVIANI Guglielmo	* 16 IV 1904 Monte San Giovanni Campo (Frosinone)	+ 25 II 1988 Addis Ababa
No.17 LISOTTI Salvatore	* 3 V 1915 Limbadi	+ 25 II 1988 Addis Ababa
No.18 CAPPONI Giovanni	* 3 IX 1897 San Felice Circeo	+ 18 I 1988 Bahir Dar
No.19 NOCE Salvatore	* 1912	+ 1987

Campo N. XII

tombs: 21, names that can be read: 20

No. 1 CAMMARANA Dott. Giovanni	* 1951 Addis Ababa	+ 1989 Addis Ababa
No. 2 BENIAMINO Stefano	* 19 II 1902 Pola	+ 21 VII 1989 Addis Ababa
No. 3 AZZURRO Agostino	* 15 X 1910 Telese (Benev.)	+ 9 VIII 1989

No. 4 PEDROTTI Giuseppe	* 12 VI 1914	+ 10 VIII 1989
No. 5 VERGINELLA Benedetto	* 24 VII 1911 Trieste	+ 21 VIII1989Addis Ababa
No. 6 CARPANELLI Giovanni	* 25 IV 1902 Venzone (Udine)	+ 26 IX 1989 Asella
No. 7 PIERUCCI Giuseppe	* 1 IX 1911 Napoli	+ 24 X 1989 Debre Zeyt
No. 8 LEGGIO Giovanni	* 1 I 1908	+ 8 XII 1989
No. 9 TAMBORRINI Mario	* 2 I 1906 Matino (Lecce)	+ 9 I 1990 Addis Ababa
No.10 MELETIS Violettis	* 27 IV 1927 Mekele	+ 3 II 1990 Addis Ababa
No.11 CHINAIA Giancarlo	* 21 III 1922	+ 4 II 1990
No.12 SGOLOMBIS Stamatia	* 24 XII 1914	+ 22 VI 1990
No.13 MANCUSO Ubaldo	* 20 IX 1917	+ 14 II 1990
No.14 MANSTRANGELO Nicola	* 19 IX 1914 Panni	+ 23 II 1990 Addis Ababa
No.15 ROCCO Cliberto	* 26 III 1914 Jacurso (CZ)	+ 3 IV 1990 Addis Ababa
No.16 GRISON Giorgio	* 20 XII 1959	+ 2 VII 1990
No.17 GRISON Ulderico	* 17 VI 1904 Trieste	+ 15 XI 1995 Addis Ababa
No.18 SPARTACO Bruna	* 6 XI 1904	+ 24 XII 1990 Addis Ababa
Gioilleria Svizzera (Swiss Jewelry), Optics, General de Gaulle Square		
No.20 Mascaro Cav. Salvatore	* 23 XII 1898	+ 28 II 1991
No.21 ARVANITO Poulos Mario	* 1932	+ 1990

Campo N. XIII

tombs: 21, names that can be read: 19

No. 1 LONGO Eugenio	* 21 XI 1907 Diamante	+ 10 IV 1995 Addis Ababa
No. 2 VANCINI Evaristo	* 20 VII 1906 Finale Emilia	+ 29 I 1995 Addis Ababa
No. 3 LINZITTO Salvatore	* 28 V 1909	+ 26 II 1995
No. 4 DE BENEDETTO Arduino	* 14 IV 1909 Toscana	+ 15 XII 1994
No. 5 CARGNELUTTI Giovanni	* 5 IV 1959	+ 26 XI 1994
No. 6 TESSEMA Temegne in CARGNEUTTI	* 18 VII 1943	+ 22 V 1995
No. 8 VERZI Giovanni	* 21 VI 1949 Addis Abab	+ 29 VIII 1994 Addis Ababa
No. 9 VIANELLI Beniamino	* 15 II 1938	+ 9 VI 1994 Addis Ababa
No.10 CAVALLI Giuseppe	* 16 VII 1938 Adigrat	+ 13 III 1994 Addis Ababa

No.11 ZATTA Luigi	* Padova	+ 3 V 1994
No.12 CRESCIMBENI Aurelio	* 23 IX 1912 Cingoli (Macerta – Marche)	+ 23 III 1994 Addis Ababa
No.13 CASTELLI Renato	* 8 V 1913 Lama Mocogno	+ 15 III 1994 Nazareth
No.14 SAZZINI Giovanni	* 14 VIII 1914 Asmara	+ 27 XII 1998 Addis Ababa
No.15 TUSTRIA Ing. Joseph	* XII 1903 Austria	+ 1 XI 1993 Addis Ababa
No.17 MAZZOLI Armando	* 16 XI 1911 Senigallia	+ 12 VII 1993 Addis Ababa
No.18 KASSA in MORANDI Maria	* 21 VIII 1921	+ 7 VI 1993
No.19 LOMBARDI Samerwit	* 24 V 1984	+ 19 I 1993 Addis Ababa
No.20 CIRIANI Guglielmo	* I 1913 Pinzano al Tagliam.	+ 10 I 1993
No.21 MALGARI Fabio	* 8 VII 1972	+ 6 I 1993

Campo N. XIV

tombs: 20, names that can be read: 19

No. 1 PERRET HABTEMARIAM Edouard	* 13 VIII 1919	+ 21 XII 1992

Architect, built i.a. Jubilee Palace and Clock Tower of Parliament, Mitchell Cotts Building and Moenco-Building.

No. 2 GRASSO Francesco	* 4 X 1907 Zafferana	+ 2 XII 1992 Addis Ababa
No. 3 FERRARESI Vittorio	* 6 IV 1970 Dire Dawa	+ 29 XI 1992 Hararghe
No. 4 LOMBARDO Paolino	* 9 IV 1912 Sutera	+ 17 XI 1992 Addis Ababa
No. 5 GROPPA Leonzito Luigi	* 7 IV 1909 Dornak (France)	+ 15 III 1992 Addis Ababa
No. 6 RESI Roberto	* 25 V 1915 Boudeno, Ferrara	+ 19 II 1992
No. 7 DI FABIO Amedeo	* 11 V 1911 Monteferrante (Chieti)	+ 15 XI 1991 Addis Ababa
No. 8 BOCCARANI Marino	* 6 IX 1901 Rubiera	+ 5 X 1991 Addis Ababa
No. 9 MOLENDI Francesco	* 25 XII 1907 Pescia Pistoia	+ 17 VIII 1991 Addis Ababa
No.10 ZIANTONA Angela in VECCHIA	* 25 X 1915 Asmara	+ 4 VIII 1991 Addis Ababa
No.11 MATTEI Mario	* 16 III 1915 Pietrasanta	+ 8 VII 1991 Addis Ababa
No.13 VALLE Armando	* 22 IX 1943 Asmara	+ 22 VI 1991 Addis Ababa
No.14 GALLIAN Domenico	* 6 VIII 1914 Polesella	+ 6 VI 1991 Addis Ababa
No.15 DIVITO Rosaria in FRACASSO	* 4 XI 1909 Sulmona (Aquila)	+ 30 V 1991 Addis Ababa

No.16 PESSONIPIERO Mario	* 17 VII 1993 Massawa	+ 17 V 1991 Addis Ababa
No.17 DE VALERIO Luigi	* 10 X1913 Falla Scoso (CH)	+ 7 V 1991 Dire Dawa
No.18 GAETANO Marino	* 7 VI 1908 Cerignola (FG)	+ 1 V 1991 Addis Ababa
No.19 DALLORTO Enzo		+ 9 IV 1991
No.20 PASTACALDI Pietro	* 20 IX 1914 Harar	+ 3 III 1991 Addis Ababa

Campo N. XV

tombs: 16, names that can be read: 13

No. 1 BAREGI Gino	* 9 VII 1911	+ 29 IX 1999
No. 2 GRIO Vincenzo	* 2 VI 1946 Asmara	+ 6 VIII 1999 Addis Ababa
No. 3 SOGIU Antonio	* 27 X 1911	+ 8 VI 1999
No. 4 CHECCHIN Pietro	* 2 IV 1911 Spinea	+ 20 V 1999 Addis Ababa
No. 5 GIAQUINTO Giuseppe	* 20 VIII 1942 Asmara	+ 24 III 1999 Addis Ababa
No. 6 TOMBORRINI Lucia Vincenzo	* 29 XII 1943 Asmara	+ 16 II 1999 Addis Ababa
No. 8 BERNARDONI Giuseppe	* 5 XI 1932	+ 17 I 1999
owner of Bernardoni Delicatessen-supermarket		
No. 9 MELLONI Vincenzo		
No.10 MANNA Giuseppe	* 7 IV 1953 Asmara	+ 1 XI 1998 Addis Ababa
No.11 ROSSI Vittorio	* 17 IV 1950 Addis Ababa	+ 4 VII 1998
No.13 BUFALINI Mario	* 21 ? 1912	+ 20 ? 1998
No.14 LAMBRUSCHI Giovanni		+ 1998
No.16 SORDINA Rosa Maria	* 2 IV 1996 Addis Ababa	+ 25 IV 1997 Bergamo

Campo N. XVI

tombs: 21, names that can be read: 20

No. 1 CORSALINI Olinto	* 26 IV 1912 Santa Croce di Magliano C.B.	+ 8 II 1997 Addis Ababa
No. 2 MASSA Giovanni	* 5 I 1934 Massawa	+ 8 XI 1996 Addis Ababa
No. 3 DOMENICO Giovanni	* 10 X 1955 Senafe	+ 7 XI 1996

No. 4 SCIOLINI Aurelio	* 25 XI 1926 Asmara	+ 29 X 1996 Lodi
No. 5 DI STEFANO Romano	* 12 IX 1941 Asmara	+ 3 X 1996 Addis Ababa
No. 6 RICCI Romano	* 15 IV 1945 Bati	+ 23 IV 1996 Addis Ababa
No. 7 COLORITO Mima	* 22 II 1946	+ 10 IV 1996
No. 8 CAMINITO Valeria Riva	* 14 V 1964 Addis Ababa	+ 15 II 1996 Addis Ababa
No. 9 BALSAMO Rita	* 5 X 1949	+ 4 II 1996 Addis Ababa
No.10 TARTAGLIA Giulio Cesare	* 3 XII 1924 Livorno	+ 29 I 1996 Addis Ababa
No.11 DI NOIA Enrico	* 1925	+ 12 I 1996
No.12 DI PEDE Ugo	* 2 XII 1943 Woldia	+ 2 XI 1995 Addis Ababa
No.14 COSENTINO Aldo	* 19 X 1950 Addis Ababa	+ 5 X 1995 Addis Ababa
No.15 CIGANA Roberto Guido	* 2 X 1944 Hararghe	+ 17 XI 1987 Addis Ababa
No.16 CIGLIANI Michele	* 7 III 1946 Asmara	+ 22 VII 1995 Addis Ababa
No.17 SCARPINO Michele	* 11 XI 1912 Cosenza	+ 26 VI 1995 Addis Ababa
No.18 PANA Giovanni	* 14 XII 1932 Massawa	+ 17 VI 1995 Addis Ababa
No.19 CANNISTRA Antonio	* 10 XII 1942 Addis Ababa	+ 16 VI 1995 Addis Ababa
No.20 BENEDETTO Andrea	* 15 V 1912 Motto San Giovanni (RG)	+ 3 VI 1995 Addis Ababa
No.21 DECONI Daniele	* 13 I 1956 Dire Dawa	+ 18 VI 1996 Addis Ababa

Campo N. XVII

tombs: 18, names that can be read: 15

No. 1 DI LORENZO Peppino	* 1928	+ 18 IV 2006
No. 2 DURETTI Yota	* 1930	+ 8 V 2006
No. 3 PETRATOS John		
No. 4 TEGEGNE in ANGELINI	* Addis Ababa I XI 1934	+ 16 IX 2006
Tiruwork		
No. 5 MINI Marcello E. *money-lender*	* 29 IV 1923	+ 14 I 2007
No. 6 no inscription		
No. 7 BORIONI Davide	* 10 XII 1958	+ 15 IV 2007
No. 8 MEDICI Giorgio	* 18 XI 1942	+ 5.6.2007
No. 9 CARPACCI PACHIDOU Elena	* 5 V 1930	+ 12 VI 2007

No.10 BUCCI Carlo	* Addis Ababa 25 IX 1938	+ Addis Ababa 1 VIII 2007
No.11 no inscription		
No.12 no inscription		
No.13 NUNZIO Silvestri	* 1957	+ 29 XI 2007
No. 14 LORENZO Vincenzo di		
No.15 BERTILLI Raimundo *maker of Cacciamali-Busses*	* Asmara 28 XI 1947	+ Addis Ababa 6 III 2008
No.16 DOSIO Margarita	* 4 V 1943	+ 22 III 2008
No.17 TOCCI Yolanda	* 10 XI 1022	+ 25 III 2008
No.18 PASQUA Giuseppe	* Asmara 2 III 1932	+ 18 VI 2008

Campo N. XVIII

tombs: 17, names that can be read: 16

No. 1 CAPOGROSSO Arturo	* Dire Dawa 9 III 1947	+ 12 III 2006
No. 2 ROSSETTO Giuseppe *mechanic*	* Limena (PD) 5 III 1927	+ Addis Ababa 22 II 2006
No. 3 ULETAW COSTANTINI Elfinese Carla	* 4 XI 1926	+ 9 XII 2005
No. 4 RENATO PROTA Giovanni	* 19 I 1930	+ 22 XI 2005
No. 5 BASSANO Mario	* 15 VII 1943	+ 18 X 2005
No. 6 CAPOSACQUA Benito	* 1936	+ 6 X 2005
No. 7 SHAROVA Tatiana	* 12 I 1950	+ 5 VII 2005
No. 8 FOCACCIA Teresa	* 4 XII 1961	+ 8 XII 1961 child
DOMENICO Romeo	* 1937	+ 10 IV 2005
No. 9 PEREZ Pedro	* Palermo III 1912	+ Addis Ababa II 2005
No.10 ASTATKE Paolo	* Harar 10 X 1942	+ Addis Ababa 10 II 2005
No.11 DIXON Paul	* 21 II 1946	+ 17 I 2005
No.12 FOCACCIA Federico	* Cervia 13 II 1918	+ Addis Ababa 21 XII 2004
No.13 MORANO Angelo	* 1939	+ 12 III 2004
No.14 no inscription		
No.15 VALERIANI Giovanni Pado	* 17 VII 1946	+ 13 X 2004

No.16 CORRA Dr. Michele	* 22 IX 1945	+ 23 IX 2004
No.17 MENGESCIA in VERZI Atzde	* 16 VII 1926	+ ?

Campo N. XIX

tombs: 4, names that can be read: 3

No. 1 BORSATTI Carla	* 12 X 1939	+ 27 VII 2008
No. 2 Mamet GHEBRAB in CIRILLO	* Asmara 1927	+ 18 III 2009
No. 3 MORANDI Marco	* Schilpario 5 XI 1916	+ 2 V 2009

Colombaia I (24)

No. 1 VALENTINI Famiglia Luigia Maria Gianluigi

No. 2 TOMONIERI Annunziata	* 24 IV 1914	+ 23 VI 1978
No. 3 CAVALLERA Lorenzo *Missionario della Consolata*	* 22 XI 1921 Italia	+ 4 X 1973 Addis Ababa
No. 4 PECCHIDLI Silvio	* 10 IX 1900 Italia	+ 4 X 1973 Addis Ababa
No. 5 LACAMERA Bernardo		+ 23 VI 1974 Addis Ababa
No. 7 BATTISTI Felice	* 17 XII 1899 Roma	+ 22 V 1971 Addis Ababa
No. 8 BATTISTI Maria	* 3 VII 1903 Roma	+ 10 VII 1981 AddisAbaba
No. 9 PANI Domenico	* 1914	+ 1974
No.10 RIGOLI Filippo	* 4 VII 1913 S.Piero Pattime	+ 6 VIII 1967 Addis Ababa
No.11 FONDACCI Alfredo	* 10 V 1915 Gubbio	+ 3 II 1978 Addis Ababa
No.12 FERRARI Ca. Nicola	* 15 II 1885	+ 30 V 1972
No.13 REALE Elena	* 16 VIII 1933	+ 18 X 1970
No.14 NODARI Antonio	* 6 X 1908	+ 16 XI 1970
No.15 TIMONIERE Emanuele	* 8 V 1907 Comiso	+ 18 VI 1978 Addis Ababa
No.16 MARCHETTI Maria in MORGAVIO	* 28 VIII 1911 Vochera	+ 16 XII 1970 AddisAbaba
No.17 FAVIA Marcella	* 24 IX 1920 Asmara	+ 4 I 1971 Addis Ababa
No.18 LOMBARDI Nello	* 18 IX 1911 Ponte a Poppi Arezzo	+ 9 XI 1971
No.19 TARO Battista Giovanni	* 8 III 1882	+ 29 VI 1969

No.20 SALVI Lucia in NASSO	* 19 V 1942	+ 19 X 1978
No.21 PIASTRA Donatella	* 12 VII 1946	+ 5 V 1970
No.22 GIOSTRA Benite	* 11 XI 1885	+ 22 V 1970
No.23 RICCIO Angela in GIOSTRA	* 24 VIII 1888	+ 11 VII 1970
No.24 SARDINI Aldo	* 20 II 1908 Roma	+ 7 VIII 1970 Addis Ababa

Colombaia II A

Colombaia IIA (30)

No. 1 BRANCA Comm. Ing. Cesare	* 1901	+ 1987
No. 2 BRANCA Giuseppina	* 14 X 1908	+ 27 V 1985
No. 3 SANTILLI Ermanno	* 3 I 1910 Pescosansonesco	+ 10 VIII 1986 Addis Ababa
No. 4 SANTILLI Vittoria	* 27 XI 1918 Gravedona	+ 10 VIII 1984 Addis Ababa

No. 5 BRUSCHI Mario	* 31 III 1908 Piacenza	+ 10 X 1988 Ischia
No. 6 PERUZZI Bice	* 1901	+ 14 VIII 1980
No. 7 SOLIGO Gino	* 14 II 1910 Vedelago	+ 31 I 1978 Addis Ababa
No. 9 NUTI Ugo	* 1 V 1912	+ 7 X 1980
No.10 CAMAGGI Ter. in BELTRAMI	* 3 X 1942	+ 19 XI 1980
No.11 FARINA Angelo	* 21 V 1914 Cagliari	+ 30 IV 1977 Addis Ababa
No.13 GIAQUINTO Cav. Filippo	* 30 VI 1899	+ 23 VII 1977
No.14 PROTA Aniceto	* 1 IX 1927	+ 25 VII 1977
No.15 CASI Giovanni	* 5 VII 1912 Asmara	+ 17 X 1977 Addis Ababa
No.16 TEKLE Anna	* 1903	+ 1974
No.17 GRISENTI Cav. Albino	* 20 XI 1909 Baselga di Pine	+ 4 VI 1974 Addis Ababa
No.18 NEGRIN Roberto	* 5 XII 1946 Keren	+ 17 VI 1974 Padova
No.19 ROSSI Dante	* 23 VII 1911 Montefalcone Del Sanio Campobasso	+ 14 XI 1974 Addis Ababa
No.20 BELLATTI Attilio	* 24 IX 1903 Ferrara	+ 26 V 1974 Addis Ababa
No.21 NAZZARENO Petriccia	* 9 XI 1908 Sora	+ 23 XII 1971 Addis Ababa
No.22 MOI Mario	* 12 VII 1910	+ 28 I 1973
No.23 TIMONIERI Biagia	* 19 VIII 1913 Comiso	+ 14 II 1973 Addis Ababa
No.24 CROCIS Giovanni	* 4 III 1904 Asmara	+ 21 X 1973 Addis Ababa
No.25 PALECO Dante	* 23 VII 1907	+ 28 X 1973
No.26 CANTORI Padre Anastasio G. *Missionario Cappuccino di Bologna*	* 27 IX 1917 Cento	+ 19 XII 1971 Butagira
No.27 VITALE Giuseppe	* 1 I 1912 Modugno	+ 31 I 1972
No.28 DALLORTO Bernardo	* 2 VI 1906 Vezza D'Alba	+ 30 VI 1973 Addis Ababa
No.29 DALLORTO Tersilla	* 19 III 1908 Vezza D'Alba	+ 4 VII 1973 Addis Ababa
No.30 BAGNI Gino	* 19 IV 1903	+ 16 VII 1973

Colombaia IIB (15, mostly infants)

No. 1 JALOUX Beppe	* 1938	+ 1945
No. 2 VALLE Elisabetta	* 2 VIII 1973 Asmara	+ 23 I 1983 Addis Ababa
No. 3 LEGGIO Adriana	* 22 VII 1960	+ 19 VII 1961
No. 4 LEGGIO Alba	* 21 X 1967	+ 19 XI 1967

No. 5 DIANO Rita	* 22 V 1961	+ 30 VI 1961
No. 6 TESTA Gianfranco	* 20 XI 1946	+ 2 XII 1946
No. 7 de FRANCO Giuseppe	* 13 VI 1948	+ 25 IV 1949
No.8 CASERTA Amadeo	* 23 VII 1943	+ 30 XII 1943
No. 9 di FABIO Gabriele	* 26 XII 1957	+ 27 VII 1959
No.10 SACCONI Fausto	* 5 VIII 1968	+ 10 VIII 1968
No.11 ALBERTINI Alfredo	* 3 IX 1905 Genova Sestri	+ 16 VI 1949
No.12 RIVA Adriana	* 30 V 1941 Asmara	+ 13 VII 1949 Dire Daua
No.13 LOMBARDO Serafina	* 1 IV 1956	+ 15 VIII 1956
No.14 RIVA Ca. Alessio	* 17 VII 1884	+ 3 II 1959
No.15 SANFELICE in RIVA Angela	* 11 X 1888	+ 16 VII 1975

Colombaia IIC (31)

No. 1 DE PASQUALE Francesco	* 1914	+ 1986
No. 2 CONTE Pietro	* 1910	+ 1987
No. 3 FUMO Vittore (Pittore)	* 20 I 1907	+ 18 II 1986
No. 4 BELTRAMI Viliam	* 2 VIII 1926	+ 24 X 1997
No. 5 RADA Tibero	* 1914	+ 2000
No. 6 PICCOLO D.R.	* 1 X 1907 Cacuri (CZ)	+ 3 II 1982 Addis Ababa
No. 7 FIORANI Maria BELTRAMI	* 16 I 1901	+ 30 II 1982
BELTRAMI Erio		+ 10 XI 1957 Aden
No. 8 BELTRAMI Adelmo Cav.	* 9 IV 1897	+ 27 VII 1983
No. 9 SERVARA Giovanni	* 18 V 1941 Decamere	+ 10 IX 1983
No.10 LEGATO Giusepp. in FRATTA	* 1928	+ 1986
No.11 GUERRISI Rinaldo	* 21 V 1899 Tanova	+ 3 VII 1976
No.12 MOSCATELLI Giovanni	* 22 V 1911 Pontremoli	+ 4 VII 1976 Addis Ababa
No.13 PASSERA Carlo	* 25 XI 1907 Salso Maggiore Terme	+ 26 VII 1976
No.14 BERNARDINI Cav. Nello	* 22 I 1910 Aquila	+ 10 XII 1976 Addis Ababa
No.15 IGHZAU Anna Maria in PAGANI	* 26 VII 1927 Debre Marcos	+ 3 III 1977 Addis Ababa
No.16 FRENDA Francesco	* 28 X 1908 Port Said	+ 10 IX 1975 Addis Ababa

No.17 SERRA Dott. Pietro	* 19 VII 1899 Sarrasi Carrara	+ 27 VIII 1975 Addis Ababa
No.18 BIANCO Gaetano	* 17 I 1916	+ 11 VII 1975
No.19 CHECCHIN Ines	* 16 II 1920	+ 5 VIII 1975
No.20 PASI Enrico	* 12 III 191 Cairo	+ 25 VIII 1975 Addis Ababa
No.21 CONDOLUCI Michele	* 31 VIII 1911 Cinque Frondi, Reggio Calabria	+ 16 XI 1974 Addis Ababa
No.22 VENTO Francesco	* 1 I 1901	+ 18 XI 1974
No.23 MONTINI Maria	* 9 VIII 1910	+ 4 I 1975
No.24 MONTINI Guglielmo	* 27 I 1903	+ 22 II 1968
No.25 BAY Aldo	* 18 X 1914 Castel Varese	+ 1976 Addis Ababa
No.26 CELONA Angelina	* 4 IV 1908	+ 6 IV 1975
No.27 CAFAGNA Michele	* 25 V 1913 Barletta	+ 7 XI 1975 Addis Ababa
No.28 MILITA Giovanni	* 22 VII 1912 Catania Sicilia	+ 15 IX 1981
No.29 BRACINI Paolo	* 18 VII 1915 Perugia	+ 30 III 1976 Addis Ababa
No.30 DIERNA Antonio	* 13 VIII 1911	+ 19 V 1980

3.6. THE MILITARY CEMETERIES

3.6.1 IL CIMITERO MILITARE ITALIANO – THE ITALIAN MILITARY CEMETERY

Location: N 09° 03.423' E 038° 42.899'
Administered by:
Embassy of the Republic of Italy, Yeka Kifle Ketema – Kerbele 07, Addis Ababa, Tel. 00 251 11 1235717

The Italian Military Cemetery is administered by the Ministry of Defence of the Italian Republic and locally by the Defence Attaché of the Italian Embassy Addis Ababa. It was not possible to find the exact date the cemetery was established. As it is bordered by the New Armenian Cemetery and the Commonwealth War Graves Cemetery, a date around 1950 seems plausible.

The Cimitero Militare Italiano consists of 811 tombs of known persons, while 1662 unknown soldiers are buried there too. The cemetery is divided into 6 "riquardos" (quadrants) numbered 1 to 6; the riquardos 5 and 6 contain four mass-graves each. Within the riquardos tombs are arranged in rows A – I; within a row the graves follow alphabetical order. Riquardo1 contains a total of 196 graves, while 209 graves are in riquardo 2. Riquardo 3 has 186 tombs and the magnificent tomb of General Mariotti, riquardo 4 is made up of 172 tombs and the tomb of General Malta. On the left side there are additional tombs in sectors A to D. Sector A is made up of 51 tombs, sector B of a mass grave of 15, sector C of 51 and sector D of 60 tombs. Sectors A and C-D consist of 3 graves per row with, and sector B of a mass-grave of 15, adding up to a total of 177 burials.

The guardian of the cemetery will invite the visitor to sign a book with black cover bearing the coat of arms of the Italian Republic "Registro dei Visitatori del Cimitero Militare di Addis Ababa per firme ad eventuali annotazioni"; the present book begins in January 2006 and is a testimony to the fact that the military cemetery is not having many visitors. When checked in July 2008 there were, in 18 months barely, 5 pages of signatures and comments by visitors, obviously nearly all from Italy.

The cemetery is dominated by a cross, behind which a marble plaque with the following inscription refers to a yet to be researched massacre of Italians at Addis Alem, Holeta and Mount Managesha:

A PERENNE MEMORIA
DEI VALOROSI
DEL GRUPPO SQUADRONI CAVALIERI DI NEGHELLI
DEL 6 GRUPPO SQADRONI CAVALLERIA COLONIALE
DELLA POLIZIA AFRICA ITALIANA
DEL BATTAGLIONE MITRAGLIERI SCIOA
CADUTI
NEI COMBATTIMENTI DI ADDIS ALEM
TORRENTE BARGA HOLETTA MANNAGASCIA
2 – 7 APRILE 1941

A look at the dates of death on the graves reveals that in riquardo 1: 154 out of 196, in riquardo 2: 127 out of 209, in riquardo 3: 118 out of 186, and in riquardo 4: 14 out of 172 Italian soldiers, "blackshirts" and others died between 9 May 1936, when in Rome, from the balcony of the Palazzo di Venezia, Mussolini had proclaimed the "Impero", and 10 June 1940, when Italy entered World War II. In riquardo 4: 109 tombs out of 172 are marked "non identificato". Three graves in row G, numbers 18 to 20, are the last resting place of the crews of three Italian planes that crashed on 21 VI 1940, 11 VIII 1940 and 16 VIII 1940.

It is generally believed that during the period of General Graziani as Vice-Roy of Abyssinia (May 1936 – end of 1937) 20.000 Italians were killed; during war and occupation (October 1935 to May 1941) a total of 25.000 Italian military and civilian are assumed to have died. 17 South Tyroleans who much to their dislike had to fight for their new fatherland Italy found their death in "Africa Orientale Italiana." Two of these South Tyrolean soldiers are buried in riquardo 2: Johannes (Giovanni) Stanislaus Maria Ferdinand Ernst Antonius Romedius Count Thun - Hohenstein (* Vienna 22 XII 1913 + Monte Tight, AOI 23 VIII 1938), Second Lieutenant in the Cavalry Regiment "Vittorio Emanuele" (B-19).

The other is private Franz (Francesco) Kross of Sarnthein (+ 8 IX 1936, C-18). Nothen South Tyrolean is probably Josef (Giuseppe) Stoffner (+ 7 I 1938, G-18) in riquardo 3.

Generals Oreste Mariotti (* Rome 23 IX 1874 +Addis Ababa 2 II 1937) and Giuseppe Malta (* Pizzo di Calabria 6 II 1883 + Bonga, Ethiopia 30 V 1937) are buried in impressive sarcophagi-type tombs.

Tomb of Johannes Count Thun-Hohenstein

Tomb of Brigadier - General Giuseppe Malta

Abbreviations:

1 Av.	
1 Av Mot.	
1 Av. Marc.	
Alp.	Alpini
App. cc.	
Art.	
Att. Uff.	
Auto.	
Av. Sc.	
Av.Sc.Am.	
Bersagliere	

Camicia Nera		Black Shirt (Fascist)
Cap. Magg.	Caporale Maggiore	
Capo Sq.		Squadron Leader
Capo. Man.		
Capor.	Caporale	Corporal
Carab.	Carabinieri	
Colonello		Colonel
F. Ante		
Finanz.		
Gran.	Granatieri	Grenadier
Leg. Lavor.		
Mar. Ord.		
M.A.		
M.B.V.M.		
M.O.	Medaglie d'Oro	Gold Medal
M.O.V.M.	Medaglie d'Oro al Valore Militare	Gold Medal f. Military Valour
Magg.		Major
Marin.		
Militarizzato		
Op.	Operaio	Civil Worker
Op. Gen.		
S. Ten.	Sotto Tenente	Second Lieutenant
Sarg. Magg.	Sergeant Major	
Sold.	Soldato	Private
Ten. R.E. Oss.		
Ten. M.A.		
T. Col.	Tenente Colonello	Lieutenant – Colonel
Tenente	First Lieutenant	
Tenente Pil.	Pilot Lieutenant	
V. Brig.	Vice-Brigadiere	
Vice C.So.	Vice Capo Squadrone	Deputy Comp. Leader
V. Capo Sq.	Vice Capo Squadrone	Deputy Comp. Leader

Riquardo 1
7 rows A – F of 23 graves each (grave row A – 1 missing), rows H – I 18 graves each; total number of buried 196

Row A – 2	Soldato	ACQUISTAPACE Demetrio	5 VI 1940
Row A – 3	Op.	ADAMO Giuseppe	2 XII 1937
Row A – 4	Op.	AIDONE Salvatore	24 V 1937
Row A – 5	Cap. Magg.	ALBERIZZI Romeo	26 X 1939
Row A – 6	Cap. Magg.	ARNONE Fortunato	
Row A – 7	Cap. Sq.	ANASTASI Natale	21 VIII 1941
Row A – 8	Op.	ANGELO SANTE Cristoforo	17 IV 1938
Row A – 9	Op.	AUGUSTO Saverio	4 VIII 1937
Row A – 10	Soldato	ARLOTTA Giuseppe	3 II 1938
Row A – 11	Sarg. Magg.	AVOLIO Vincenz	5 VI 1940
Row A – 12	Soldato	AFFORTUNATO Liborio	3 X 1940
Row A – 13	Op.	BABINI Mario	1936
Row A – 14	V.Capo Sq.	BADARACCO Giuseppe	21 III 1939
Row A – 15	Soldato	BARDI Guerrando	2 V 1937
Row A – 16	Camicia Nera	BALESTROZZI Alfredo	11 X 1936
Row A – 17	Civile	BARBARA Mirella	22 V 1937
Row A – 18	Cap. Magg.	BAGNARIOL Giuseppe	14 XII 1938
Row A – 19	Gran.	BARCELLINI Natale	14 I 1937
Row A – 20	Op.	BARETTA Mario	18 VIII 1937
Row A – 21	Op.	BARONE Antoni	26 XI 1936
Row A – 22	Op.	BARONI Ugo	1936
Row A – 23	Soldato	BARISAN Marcell	19 II 1937
Row B – 1	Alp.	BASSO Gino	31 V 1939
Row B – 2	Civile	BOTTELINO Maddalena	5 IV 1937
Row B – 3	Op.	BEDOCCHI Ferdinando	30 XII 1937
Row B – 4	Tenente	BEGNA Franco	3 IX 1937
Row B – 5	Op.	BELLINI Leonardo	4 III 1939
Row B – 6	Cap. Magg.	BERGAMINI Giuseppe	I VI 1937
Row B – 7	Serg. M.O.	BIFFI Franco	17 II 1937

Row B – 8	Tenente	BIGOLA Ludovico	25 VIII 1940
Row B – 9	S. Tenente	BODO Giovanni	5 VIII 1941
Row B – 10	Op.	BOGNANNI Francesco	11 XI 1936
Row B – 11	Op.	BOINAGA Mario	25 X 1938
Row B – 12	Cap. Magg.	BOMBIERO August	22 VIII 1938
Row B – 13	Cap. Magg.	ACETO Renato	13 XII 1938
Row B – 14	Av. Sc.	BONGIOVANNI Antonio	24 IX 1938
Row B – 15	App. cc.	BONIN G. Battista	1 XII 1936
Row B – 16	Capo Sq.	BOSCHETTI Antonio	14 V 1937
Row B – 17	Op.	BOSO Ismaele	8 XII 1937
Row B – 18	Camicia Nera	BRICELLI Miro	29 XII 1937
Row B – 19	Carab.	BRIGANTE Luigi	3 I 1937
Row B – 20	Soldato	BRIGO Massimiliano	15 VIII 1941
Row B – 21	Op.	BRAMBILLA Francesco	6 VI 1938
Row B – 22	Op.	BRUNI Giovanni	21 V 1937
Row B – 23	Av. Sc.	BRUNO Vittorio	29 VII 1936
Row C – 1	Serg. Magg.	BUONGARZONE Vincenzo	5 VI 1937
Row C – 2	Op.	BUSE Benedetto	8 V 1937
Row C – 3	Op.	CAGNONI Angelo	6 IX 1941
Row C – 4	Tenente	CALABRESE Biagio	18 XI 1936
Row C – 5	Op.	CAMPO Antonio	3 VII 1937
Row C – 6	Bersagliere	CANTAFIO Giovanni	3 VI 1937
Row C – 7	Op.	CANTELLO Umberto	23 V 1937
Row C – 8	1 Av.	CAPODIFERRO Vito Donato	8 X 1938
Row C – 9	Op.	CARTA Salvatore	1 X 1939
Row C – 10	Art.	CARATTINI Remo	31 VIII 1938
Row C – 11	Soldato	CARI Felice	? 10 1937
Row C – 12	V. Capo Sq.	CARIOLATI Antonio	11 VII 1939
Row C – 13	Gran.	CARLASSARA Domenico	22 II 1939
Row C – 14	Op.	CAPITANI Corrado	3 XII 1936
Row C – 15	Op.	CARLIG Egidio	19 II 1938
Row C – 16	Serg. Magg.	CARPENTIERI Renato	2 IV 1940

Row C – 17	Colonello	CASABASSA Gierolamo	5 VI 1946
Row C – 18	Op.	CASERTA Luigi	24 IV 1938
Row C – 19	Av. Sc.	CASOLA Angelo	9 X 1938
Row C – 20	Serg. M.A.	CASSULO Maurizio	1936
Row C – 21	Op.	CASTELLI Francesco	22 XII 1936
Row C – 22	Capor.	CATTAI Andrea	1941
Row C – 23	1 Av.	CAVA Salvatore	8 X 1938
Row D – 1	Cap. Magg.	CAVAGNA Giovanni	3 X 1940
Row D – 2	Soldato	CAVALLARI Francesco	1941
Row D – 3	Op.	CHIARELLA Giuseppe	29 VI 1938
Row D – 4	Tenente Pil.	CHIAROTTO Giovanni	18 I 1941
Row D – 5		CHICCA G. Battista	15 VII 1937
Row D – 6	S. Tenente	CIUFFO Salvatore	20 IV 1937
Row D – 7	Cold.	COLANTONI Biagio	1 VII 1939
Row D – 8	Sold.	COLANTONI Biasio	1 VII 1937
Row D – 9		COMPARINI Angelo	13 VII 1938
Row D – 10	V. Capo Sq.	CONGEDO Giuseppe	15 V 1937
Row D – 11	Op.	CONGIUNTI Francesco	12 X 1938
Row D – 12	V. Brig.	CONSOLAZIONE Giuseppe	17 IV 1938
Row D – 13	Carab.	CORAPI Antonio	19 II 1937
Row D – 14	Capo Man.	CORDONI Rosario	15 VI 1937
Row D – 15	Capo Sq. Op.	CORSINI Luigi	24 V 1939
Row D – 16	Op.	CORSO Giuseppe	29 IV 1937
Row D – 17	Art.	COSTANZO Sante	16 ? 1936
Row D – 18	Gran.	CREATO Pietro	20 VI 1938
Row D – 19	Art.	CREDARO Vincenzo	22 II 1939
Row D – 20	Capo Man.	CUCCHETTO Antonio	7 IX 1937
Row D – 21		CUPPARI Raffaele	24 V 1937
Row D – 22	Av. Sc.	CURATOLO Michele	8 X 1938
Row D – 23	1 Av.	CURIEL Ruggero	18 X 1938

Row E – 1		DAGHERO Matteo	30 III 1938
Row E – 2	Cap. Magg.	DALLA LIBERA Olindo	29 IV 1937
Row E – 3	Op.	DANIELE Odoardo	6 I 1937
Row E – 4		D'AVOLIO Gino	2 V 1939
Row E – 5	Serg. Magg.	DE BASTIANI Angelo	13 VI 1939
Row E – 6	Camicia Nera	DE GASPERIS Antonio	21 XII 1938
Row E – 7	1 Av.	D'ELIA Ernesto	14 VIII 1936
Row E – 8	Serg. Magg.	DE MARIA Danilo	7 XI 1937
Row E – 9	Op.	DE PAOLI Lorenzo	31 VII 1937
Row E – 10	Op.	DE SANTI Amedeo	1 II 1939
Row E – 11	Cap. Vasc.	DE SANTIS Luciano	6 VII 1936
Row E – 12	Capor.	DE SARIO Cosimo	28 IX 1938
Row E – 13	Serg. Magg.	DI MARCO Giuglielmo	2 VIII 1941
Row E – 14	Camicia Nera	DI PERSICO Vincenzo	13 IV 1938
Row E – 15	Soldato	DOMENIS Paolino	13 VII 1940
Row E – 16	Cap. Magg.	DORLANDO Giulio	16 XI 1936
Row E – 17	Op.	DOTTORE Giuseppe	16 XII 1938
Row E – 18	Op.	DROGO Antonio	11 II 1941
Row E – 19	Capor.	ESPOSITO Gennaro	6 IX 1937
Row E – 20	Serg. P.L.	FABBRINI Raffaele	9 XII 1937
Row E – 21	Av. SC.	FABIO Vincenzo	11 II 1941
Row E – 22	Soldato	FADDA Domiziano	12 IX 1941
Row E – 23	Soldato	FANTONI Enzo	11 XI 1940

Row F – 1	Av. Sc.	FASANO Paolo	9 XII 1937
Row F – 2	Serg. Magg.	FATTORELLI Pietro	9 I 1939
Row F – 3	Centur.	FAVERO Giovanni	13 XI 1937
Row F – 4	Op.	FAVIANO Attilio	16 VI 1937
Row F – 5	Camicia Nera	FILIPPINI Angelo	18 XII 1938
Row F – 6	Capo Sq.	FLAGELLO Domenico	26 III 1938
Row F – 7	Camicia Nera	FOSSATI Giovanni	17 VI 1937
Row F – 8	Capor.	FRANZOLIN Angelo	19 VI 1936
Row F – 9	Av. Sc.	FUSCO Aldo	

Row F – 10	Op.	GALBER Samuele	3 X 1938
Row F – 11	Cap. Magg.	GASPAROLLOV Valentino	19 X 1938
Row F – 12	Soldato	GASTALDO Erminio	
Row F – 13	Soldato	GAZZOLI Angelo	21 VII 1939
Row F – 14	Serg. Magg.	GAY Giovanni	30 VII 1936
Row F – 15	Art.	GENNARO Damiano	7 XII 1936
Row F – 16	Alp.	GENRE Arturo	30 XI 1939
Row F – 17	Art.	GERMANOTTA Antoni	16 VIII 1938
Row F – 18	Cap. Magg.	GIAVEDONI Romeo	10 XII 1940
Row F – 19	Op.	GIRANIO Stefano	26 IV 1937
Row F – 20	Magg.	GIROTTO Mario	
Row F – 21		GIUSTOLISI Vincenzo	29 XII 1936
Row F – 22	G. Pol. Col.	GRANDI Gastone	3 V 1939
Row F – 23	Cap. Magg.	GRIMALD Michele	18 X 1936
Row G – 1	T. Col.	GUARINI Maria Filippo	23 XI 1940
Row G – 2	Capo Man. Medico	GUIDA Fulvio	2 I 1938
Row G – 3	Op.	IANNICELLI Francesco	28 V 1937
Row G – 4	Soldato	IESU Giovanni	6 VIII 1938
Row G – 5	Camicia Nera	INDELICATO Luciano	5 X 1936
Row G – 6	Civile	LAMBERTI Giovanni	6 VIII 1937
Row G – 7	Soldato	LANZA Amorigo	30 IX 1941
Row G – 8	Camicia Nera	LEONELLI Guido	20 VII 1939
Row G – 9	Guardia Carcer.	LAZZARO Giuseppe	8 IV 1937
Row G – 10	Art.	LIBERATORE Rocco	22 VII 1937
Row G – 11	1 Cap.	LUCCHETTI Amato	27 VII 1937
Row G – 12	V. Cap. Sq.	MAGRI Angelo	1 IV 1940
Row G – 13	Cap. Magg.	MENICUCCI Luigi	? V 1941
Row G – 14	Camicia Nera	MAGNETICO Magno	19 X 1939
Row G – 15	Op.	MANCINI Alfonso	4 VII 1938
Row G – 16	Gran.	MANCINI Michele	20 II 1937
Row G – 17	Motocicl.	MANDRA Cesare	27 I 1938
Row G – 18	Alp.	MANINI Carlo	1936

Row G – 19	Soldato	MARAGNO Giuseppe	30 VIII 1936
Row G – 20	Art.	MARCHETTI Fiore	1 I 1937
Row G – 21	Soldato	MANCUSO Arturo	23 XI 1937
Row G – 22	Cap.	MARINO Alfredo	30 X 1940
Row G – 23	Camicia Nera	MARINONI Rocco	30 V 1938
Row H – 1		MARTINELLI Giovanni	16 II 1938
Row H – 2	Op.	NARTORANO Antonio	11 X 1936
Row H – 3	Aut.	MASETTI Alcibiade	1 V 1937
Row H – 4	Soldato	MESITI Domenico	
Row H – 5	Art.	MILANO Pietro	1936
Row H – 6	Soldato	MILLIMACI Giuseppe	22 V 1941
Row H – 7	Soldato	MIOTTI Nilo	18 III 1938
Row H – 8	Op.	MIRAFLORES Pancrazio	27 IX 1937
Row H – 9	Op.	MOLINARI Giovanni	14 XII 1936
Row H – 10		MONZINALI Carlo	30 IV 1937
Row H – 11	Op.	MORANDI Antonio	26 X 1936
Row H – 12	Op.	MORIELLO Angelo	14 XI 1937
Row H – 13	Generale	MÜLLER Giuseppe	
Row H – 14	Serg. Magg. Pil.	MUSANTE Franco	8 X 1938
Row H – 15	F. Ante	NANNI Domenico	
Row H – 16	Serg.	NARDIELLO Rodolfo	17 VI 1941
Row H – 17	Art.	OBINO Agostino	18 III 1938
Row H – 18	Art.	OCCHIPINTI Salvatore	23 IV 1937
Row I – 1	Soldato	OSPARTELLI Giuseppe	18 XI 1940
Row I – 2	Camicia Nera	OSTINELLI Giuseppe	18 VIII 1936
Row I – 3		OTTONI Costantino	28 VII 1936
Row I – 4	Op.	PACERA Alfonso	17 XII 1936
Row I – 5	Mar.	PALMINTERI Salvatore	4 IV 1941
Row I – 6	Tenente	PANEGROSSI Luigi	22 X 1937
Row I – 7	Soldato	PANICHELLA Giuseppe	
Row I – 8	S. Tenente	PATTARELLI Aldo	19 VIII 1940

Row I – 9	Camicia Nera	PASQUALE Aldo	25 III 1939
Row I – 10	Serg. Magg.	PATRUNO Rocco	26 VI 1941
Row I – 11	Serg.	PEDRAZZI Amedio	4 III 1939
Row I – 12	Camicia Nera	PERSANO Giuseppe	19 III 1940
Row I – 13	Op.	PERSICO Francesco	25 X 1937
Row I – 14		PERUZZO Emilio	13 XI 1937
Row I – 15	Op.	PETRINELLI Giovanni	1 I 1937
Row I – 16	Tenente M.O.	PETROPOLI Guido	21 VI 1938
Row I – 17	Cap. Magg.	PINI Ugo	26 V 1939
Row I – 18	Aut.	PIOTTI Angelo Domenico	19 V 1937

Riquardo 2
6 rows A – F of 23 graves each, row G including 3 mass graves of 4, 5 and 6 graves respectively, rows H – I 18 graves each; total number of buried 209

Row A – 1	Op.	PISTORIO Vincenzo	8 IV 1941
Row A – 2	Att. Uff.	POMATI Gian Luigi	31 V 1939
Row A – 3	Gran.	PRINCIPIANO Bartolomeo	18 XI 1940
Row A – 4	Carab.	PROFETI Amos	9 VIII 1938
Row A – 5	Op.	RAGONESI Antonio	20 III 1937
Row A – 6	Capo Sq.	RECCHIA Florindo	2 VI 1937
Row A – 7	Camicia Nera	REZZANO Alberto	5 IV 1939
Row A – 8	Soldato	RICCARDO Vincenzo	15 V 1937
Row A – 9	Tenente	RODDA Benvenuto	7 I 1938
Row A – 10	Tenente	RODDOLO Carlo	25 II 1937
Row A – 11	Soldato	BOSASTRA Giuseppe	5 IX 1937
Row A – 12	Aiutante	ROSSO Antonio	3 VIII 1936
Row A – 13	Op.	REBECCHI Francesco	
Row A – 14	Carab.	RUGGIERO Luigi	6 VII 1940
Row A – 15	Op.	RUIZ Baldessare	28 VI 1938
Row A – 16	Soldato	RUSSO Giovanni	5 ? 1937
Row A – 17	Magg.	SALA Achille	8 I 1942
Row A – 18	1 Av.	SALVARESE Alessandro	8 X 1938

Row A – 19	Camicia Nera	SAVO Aracangelo	9 VI 1937
Row A – 20	Soldato	SBARRA Vincenzo	20 VII 1936
Row A – 21	Camicia Nera	SCAGLIARINI Vittorio	1 V 1938
Row A – 22	Cap. Magg.	SANGALLI Aquilino	27 I 1939
Row A – 23	Capo Sq.	SCALIA Matteo	6 I 1938
Row B – 1	Camicia Nera	SEGATO Antonio	1936
Row B – 2	Av. Sc.	SELLE Achille	8 X 1938
Row B – 3	Gran.	SERGI Salvatore	1 VII 1938
Row B – 4	Soldato	SERGIO Domenico	8 V 1937
Row B – 5	1 Av.	SEVERI Francesco	8 X 1938
Row B – 6	Av. Sc.	SIRISCHEWICH Narcisio	11 V 1938
Row B – 7	Marin.	SMILOVICH[52] Giovanni	8 VII 1936
Row B – 8	Tenente	SOLLAZZO Giovanni	15 V 1939
Row B – 9	Caporale	SOLDATINI Alfio	7 XI 1937
Row B – 10	Carab.	SOLITRO Pasquale	22 XI 1937
Row B – 11	1 Centur.	SOLINAS Giovanni	
Row B – 12	Soldato	SPAGNOLETTI Antonio	15 II 1938
Row B – 13	Op.	SPAGNOLO Nicolo	7 V 1938
Row B – 14	Op.	SPINA Antonio	25 II 1937
Row B – 15	Op.	SUSANI Emilio	11 X 1937
Row B – 16	Capo. Man.	TADDEUCCI Giovanni Dionisio	22 VIII 1938
Row B – 17	Aut.	TANONI Luigi	5 VI 1940
Row B – 18	Camicia Nera	TESTASECCA Luigi	1941
Row B – 19	S. Ten. M.O.	THUN v HOHENSTEIN Giovanni[53]	23 III 1938
Row B – 20	Soldato	TOLEDO Pierino	4 VI 1940
Row B – 21	Cap. Magg.	TOLFO Giovanni	3 XI 1937
Row B – 22	Magg.	TONELLI Carlo	28 VIII 1940
Row B – 23	Op.	TORRE Antonio	25 IX 1937

[52] Slovene from Istria.

[53] Johannes Stanislaus Maria Ferdinand Ernst Antonius Romedius Count Thun-Hohenstein (* Vienna 22 XII 1913 + Monte Tight, AOI 23 VIII 1938), Second Lieutenant in the Cavalry Regiment "Vittorio Emanuele".

Row C – 1	V. Cap. Sq.	TREPPO Arturo	24 X 1937
Row C – 2	Op.	TREVISANI Augusto	3 X 1937
Row C – 3	S.Ten.Pil.	TREVISANELLO Eugenio	9 XII 1937
Row C – 4		TADEI Teodoro	1 VIII 1941
Row C – 5		TROTTA Amilia	20 III 1937
Row C – 6	Centur.	VACCARO Michelangelo	31 V 1938
Row C – 7	Op.	VALCAVI Carlo	15 VII 1937
Row C – 8	Op.	VANELLO Emilio	6 XII 1937
Row C – 9	Alp.	VISENTIN Natale	5 III 1938
Row C – 10	Ten. M.A.	VITALI Massimiliano	23 II 1937
Row C – 11	Soldato	VITALI Nullo	
Row C – 12	Camicia Nera	ZAMOLO Leonardo	11 IV 1938
Row C – 13	Serg. Magg.	ZANNI Salvatore	2 X 1940
Row C – 14	Op.	ZOZZOLI Natale	30 V 1937
Row C – 15	Soldato	ZITO Michele	29 VII 1936
Row C – 16	Tenente	ZOLI Lauro	9 II 1940
Row C – 17	Soldato	ZONA Arcangelo	6 VII 1937
Row C – 18	Soldato	KROSS[54] Francesco	8 XI 1936
Row C – 19	Soldato	COGOI Speridio	3 II 1938
Row C – 20	Carab.	DAL GRANDE Giuseppe	26 X 1936
Row C – 21	Soldato	FABRIZI Gerardo	22 II 1937
Row C – 22	Op.	FALDI Francesco	13 V 1938
Row C – 23	Op.	GOZZI Francesco	10 II 1937
Row D – 1	Op.	IELLINA Michele	31 X 1937
Row D – 2	Finanz.	LOPEZ Vittorio	22 VI 1940
Row D – 3	Soldato	MESSINA Alfio	26 VII 1938
Row D – 4	Op.	SARTORI Dario	3 I 1939
Row D – 5	Camicia Nera	SCHIRO Giuseppe	4 VIII 1939
Row D – 6	Op.	BERTANZA Silvio	1 VI 1938
Row D – 7	Soldato	CASSIDEI Giuseppe	13 IX 1938

[54] Franz Kross from Sarnthein; siehe Gerald Steinacher (Hrsg.) "Zwischen Duce und Negus - Südtirol und der Abessinienkrieg 1935 – 1941", Bozen 2006, p.17.

Row D – 8	Op.	FAUSTINELLI G. Battista	15 XI 1936
Row D – 9	Camicia Nera	D'ORAZIO Antonio	6 III 1939
Row D – 10	Op.	FOGATO Primo	10 X 938
Row D – 11	Op.	FRAZONI Pietro	11 II 1938
Row D – 12	S. Ten.	FRENI Gaetano	7 X 1937
Row D – 13	Camicia Nera	GASPARRO Dante	23 III 1937
Row D – 14	Aiut. Col.	GUTTIERI Luigi	16 XI 1938
Row D – 15	V. Capo. Sq.	MEZZAPESA Giovanni	7 V 1938
Row D – 16	Soldato	NANIA Giovanni	11 VII 1939
Row D – 17	Capo Sq.	NICOLETTI Emilio	21 X 1938
Row D – 18	S. Ten.	RANCATI Rodolfo	11 XI 1938
Row D – 19	Op.	SASSI Mario	19 VIII 1938
Row D – 20	Serg. Magg.	VASSALLO Benedetto	24 VIII 1937
Row D – 21	Magg,	ALLIETTA Giovanni	
Row D – 22	Cap.	BARONE Giuseppe	2 I 1938
Row D – 23	Ten.	BARRA Gennaro	27 VIII 1937

Row E – 1		BERTUZZI Mario	5 II 1946
Row E – 2		BODO Giovanni	1938
Row E – 3	Carab.	BRIGLIOZZI Tommaso	
Row E – 4		BUONASSISI Antonio	8 II 1942
Row E – 5	Soldato	BUSTO Carmine	18 XII 1936
Row E – 6		CANANO	
Row E – 7	Serg. Magg. Pil.	CANIATO Luigi	21 VI 1940
Row E – 8	Camicia Nera	CATALANO Gandolfo	16 XI 1940
Row E – 9		CEREDA Egidio	7 IX 1941
Row E – 10	S. Ten. M.O.	CORSI DI TURRA Antonio	21 IX 1939
Row E – 11		CROCI Giuseppe	13 III 1947
Row E – 12	Tenente	COSI Bruno Ernesto	29 IX 1936
Row E – 13	Soldato	COSTANTINO Domenico	23 IV 1941
Row E – 14	Tenente	COTTI Mario	13 III 1939
Row E – 15	S. Tenente	DA CRUZ Giuseppe	29 VIII 1940
Row E – 16	1 Av.	DALL'ORO Dario	29 XI 1938

Row E – 17		D'AMICO Alberto	13 XII 1941
Row E – 18		DE BARTOLI Demetrio	
Row E – 19	Op.	DURANTE Silvio	1939
Row E – 20	Ten. M.A.	FENZI Gianfranco	18 VI 1938
Row E – 21		FOCICCHIA	16 I 1942
Row E – 22	Soldato	FOPPOLI Lorenzo	27 IV 1937
Row E – 23	Op.	FUMAGALLI Gaetano	19 II 1938
Row F – 1	Aut.	GAMBARINI Araldo	7 IX 1938
Row F – 2	Camicia Nera	GALLELLA Mario Antonio	14 I 1939
Row F – 3	Op.	GARIUP Antonio	3 I 1939
Row F – 4		GARRECINAIO Riccard	1938
Row F – 5		GASPARO Paolo	
Row F – 6	Aut.	GENTILE Gino	12 I 1938
Row F – 7	Op.	GRECO Pasquale	29 IV 1937
Row F – 8	Tenente	LEGA Paolo	6 VIII 1941
Row F – 9	Soldato	LOLLANO Luigi	29 III 1939
Row F – 10	Leg. Lavor.	LOMAZZO Vito	8 VII 1937
Row F – 11	Camicia Nera	LUCCHESI Giorgio	8 VI 1938
Row F – 12		MARONI Carlo	15 VII 1940
Row F – 13	Soldato	MARTINO Vito Domenico	
Row F – 14		MONREALE Domenico	
Row F – 15	Op.	MORA Dante	11 VII 1939
Row F – 16		MUZZARELLI Attilio	28 VII 1940
Row F – 17	S. Tenente	OLIVETTI Ermanno	6 XII 1938
Row F – 18		OSSOLA Oleone	
Row F – 19	Serg. Magg.	PECCHIA Nazzareno	11 I 1943
Row F – 20		PERRONE Alberto	1938
Row F – 21		PIUBELLO Carlo	17 VI 1941
Row F – 22	1 Capo Sq.	PRAT Rolando	11 VII 1942
Row F – 23	S. Tenente M.O.V.M.	PROLA Lorenzo	
Row G – 1	Cap. M.O.	PROTTI Arrigo	

Row G – 2	C. Cepor.	PUCCI Giuseppe	18 IX 1936
Row G – 3	1 Av.	QUINCI Giovanni	24 V 1940
Row G – 4	Soldato	SANTALUCIA Vincenzo	22 II 1942
Row G – 5	Cap. M.O.	SAVARECONELLI Manlio	24 VIII 1940
Row G – 6		SCARABELLI Francesco	16 VI 1942
Row G – 7		SCIORTINO Stefano	15 IV 1941
Row G – 8	Serg. Pil.	SGAMBATI Osvaldo	2 XII 1936
Row G – 9	S. Tenente	SPAGNA Ermanno	18 X 1936
Row G – 10	Magg.	TAUSICH	23 I 1938
Row G – 11		TOSI Francesco	
Row G – 12		TURCHETT Giuseppe	
Row G – 13		VITTORIO Vincenzo	22 IX 1938
Row G – 14	Soldato	VIVAQUA Orlando	13 II 1942
Row G – 15		ZASSO Lodovico	24 VIII 1940
Row G – 16	Camicia Nera	ZIDDA Antonio	14 IV 1936
Row G – 17	Capor.	ACCANTINO Vincenzo	8 IV 1936
Row G – 18	Equipaggio di Volo		11 VIII 1940
	S.Tenente Pil.	D'AMICO Emmanuele	
	S. Tenente Pil.	SASSI Sergio	
	Ten.R.E.Oss.	PAGANINI Emilio	
	1 Av. Marc.	RECCHIA Giovanni	
	Av.Sc.Arn.	CANONICO Antonio	
	Av.Sc.Mot.	PANTAROTTO Angelo	
Row G – 19	Equipaggio di Volo Velivolo S-79 M.21940		16 VIII 1940
	S. Tenente Pil.	CONTI Luigi	
	Serg.Magg. Pil.	SCANNAVINI Leon	
	1 Av. Marc.	CAPPUCIO Mario	
	1 Av. Arm.	IOVONE Elia	
	Av.Sc.Mot.	TESTOLINI Maurizio	
Row G – 20	Equipaggio di Volo Velivolo S-81 M.20610 4 GR.B.I		21 VI 1940
	Ten. Col.	GORELLI Gastone	
	1 Av. Mot.	FONTANELLA Eligio	
	1 Av. Marc.	LEONI Marioa	

	Av. Sc. Arm.	RAGNI Agostino	
Row G – 21	V. Capo Sq.	ARORI Cesare	21 I 1936
Row G – 22	Aut.	ASSANDRI Giacomo	
Row G – 23	Tenente M.O.	BECCARIA Inciso	19 II 1938
Row H – 1	Soldato	BOLOGNESI Antonio	13 IV 1940
Row H – 2	Soldato	BUCEOLI Umberto	21 IX 1938
Row H – 3	Soldato	BENVENUTI Settimo	1939
Row H – 4	Soldato	CAMPISI Salvatore	
Row H – 5	Aut.	CASTELLANO Galileo	17 IX 1938
Row H – 6	S.Tenente M.O.	CASTELLACI Pietro	19 V 1936
Row H – 7	Capo Sq.	CASOLARI Aldo	14 VI 1936
Row H – 8	Op.	CATALANO Nicola	28 VI 1936
Row H – 9	Serg.	CELLI Adalberto	18 VIII 1936
Row H –10	1 Cap.	CERRUTI Luigi	16 X 1936
Row H –11	Camicia Nera	DE LELLIS Michele	28 VII 1936
Row H – 12	Ten. M.O.	DALLA NOCE Adolfo	19 V 1936
Row H – 13	Cap. M.O.V.N.	DE REGE Thesauro Amadeo	2 II 1936
Row H – 14	Alp.	TOBIA Franzino	15 V 1936
Row H – 15	Lanciere	GIANDINI Gino	8 IV 1936
Row H – 16	Civ.	GHIGLIETTI Giuseppe	4 VII 1940
Row H – 17	Op.	CORRINI Francesco Faustino	3 V 1937
Row H – 18	Camicia Nera Sc.	GIANNICO Vito	15 VI 1941
Row I – 6	Soldato	LEO Giuseppe	18 V 1936
Row I – 7	Camicia Nera	MAGRI Giuseppe	9 IV 1936
Row I – 8	Cap. Magg.	MARCHESE Francesco	
Row I – 9	S. Tenente M.O.V.M.	MERICUCCI Lodovico	8 IV 1936
Row I – 10	Fante.	MENISSALE Costantino	25 XII 1936
Row I – 11	Dragone	MICCO Luigi	23 I 1938
Row I – 12	Soldato	MORGESE Salvatore	2 VI 1937
Row I – 13	Soldato	OLIVA Francesco	14 V 1938
Row I – 14	Dragone	PAGANINI Bruno	17 VI 1936

Row I – 15	Legion.	PAGANO Mario	31 VII 1937
Row I – 16	Alp.	PIANA Giacomo Anacleto	27 VII 1937
Row I – 17	Legion.	PILLININI Massimo	5 V 1938
Row I – 18	Magg.	RIGHETTI Giuseppe	2 II 1936
Row I – 19	Lanciere	RINALDI Giuseppe	2 II 1936
Row I – 20	Camicia Nera	RONGHI Walter	21 I 1936
Row I – 21	Soldato	ROSSI Carlo	31 V 1936
Row I – 22	Camicia Nera	SCHIAVONE Antonio	4 XI 1940
Row I – 23	Lanciere	SCOPETTI Ottavio	8 IV 1936

Riquardo 3
9 rows; rows A – C 18 graves each, rows D – E 20 graves each, rows F – I 23 graves each; tomb of General Mariotti), total number of buried 186 plus 1

Oreste MARIOTTI
* Rome 23 IX 1874
+Addis Ababa 2 II 1937
11th Infantry Regiment 1892; Caporale 1893; Sergente 1894; 53rd Infantry regiment "Umbria" 1895; Military School of Modena 1895-1899; 2nd Lieutenant 47th Infantry Regiment in Messina 1899; Lieutenant 1903; Captain 1912; 82nd Infantry Regiment; 2nd Indigenous Battalion Eritrea 1912, commanding officer 4th company of 3rd Indigenous Battalion 1912, served in the conquest of Libya 1912/1913, returned to Massaua 1913; served in Cirenaica 1914; AdC of Commanding General "Alpi" Brigade 1915; served at the front 1915, major 1916; took part in the attack on the Col di Lana 1916; Battalion Commander 46th Infantry Regiment; Lt. Colonel 1917; served several times in Libya 1921-1928; Colonel 1926; Commander 46th Infantry Regiment; Brigadier General 1935; Commander of Troops of Eastern Eritrean Lowlands 1935; took part in conquest of Ethiopia; head of sector Agamé; Division General 1937.

Row A – 1		ACCORSI Ottavio	12 VI 1992
Row A – 2	Serg. Magg.	ALAIMO Annibale	3 XII 1936
Row A – 3	Op.	ALEOTTI Alfonso	6 VIII 1941
Row A – 4	Aut.	ANGELINI Federico	27 VII 1937
Row A – 5	Aut	ANDINO Pier Franco	24 VIII 1937
Row A - 6	1 Pil.	ARCHETTIG. Battista	22 VIII 1937
Row A – 7	Sold.	ARCIONI Luigi	22 XII 1936

Row A - 8		AVALA Eustacchio	24 VII 1941
Row A - 9	Sold.	BACER Lionello	4 IX 1936
Row A -10	Op.	BARBASSO Alberto	13 VIII 1937
Row A -11	Camicia Nera	BARBIERI Luigi	19 III 1937
Row A-12	Op.	BARDELLA Adriano	26 V 1938
Row A-13	Camicia Nera	BARRERI Evaristo	21 VI 1941
Row A-14	Tenente	BATTAGLIA	
Row A-15	Op.	BELLADON NA Gaetano	29 X 1936
Row A-16	Camicia Nera	BELTRAMINI Adelchi	29 XI 1941
Row A-17	Op.	BERNASCONI Ambrogio	13 XI 1938
Row A-18	Op.	BERTONI Antonio	2 XI 1939
Row B- 1	Carab.	BIUNDO Vincenzo	1 II 1937
Bow B- 2	Op.	BLASONE Antonio	24 XII 1936
Row B- 3	Sold.	BONA Secundo	9 XI 1936
Row B- 4	Op.	BORTOLUZZI Mario	25 X 1936
Row B- 5	Tenente	BOTTICHIO Francesco	30 IX 1940
Row B- 6	Aut.	BRAIDO Bartolo	26 VIII 1939
Row B- 7	Camicia Nera	BRUNELLI Cirillo	
Row B- 8	S. Tenente	BRUNO Cesare	26 IV 1939
Row B- 9	Capor.	BRUSA Arturo	13 II 1940
Row B-10	Sold.	BRUSATI Giuseppe	16 VIII 1936
Row B-11	Camicia Nera	BUSSO Giuseppe	6 XI 1938
Row B-12	Camicia Nera	CAMERINI Vittorio	21 I 1936
Row B-13	Cap. Magg.	CALLIGARIS Angelo	16 VIII 1940
Row B-14	Aut.	CANEPALuigi	5 IV 1938
Row B-15	Aut.	CANTATORE Giovanni	24 VIII 1937
Row B-16	Op.	CORDONE Vincenzo	16 VI 1937
Row B-17	Sold.	CASE Enrico	17 VI 1936
Row B-18	Op.	CASONI Giovanni	31 X 1937
Row C- 1	Aut.	CASTELLI Francesco	2 VII 1940
Row C- 2	Op.	CAVALLIERI Ilario	7 IV 1937

Row C- 3	Op.	CAVAZZI Prospero	13 I 1938
Row C- 4	S. Tenente	CERASI Virgilio	26 IV 1941
Row C- 5	Sold.	CHIANESE Antonio	22 I 1937
Row C- 6	Sold.	CHIAPPA Giovanni	11 IX 1940
Row C- 7	Sold.	COLETTI Vito	2 II 1937
Row C- 8		COSTA Gino	26 VII 1940
Row C- 9	Aut.	COSTA Giuseppe	16 XI 1938
Row C-10	Op.	COTARDO Antonio	19 V 1937
Row C-11	Serg.Magg.	CRABU Giovanni	26 IV 1941
Row C-12	Op.	CUNEO Agostino	11 XI 1937
Row C-13	Op.	DANTE Vincenzino	25 VII 1941
Row C-14	Op.	D'ARCANGELO Teodorico	23 X 1936
Row C-15	Op.	DA RECH Luigi	30 XII 1936
Row C-16	Camicia Nera	DI DEO Nicola	28 IX 1940
Row C-17	Soldato	DIMARCOBERARDINONicola	26 II 1937
Row C-18	Capor.	DI MICELI Giuseppe	6 XI 1936

Row D- 1	Soldato	DIPANEAttilio	26 IV 1941
Row D- 2		DONATI	
Row D- 3	Op.	DONZELLI Giuseppe	28 IX 1937
Row D- 4	Op.	DORDOLOLuigi	18 XII 1936
Row D- 5	Op.	ELLERO Giovanni	21 VI 1937
Row D- 6		FAGARAZZI Antonio	8 III 1941
Row D- 7	Cap. Magg.	FASCIANA Giuseppe	28 X 1936
Row D- 8		FASSA Elio	26 III 1938
Row D- 9	Magg.	FERRANTE Mario	18 I 1936
Row D-10	Op.	FIOR Raffaele	4 VIII 1937
Row D-11	Op.	FOGLIAME Giuseppe	22 XI 1938
Row D-12	Sold.	FRANI Giovanni	17 XII 1937
Row D-13	Sold.	GAIBA Pietro	22 XII 1936
Row D-14	Aut.	GALLIZIA Mario Napoleone	4 XI 1938
Row D-15	Op.	GARMI Primo	10 I 1937
Row D-16	Op.	GASPERINI Pietro	19 V 1937

Row D-17		GATTI Salvatore	23 V 1941
Row D-18	Op.	GESSAGA Rodolfo	15 XI 1938
Row D-19	Op.	GHIA Luigi	10 II 1939
Row D-20		GIACOMINI Giovanni	15 III 1939
Row E- 1	Serg.	GIAQUINTO Vincenzo	
Row E- 2	V.Capo.Sq.	GOBBER Alberto	21 IV 1941
Row E- 3	Camicia Nera	GRAZIETTO Francesco	2 III 1939
Row E- 4	S. Tenente Med.	GRECO Matteo	31 I 1940
Row E- 5	Op.	GRENZI Edouardo	3 XI 1939
Row E- 6		CIRILLO Lucio	4 V 1941
Row E- 7	Op.	GRIMALDI Francesco	3 I 1939
Row E- 8	Op.	GRISALLI Giuseppe	26 VI 1941
Row E- 9	Aut.	LESA Ferruccio	24 VIII 1939
Row E-10	Soldato	LEVATO Domenico	29 IV 1939
Row E-11	Soldato	LOMBARDO Tommaso	11 VIII 1936
Row E-12	Op.	LONGO Angelo	23 IV 1937
Row E-13	Soldato	LONGO Luigi	14 II 1936
Row E-14	Marin.	LOPEZ Giacomo	23 X 1940
Row E-15	Cap. Magg.	LUCARELLI Guglielmo	6 IV 1941
Row E-16	Soldato	MADDALONI Giuseppe	23 IV 1941
Row E-17	Op.	MAESTRI Francesco	28 V 1937
Row E-18	Op.	MAISTRO Guerrino	26 I 1941
Row E-19	Op.	MANFRO Giuseppe	20 IV 1937
Row E-20	Soldato	MARCENARO Emilio	8 VII 1936
Row F- 1	Soldato	MARCOLONGO Mario	8 I 1938
Row F- 2	Camicia Nera	MAROCCO Nicola	26 IV 1941
Row F- 3	Soldato	MARTINELLI Ilario	24 V 1940
Row F- 4	S. Tenente M.O.	MERCATI Giovanni	4 VIII 1940
Row F- 5	Soldato	MICHELE Giuseppe	29 VI 1936
Row F- 6	Op.	MORINI Pietro	7 VII 1937
Row F- 7	Op.	MORO Ermengildo	30 I 1940

Row F- 8	Aut.	MUNTONI Vincenzo	23 I 1939
Row F- 9	Op.	NEGRO Valentino	7 IV 1937
Row F-10	Aut.	NESCETTI Angelo	16 V 1936
Row F-11	Soldato	NOTARO Giuseppe	3 X 1937
Row F-12	Mann.	NOVACCO Giuseppe	30 X 1940
Row F-13	Carab.	OTTAVI Nicolo	
Row F-14	Op.	PALAZZI Olivo	1 XII 1937
Row F-15	Capor.	PALMA Rinaldo	12 XII 1936
Row F-16	Op.	PARA Salvatore	6 IX 1936
Row F-17	Op.	PARMEGGIANI Civo	15 IX 1938
Row F-18	Geometre	PASSARINI Cesare	27 V 1937
Row F-19		PASTRONE Giuseppe	20 XI 1944
Row F-20	Aut.	PEDRALI Giulio	21 IV 1937
Row F-21	Camicia Nera	FES Pietro	15 I 1938
Row F-22		PETRICCIONE Paolo	22 VIII 1937
Row F-23	Op.	PICCINATO Antonio	6 VIII 1937
Row G- 1	Op.	POZZI Carlo	17 I 1937
Row G- 2	Tenente M.O.	PUCCI Marcello	29 IX 1937
Row G- 3	Aut.	RANCHINO Giuseppe	26 III 1937
Row G- 4	Soldato	RAVIOLA Severino	28 VII 1936
Row G- 5	Soldato	RAN Ugo	I VIII 1936
Row G- 6	Camicia Nera	SCICLONE Emanuele	10 VI 1936
Row G- 7	Op. Genio	SANNO Lorenzo	2 III 1937
Row G- 8	S. Tenente	SANTA ANDREA Roberto	23 IV 1941
Row G- 9	Alp.	SASIA Giovanni	4 VII 1936
Row G-10	Op.	SCIACCA Giuseppe	14 I 1939
Row G-11	Cap. Magg.	SCANDURA Sante	1937
Row G-12		SERRA Dante	27 I 1938
Row G-13	Op.	SIMONITTI G. Battista	23 I 1939
Row G-14	Lanciere	SONCINI Alfeo	8 IV 1936
Row G-15	Soldato	SOSTERO Giovanni	22 IV 1941
Row G-16	Camicia Nera	SPATICCHIA Francesco	29 XI 1941

Row G-17	Op.	SANTE Michele	3 XI 1937
Row G-18		STOFFNER Giuseppe	7 I 1938
Row G-19	Op.	STOLFA Giuseppe	25 XII 1936
Row G-20	Aut.	TIBALDI Giuseppe	1 XI 1939
Row G-21	Op.	TOCALLI Albino	2 XII 1938
Row G-22	Aut.	TOLU Salbatore	31 X 1938
Row G-23	Soldato	TRANCHITA Vincenzo	21 III 1937
Row H- 1	Op.	TREVE Cirillo	12 V 1939
Row H- 2	Op.	TUDISCA Castrense	1 VI 1938
Row H- 3	Aut. civ.	TAFFURELLI Antenore	13 VII 1937
Row H- 4	Op.	VALTESI Amedeo	18 III 1937
Row H- 5	Legionario	VIANELLO Cherubino	20 VII 1937
Row H- 6	Soldato	VANTURA Salvatore	15 III 1936
Row H- 7	Capor.	VIRGENTI Giovanni	27 VIII 1940
Row H- 8		ZANETTI Guglielmo	23 III 1941
Row H- 9	Op.	ZENI Giuseppe	18 IV 1937
Row H-10	Op.	BASSA Paolo	27 VI 1937
Row H-11	Op.	BASSONELO Giovanni	7 VII 1937
Row H-12	Av Sc.	BUCCELLA Salvatore	4 IV 1936
Row H-13	Carab.	CANAVARA Paolo	24 IV 1936
Row H-14	Tenente	CANTONI Bruno	20 IV 1936
Row H-15	Op.	CAPUZZELLI	1937
Row H-16	Op.	CAPUZZELLO	
Row H-17	Camicia Nera	COIA Rinaldo	24 IV 1936
Row H-18	Carab.	DIDDIO Giovanni	29 IV 1936
Row H-19	Op.	DIPRIMA Michele	26 VI 1937
Row H-20	Carab.	DI STEFANO Luigi	24 IV 1936
Row H-21	Op.	FERNE Aldo	15 VI 1936
Row H-22	Op.	GRUPPONI Gelso	10 XI 1937
Row H-23	Op.	LAZZARI Valerio	1 VI 1937
Row I- 1	S. Tenente	MAGNANI Giuseppe	24 IV 1936

Row I- 2	Soldato	MAGRIS Aronne	16 IV 1936
Row I- 3	1 Cap.	MORELLO Domenico	4 III 1937
Row I- 4	Cap. M.O.	PAGNOTTINI Dante	24 IV 1936
Row I – 5	Carab.	PATTARO Aurelio	24 IV 1936
Row I- 6	Soldato	PRINCIPATO Salvatore	15 V 1936
Row I- 7	Op.	TANGAVI Michaele	14 VI 1936
Row I- 8	Cap.	TROMBY Giovanni	14 IV 1936
Row I- 9	Carab.	VITTORI Renato	24 IV 1936
Row I-10	Tenente M.O.	ZUCCHI Aldo	24 III 1936
Row I-11	Camicia NeraSc.	ADRODEGARI Guglielmo	27 II 1936
Row I-12	Camicia Nera	BARDELLA Domenico	27 II 1936
Row I-13	Camicia Nera	BENENTI Silvestro	27 II 1936
Row I-14	Soldato	CAVALLERI Pietro	17 IV 1936
Row I-15	Alp.	DAMELE Giovanni	
Row I-16	Capo Sq.	FIORIT Carlo	23 I 1936
Row I-17	Sergente	GAVARDO	
Row I-18	Leg. Lavor.	LIPPI Giovanni	
Row I-19	Camicia Nera	ZANOTTI Renzo	14 XI 1938
Row I-20	Camicia Nera	RAMONDI Remo	21 I 1936
Row I-21	S. Tenente	SAVARE Gioacchino	
Row I-22	Capo Sq.	TAMBURINI Massimiliano	21 I 1936
Row I-23	Soldato	VIVALDA Lorenzo	

Riquardo 4
9 rows; rows A – D 15 graves each, row E 20 graves, rows F – I 23 graves each; tomb of General Maltai, total number of buried 172 plus 1, of which unidentified 109

Giuseppe MALTA
* Pizzo di Calabria (Monteleone, CZ) 6 II 1883
\+ Bonga, Ethiopia 30 V 1937 (in service)
Soldier in the Military District of Catanzaro; 8th Bersaglieri Regiment 1900, corporal resp. sergeant 1901; NCO; Military School Modena 1904-1906; Secind Lieutenant (Infantry) 1906 with 9th Bersaglieri Regiment; participated in Libyan Campaign 1911 -1912; served in Somalia 1913-1914; captain with 9th Bersaglieri Regiment 1915; commanding officer of a company in 1st Bersaglieri Regiment

1915; served in Libya 1915; served at the front in Venezia Giulia 1915/16; assigned to General Staff of 4th Army Corps 1916; General Staff 63rd Division 1917; major and battalion commander 1917; served in Libya 1919-1920; School of War Torino 1920-1921; 7th Bersaglieri Regiment 1921; served in Libya 1921-1929; lieutenant-colonel 1926; served in Cyrenaica 1930-1933 as military commander of Gebel Cyrenaica; commander 7th Bersaglieri Regiment 1933-1935; War Ministry 1935; served in Eritrea 1935; commander of a colonial brigade 1935; participated in Ethiopian campaign 1935-1937 where he occupied the West of Ethiopia, in particular Gore and Bonga; promoted posthumously to rank of Brigadier General.

Row A- 1	Camicia Nera	AMODDIO Edouardo	21 I 1936
Row A- 2	V. Capo Sq.	AMODEO Damiano	21 I 1936
Row A- 3	Camicia Nera	COLZI Amedeo	
Row A- 4	Art.	BISSOLOTTI Giacomo	
Row A- 5		BOGO Luigi	27 II 1936
Row A- 6	Camicia Nera	BONETTI Guido	27 II 1936
Row A- 7	Serg. Magg.	BOTTICELLI Enrico	12 V 1941
Row A- 8	Camicia Nera	CASAGRANDE Antonio	21 I 1936
Row A- 9	Camicia Nera	CICCONE Donato	19 X 1939
Row A-10	S. Tenente	CICCIRELLO Antonio	27 II 1936
Row A-11	Op.	COMPARIN Paolo	17 III 1938
Row A-12	Soldato	CRISTIANI Alfredo	
Row A-13	Centur.	DAL FIUME Ciro	21 I 1936
Row A-14	Soldato	DAL MASCHIO Amedeo	24 VIII 1936
Row A-15	Tenente	DALZINI Corrado	

Row B- 1	Alp.	DEMARI Marino	27 II 1936
Row B- 2	Camicia Nera	DERNI Amedeo	28 II 1936
Row B- 3	V. Capo Sq.	DE TOFFOLI Pietro	18 VI 1941
Row B- 4	Camicia Nera	DODERO Giuseppe	21 I 1936
Row B- 5	Capo Sq.	ERMACORA Domenico	21 I 1936
Row B- 6	Capo Sq.	FICADELLI Renato	22 I 1936
Row B- 7	Carab.	FOIS Paolo	29 X 1938
Row B- 8	S. Tenente	FUSETTI Giovanni	19 II 1938
Row B- 9	Camicia Nera	GALLI Carlo	23 I 1936
Row B-10	Camicia Nera	GASPARETTI Giacomo	27 II 1936

Row B-11	Camicia Nera	GENTILINI Arturo	28 II 1936
Row B-12	M.V.S.N.	GHETTI Ruffilo	1940
Row B-13	Camicia Nera	GIGANTI Mario	25 I 1936
Row B-14	Camicia Nera	LEONARDO Giovanni	21 I 1936
Row B-15	Cap.	LOVISETTI Giuseppe	18 I 1939
Row C- 1	1 Centur.	MANNI Manno	
Row C- 2	1 Capo Sq.	MANZI Salvatore	17 IV 1938
Row C- 3	Camicia Nera	MARRA Giovanni	23 I 1936
Row C- 4	Tenente	MASTRODICASA Marcello	25 VI 1941
Row C- 5	Camicia Nera	MAZZOCCHI Rosolino	
Row C- 6	Op.	MILAZZO Giuseppe	18 I 1937
Row C- 7	Art.	MOCCI Enrico	
Row C- 8	Serg. Pil.	MONTI Mario	5 II 1937
Row C- 9	Camicia Nera	PAGANELLI Umberto	21 I 1936
Row C-10	Cap. Magg.	PALERMO Antonio	4 VII 1941
Row C-11	Camicia Nera	PAPPADA Lucio	
Row C-12	Magg.	PASSERINI Galliano	12 IV 1941
Row C-13	Camicia Nera	PARUSSINI Sante	22 I 1936
Row C-14	Op.	PIACENTINI Domenico	10 IX 1939
Row C-15		PIRAS Raffaele	
Row D- 1	Alp.	QUARANTA Giacomo	27 II 1936
Row D- 2	Op.	REOLON Massimiliano	
Row D- 3		ROSSELLO Giuseppe	
Row D- 4	Soldato	SARTINI Primo	6 IX 1937
Row D- 5	Alp.	SECCHIANTI Gino	
Row D- 6	Tenente	SEDDA Luigi	
Row D- 7	Camicia Nera	SERRA Aurelio	
Row D- 8	Cap.	SINI Severo	5 V 1944
Row D- 9	Camicia Nera	TERFONE Giovanni	1939
Row D-10	Camicia Nera	TESTA Sante	17 VI 1941
Row D -11	Camicia Nera S.C.	TUBERONI Vaiflo	21 I 1939

Row D-12	Camicia Nera	ULISSI Ezio	
Row D-13	Camicia Nera	VINCENZI Giuseppe	21 I 1936
Row D-14	CAV	ZANIUCCHI Altilio	12 VII 1938
Row D-15	Capo Sq.	CECCANGELI Ernesto	15 VI 1941
Row E- 1		PICUS Giovanni	1 I 1939
Row E- 2	Cap.	SCOPACASA Salvatore	
Row E- 3		Militare non identificato/unidentified soldier	
Row E- 4		Militare non identificato unidentified soldier	
Row E- 5	Ten.Col.M.O.V.M.	MERCANTI Arturo	6 III 1936
Row E- 9 – 23		Militare non identificato/unidentified soldier	
Row F- 1 – 23		Militare non identificato/unidentified soldier	
Row G- 1 – 23		Militare non identificato/unidentified soldier	
Row H- 1 – 23		Militare non identificato/unidentified soldier	
Row I 1 – 23		Militare non identificato/unidentified soldier	

Riquardo 5

Mass grave 1 (upper left)

In questo riquardo riposano militari non identificati provenienti da

Bahir Dar

Burie

Dangila

Debra Markosd

Engiabara

Mass grave 2 (upper right)

In questo riquardo riposano militari non identificati provenienti da

Cinghi
Dembidollo
Ghimbi
Lechemti
Ordemule

Mass grave 3 (lower left)

In questo riquardo riposano militari non identificati provenienti da

Debarec

Ducam

Metemma

Nefas Mocia

Moggio

Mass grave 4 (lower right)

In questo riquardo riposano militari non identificati provenienti da

Afdem

Aiscia

Asba Tafari

Giggia

Harar

Riquardo 6

Mass grave 5 (upper left)

In questo riquardo riposano militari non identificati provenienti da

Biscioftu

Dessie

Quoram

Sardo

Ualdie

Mass grave 6 (upper right)

In questo riquardo riposano militari non identificati provenienti da

Wolkefit

Adi Arcai

Debra Tabor

Debivar

Arb Ghebie

Torachedam

Dolo

Malca Uacanna

Soddu

Gondar

Celga

Debarek

Mass grave 7 (lower left)

In questo riquardo riposano militari non identificati provenienti da

Addis Ababa

Biscioftu

Dessie

Quoram

Sardo

Ualdie

Mass grave 8 (lower right)

In questo riquardo riposano militari non identificati provenienti da

Abalti

Amba Alagi

Aselle

Giumme

Nazareth

Sector A
17 rows of 3 graves of "Civile" only

Row 1 – 1	Civile	NARDI Francesco	1 IV 1940
Row 1 – 2	Civile	PAONE Domenico	24 VI 1939
Row 1 – 3	Civile	TESTONI Paolo	13 I 1939
Row 2 – 1	Civile	PELTRI Felice	28 V 1940
Row 2 – 2	Civile	OREFICE Angelo	29 XI 1939
Row 2 – 3	Civile	MUCCHIUT Vittorio	22 V 1939
Row 3 – 1	Civile	FEDERICI Cosmio	3 XI 1938
Row 3 – 2	Civile	GAMBASO Giuseppe	16 III 1939
Row 3 – 3	Civile	LUCI Corrado	24 I 1940
Row 4 – 1	Civile	BERRUTO Elio	
Row 4 – 2	Civile	LORENZI Vittorio	15 XI 1940
Row 4 – 3	Civile	DUCCOLI Francesco	12 III 1939
Row 5 – 1	Civile	PATERA Gregorio	
Row 5 – 2	Civile	PITALUGA Pietro	5 V 1939
Row 5 – 3	Civile	PISCITELLI Vito	23 IV 1939
Row 6 – 1	Civile	VIOLA Francesco	28 III 1939
Row 6 – 2	Civile	DI PASQUALE Francesco	6 XI 1939
Row 6 – 3	Civile	BERTUCCIO Nicola	7 III 1941
Row 7 – 1	Civile	BOCCHINI Salvatore	26 IV 1938
Row 7 – 2	Civile	PREDIERI Anna	17 V 1940
Row 7 – 3	Civile	CERASI Giovanni	30 XI 1939

Row 8 – 1	Civile	CILIBERTI Giuseppe	7 V 1939
Row 8 – 2	Civile	ANGIOLETTI Pietro	22 XII 1940
Row 8 – 3	Civile	ZANOTTI Adolfo	3 X 1940
Row 9 – 1	Civile	BOSCHETTO Giovanni	27 IX 1939
Row 9 – 2	Civile	GIANUZINI Francesco	30 IV 1939
Row 9 – 3	Civile	CONELELLO Antonio	14 III 1941
Row 10 – 1	Civile	CANNAVO Roberto	
Row 10 – 2	Civile	SALARIS Giovanni	26 X 1939
Row 10 – 3	Civile	SERAFINO Domenico	
Row 11 – 1	Civile	CASTORI Dante	6 II 1941
Row 11 – 2	Civile	SCHENONE Luigi	11 IX 1940
Row 11 – 3	Civile	LA DELFA Carmelo	31 I 1939
Row 12 – 1	Civile	DEL SANTO Giuseppe	7 IX 1941
Row 12 – 2	Civile	SACCONE Ugo	29 IX 1941
Row 12 – 3	Civile	COSTANTINI Giovanni	31 I 1940
Row 13 -1	Civile	AMERINI Rosetta Maria	2 III 1941
Row 13 – 2	Civile	ROBERTI Luigi	10 XII 193
Row 13 – 3	Civile	LO PRESTI Giuseppe	5 VI 1937
Row 14 – 1	Civile	COCUZZI Domenico	23 X 1939
Row 14 – 2	Civile	BALIERI Giuseppe	4 XII 1932
Row 14 – 3	Civile	MAGGI Enrico	20 X 1940
Row 15 – 1	Civile	CONTI Ida Olimpia	11 VII 1940
Row 15 – 2	Civile	GUGLIANDRO Filippo	7 VII 1939
Row 15 – 3	Civile	CANIPAROLI Ettore	22 IV 1941
Row 16 – 1	Civile	DELSANTO Andrea	7 VI 1941

Row 16 – 2	Civile	PROFILI Italo	28 XII 1939
Row 16 – 3	Civile	FABBRI Eugenio	3 XII 1940
Row 17 – 1	Civile	ASQUINI Dante	1 IX 1941
Row 17 – 2	Civile	SOLLEVANTI Antonio	6 XIII 1938
Row 17 – 3	Civile	PAUSIO Giacomo	23 II 1940

Sector B
1 mass grave with 15 burials

La Sorte Che Li Uni In Vita
In Un Comune Ideale
Li Volle Insieme
Anche Dopo
Il Supremo Sacrificio

Capo. Man. M.O.V.M.	BENINI Corrado
C.N.	BUTTIGNOL Olinto
C.N. M.B.V.M.	CALTI Emilio
V. Capo. So. M.B.V.M.	COZZI Guido
Sold.	DELLAMORA Giuseppe
V. Capo. So. M.B.V.M.	DI STEFANO Salvatore
Capo So. M.A.V.M.	FACINI Paolo
C.N. M.B.V.M.	FORNO Domenico
C.N. M.B.V.M.	GIMONDI Antonio
V. Capo. So. M.B.V.M.	INCONTRO Francesco
C.N. M.B.V.M.	NICOLI Francesco
Sold.	PAGNAN Innocente
C.N.	PILOTTI Giorgio
Capor.	PUGLIESE Stefano
C.N. M.B.V.M.	ZECCHINEL Umberto

Sector C
17 rows of 3 graves

Row 1 – 1	Civile	GHIROLDI Antonio	10 IV 1938
Row 1 – 2	Civile	GASPARI Rino	2 IV 1940
Row 1 – 3	Civile	GUERRERA Rosa Maria	28 VI 1940
Row 2 – 1	Civile	RADOMILLA Attilio	8 III 1939
Row 2 – 2	Civile	DISCAN DI	7 I 1940
Row 2 – 3	Civile	PLATANIA Umberto	5 V 1939
Row 3 – 1	Civile	PENGUE Luigi	27 VI 1940
Row 3 – 2	Civile	RICCARDI Eugenio	6 VII 1939
Row 3 – 3	Civile	SBARDELLATI Pietro	22 VIII 1939
Row 4 – 1	Civile	RICCI Antonio	27 V 1940
Row 4 – 2	Civile	GRANATO Angelo	13 V 1941
Row 4 – 3	Civile	PEDERZINI Valerio	6 XI 1939
Row 5 – 1	Civile	PERGAMENO Nicola	25 V 1939
Row 5 – 2	Civile	SORLINI Mario	15 IX 1940
Row 5 – 3	Civile	RAVIOLO Fedele	1 VI 1939
Row 6 – 1	Militarizzato	TORRI Alfeo	30 VIII 1936
Row 6 – 2		TOMAI Tarciso	21 XI 1938
Row 6 – 3		BAZZO Luigi	18 V 1937
Row 7 – 1		ZULLO Gaetano	2 VIII 1937
Row 7 – 2		BONOMI Vittorio	23 I 1938
Row 7 – 3		PAPI Germinal	4 IV 1938

Row 8 – 1		DEL BARBA Luigi	18 IV 1937
Row 8 – 2		FICAZZA Vincenzo	23 VII 1937
Row 8 – 3		MARANGONI Giuseppe	2 IV 1938
Row 9 – 1		BIANCHI Emanuele Fileberto	15 IV 1938
Row 9 – 2		DI SALVO Alfio	25 XII 1938
Row 9 – 3		PLEBANI Giovanni	2 XII 1939
Row 10 – 1		MARINI Settimo	26 II 1938
Row 10 – 2		CAMPANER Claudio	19 III 1938
Row 10 – 3		PORCARO Antonio	21 XI 1937
Row 11 – 1		BOSCHETTI Luigi	13 XI 1937
Row 11 – 2		CECCHINI Umberto	6 III 1938
Row 11 – 3		MINISCHETTI Vincenzo	21 I 1938
Row 12 – 1		RUGGERI Sebastiano	9 III 1939
Row 12 – 2		MULE Giuseppe	13 III 1937
Row 12 – 3		GALVANI Giovanni	
Row 13 – 1		TABUSSO Fedele	2 IV 1938
Row 13 – 2		BUSICO Raffaele	6 III 1938
Row 13 – 3		GIUGNO Giuseppe	15 II 1937
Row 14 – 1		DI PLACIDO Valentino	26 II 1938
Row 14 – 2		NATALE Giuseppe	10 XI 1938
Row 14 – 3		FARAONI Giuseppe	24 III 1937
Row 15 – 1	Soldato	RORBERI Augusto	18 IX 1941
Row 15 – 2	Soldato	NESCI Vincenzo	11 II 1941
Row 15 – 3	Soldato	CALSOLARO Oreste	27 VIII 1940

Row 16 – 1	Soldato	CATALANO Angelo	6 IX 1941
Row 16 – 2	Soldato	NEGRO Angelo	6 IX 1936
Row 16 – 3	Soldato	SCARDINO Ernesto Dante	26 I 1941
Row 17 – 1	Soldato	SIMSIC Pietro	6 IX 1941
Row 17 – 2	Soldato	GRECO Emanuele	22 XII 1938
Row 17 – 3	Soldato	GRASSINI Vincenzo	22 XII 1938

Sector D
20 rows of 3 graves

Row 1 – 1	Soldato	VIO Giovanni	1 VIII 1936
Row 1 – 2	Soldato	SALVI Enrico	4 XII 1940
Row 1 – 3	Soldato	TREVISAN Guido	24 XI 1940
Row 2 – 1	Soldato	PIVETTI Cesare	22 XII 1938
Row 2 – 2	Soldato	MARA Vincenzo	6 VI 1941
Row 2 – 3	Soldato	TERPOLILLI Alfredo	31 III 1937
Row 3 – 1	Soldato	DI GILIO Pasquale	2 IV 1941
Row 3 – 2	Soldato	ZINZI Filippo	22 VI 1940
Row 3 – 3	Soldato	AQUAFONDATA Arturo	13 VI 1938
Row 4 – 1	Soldato	MACCAGNI Eugenio	19 IV 1939
Row 4 – 2	Soldato	VANIN Giovanni	20 XII 1926
Row 4 – 3	Soldato	TOSONI Giordano	21 IX 1941
Row 5 – 1	Soldato	POLVERINO Giuseppe	14 II 1941
Row 5 – 2	Camicia Nera	PISCOPIELLO Palmiero	24 X 1940
Row 5 – 3	Camicia Nera	CUNDARI Antonino	14 V 1941

Row 6 – 1	Camicia Nera	MATERA Filippo	21 I 1938
Row 6 – 2	Camicia Nera	DI TOLVE Alfredo	27 X 1940
Row 6 – 3	Camicia Nera	NEGRO Guglielmo	6 IX 1936
Row 7 – 1	Camicia Nera	VALVASORI Pietro	31 I 1939
Row 7 – 2	Camicia Nera	FRATI Edilio	16 III 1937
Row 7 – 3	Camicia Nera	TALARICO Filippo	22 XI 1940
Row 8 – 1	Camicia Nera	LO CICERO Benedetto	23 IV 1937
Row 8 – 2	Camicia Nera	CARTELLI Giovanni	20 V 1938
Row 8 – 3	Camicia Nera	GERARDI Giuseppe	4 V 1936
Row 9 – 1	Camicia Nera	COVACCI Gino	10 XII 1940
Row 9 – 2	Camicia Nera	ADELQUI Donato	26 III 1939
Row 9 – 3	Camicia Nera	GHIRINGELLI Amedeo	23 X 1936
Row 10 – 1	Camicia Nera	CIRIO Giuseppe	7 XII 1940
Row 10 – 2	Militarizzato	COTTILOMETTI Antonio	28 VII 1937
Row 10 – 3	Militarizzato	RICCI Luigi	25 IX 1939
Row 11– 1	1. Seniore M.O.V.M.	Luciano	10 VIII 1941
Row 11 – 2	Sergente	BROWN Alessandro	7 VI 1941
Row 11 – 3	Serg. Magg.	GIARETTON Ugo	25 III 1938
Row 12 – 1	Vice C. So.	PIRRO Francesco	29 III 1941
Row 12 – 2	Vice C. So.	VARNIERO Angelo	30 XII 1939
Row 12 – 3	Vice C. So.	PERRI Antonio	11 IX 1941
Row 13 – 1	Vice-Brigadiere	STRANO Rosario	6 IV 1940
Row 13 – 2	Caporale	MANCHINU Pietro	30 X 1941

Row 13 – 3	Caporale	DI CLAUDIO Pierino	30 IX 1941
Row 14 – 1	Caporale	ARISI Carlo	3 II 1941
Row 14 – 2	Caporale	BACCHELLI Lino	3 IX 1941
Row 14 – 3	Caporale	COHENNA Nicola	21 IV 1941
Row 15 -1	Capitano M.O.V.M.	ROSSO Giuseppe	13 IX 1941
Row 15 – 2	Capitano	NORLENGHI Alberto Guido	7 IV 1937
Row 15 – 3	Capitano	VILLA Pietro	19 IV 1939
Row 16 – 1	Capitano	SOFIO Jack	27 XI 1939
Row 16 – 2	Caporale Magg.	MISCONEL Giuseppe	4 VIII 1941
Row 16 – 3	Caporale Magg.	ARGELLI Armando	2 III 1940
Row 17 – 1	Caporale Magg.	CECCONI Luigi	6 IX 1951
Row 17 – 2	S. Tenente	DI STEFANO Pietro	19 VIII 1941
Row 17 – 3	S. Tenente	RIPANDELLI Carlo	7 VIII 1941
Row 18 – 1	S. Tenente	ARPAIA Renato	12 IV 1941
Row 18 – 2	S. Tenente M.O.V.M.	CUCCI Guido	27 XI 1939
Row 18 – 3	Tenente	FRATTI Gualteri Aldo	16 V 1941
Row 19 – 1	Tenente	BOURLOT Giulio Maurizio	24 VII 1941
Row 19 – 2	Tenente	ZANICHELLI Clorindo	16 IX 1937
Row 19 – 3	Tenente	GUGLIELMELLI Vincenzo	13 VI 1938
Row 20 – 1	Mar. Ord.	SANFEDELE Guglielmo	24 IX 1939
Row 20 – 2	Maggiore	ALISA Pasquale	30 XI 1940
Row 20 – 3	Colonello	BARBACINI Ercole	5 XII 1939

3.6.2 THE ADDIS ABABA COMMONWEALTH WAR GRAVES CEMETERY

Location: N 09° 03.439' E 038° 42.911'
Altitude: 2548 m
Administered by:
Embassy of the United Kingdom of Great Britain and Northern Ireland, Fikremariam Abatechan Street, Woreda 16, Kebele 06, Addis Ababa, Tel. 00 251 11 6612354

The history of the Addis Ababa Commonwealth War Graves Cemetery is not easily established. According to archival documents of the Commonwealth War Graves Commission, which are not overly informative, the Imperial War Graves Commission (as it was then known) appears to have provisionally taken over the cemetery on 31 December 1944 from the Directorate of Graves Registrations and Enquiries. Discussions regarding the architecture and its eventual construction then continued throughout the 1940s. The files indicate that in November 1953 a joint religious service was conducted there, attended by Admiral the Earl Mountbatten of Burma and Diplomatic representatives from America, France, Greece, Belgium and Yugoslavia, as well as the Danish Consul and a representative of the Ethiopian Army.[55] "The Ethiopian Herald" reported on Sunday, 11 November 1953, that after the religious service Lord Mountbatten "laid wreaths at the foot of the liberation monument in the British military cemetery". He then continued his voyage to Asmara and Massaua, accompanied by the Duke of Harar and Lt. Gen. Abiy Abebe, the Ethiopian Minister of War. November 1953 might indicate the official opening of the cemetery.

The Addis Ababa Commonwealth War Cemetery was bequeathed, in perpetuity, as a war cemetery by the Emperor Haile Selassie. A marble plaque at the entrance recalls that "by command of His Imperial Majesty the Emperor of Ethiopia the land on which this cemetery stands has been given for the perpetual resting place of the soldiers and airmen who are buried here." The Commonwealth War Graves Cemetery is to the right of the Italian Military Cemetery and surrounded by a wall. The central Cross of Sacrifice, made out of local sandstone, faces the main entrance. The tombstones are mostly marked with a headstone with an inscribed cross, three are inscribed with a "Magen David" (Star of David) , and some with an inscription in Arabic from the Holy Quran.

[55] The author is grateful to Mrs. Julie Somay, Commonwealth War Graves Commission, Enquiries Section for this information.

Tomb of private Hassani Ramazani

The site is maintained by the Commonwealth War Graves Commission, through the British Embassy, together with war cemeteries in Harer, where some 45 East African soldiers are buried, and at Dira Dawa where a further 70 East African soldiers are also buried. There is also one additional isolated grave at Gambella close to the Sudan border.

There are 335 known graves in the Addis Ababa cemetery of which 295 are from the Second World War when British and Commonwealth troops defeated the Italians who had invaded Ethiopia in 1936. There are 273 graves of soldiers and 24 of airmen. Seven headstones are marked "A Soldier of the 1939-1945 war".

In addition to the 42 British servicemen buried here, there are also servicemen from Sudan (1), the former Gold Coast (West Africa, 32), India, the former Rhodesia (7), Kenya, Uganda, Tanzania (East Africa, 143), the former British Somaliland, South Africa (68) and Australia (1) buried in the cemetery. Additionally, there are 3 French servicemen buried in the cemetery. 291 graves carry the names of those buried.

Behind the central Cross of Sacrifice, a recessed stone seat is set in the back wall of the cemetery facing the Cross. A plaque, set in the wall above the seat, commemorates those Ethiopians who died while serving with the British Forces. The inscription reads:

1939 1945

Here are remembered

Among their fellow fallen comrades of the

British Commonwealth and Empire

The valiant sons of Ethiopia

Who served and died with them

In the same cause"

There are, in the NE corner, 60 tombs of civilians (61 burials); they include Brigadier Sandford who died in 1972 (his wife lies beside him and it was she who founded the Sandford International School). Brigadier Sandford, together with General Orde Wingate, were both key personalities in paving the way for the Emperor's return to Addis Ababa on 5th May 1941 after his five years exile in the United Kingdom.

Tomb of Brigadier Daniel Arthur Sandford

Furthermore, five victims of the "air distaster" at Addis Ababa which took place on 18 April 1972 when an East African Airways VC-10 crashed at Bole airport killing 40 passengers found their final resting place at Gulele.[56]

Every year the British Embassy organises a Remembrance Day service at this war cemetery and there is a large diplomatic (Commonwealth and non-Commonwealth) attendance, including representatives from the Ethiopian Armed Forces. The Princess Royal visited the cemetery and laid a wreath during her visit to Ethiopia in October 2002.The most recent headstone is of Douglas George and Esher Faucher Lister, who died in 2005 and 2006 respectively.

Remembrance Sunday, 9 November 2008

[56] National Archive and Library Agency, The Ethiopian Herald of 19 and 20 April 1972.

To the left of the entrance you will find the visitor's book which visitors may wish to sign. The book reveals that between January and August 2009 a total of 49 visitors, mainly from the United Kingdom, but also from the United States, Canada, Germany, Italy and even Slovenia had visited the site and signed the book. Visitors may also wish to ask the local guard on duty to see the list of the graves, contained in a small brochure in green cover entitled

1939-1945

The War Dead of the Commonwealth

(also Non World War and Foreign Nationals burials)

Addis Ababa War Cemetery

Dire Dawa African War Cemetery

Harar War Cemetery

Ethiopia

Commonwealth War Graves Commission

This register has been re-published from the records

of the Commonwealth War Graves Commission

20 October 2005

Civilian Sector in the lower right corner:

Row A

1) SUMMERS SMITH Margareth		+29 IV 1972
2) ROBERTSGodfrey	* 18 IX 1908	+ 26 IX 1959
3) PROTOPAPPA née KING Elsie		
4) WHITTLE Timothy Patrick	* 22 X ?	+ 30 X 19 ?
5) CAFFRAY Thomas	* *Dundee,* Scotland 1 XII 1909	+ Addis A. 15 II 1994

worker at Jute-Factory in Addis Ababa 1954 - 1974

6) COLLIER Charles Saint John	* St. John, New Bruns-wick, Canada 7 I 1880	+ Addis Ababa 25 VII 1944
7) MULLEN Agnes Carus	* 19 III 1907	+ 23 VIII 1947

8) COSTIGAN George Henry	* Ireland 1905	+ Addis A. X 1951
9) DITCHBURN Jones John	* Blackburn England 4 XI 1898	+ Addis Ababa 6 XI 1951
10) JONES William	* Swansea 16 V 1888	+ A.A. 21 III 1952
11) BAILEY Elspeth Janet		+ in air disaster A.A. 18 IV 1972
12) MURPHY Robert Aitken	* Edmonton, Canada 1 IV 1918	+ 17 XI 1952
13) BAILEY Eleanor Jane		+ in air disaster A.A. 18 IV 1972
14) BENSON Joan Mary	* Oakville, Ontario 28 IX 1942	+ 25 VII 1953
15) THOMAS Harold	* London 24 I 1899	+ A.A. 8 VI 1955
16) FAULKNER Edward James	* 28 IX 1915	+ 2 IV 1971
17) GRANGE Winifred Norah	* March, England	+ 20 VI 1956
18) LAXTON Elonwy Jane	* Whitehead, Wales 20 III 1916	+ Addis Ababa 18 VIII 1970
19) DULCIE Mary née GUISE	* 26 V 1910	+ 5 X 1956
20) SCOTT Mary Frances	* 10 I 1896	+ 25 XII 1988
21) DOWNES Patrick Gregory		infant
22) BOTTO Ronald Peter Heijnes	* 3 X 1940	+ in air crash A.A. 18 IV 1972
23) Mc GREGOR WARD Ian	* 21 II 1957	+ 20 III 1957
24) MacNABB Frances David		+ in air disaster A.A. 18 IV 1972
25) STEPHENSON Katherine Torrance	* 13 IV 1873	+ 1 VII 1957
26) PANTON Bernard Joseph	* 6 VII 1906	+ in air disaster A.A. 18 IV 1972
27) BEAMENT James Reginald	* London 9 I 1915	+ A.A. 20 IX 1960

Row B)

1) SANDFORD[57] Christine	* 1893	+ 1975
2) SANDFORD[58] Daniel Arthur	* 18 VI 1882	+ AA 22 I 1972

Artillery Officer 1900-1910, then Sudan Political Service - District Ciommissioner, 1913 Sudan Liaison Officer in Addis Ababa; officer in WW I , Lt. Col, DSO; General Manager Abyssinian Trading Corporation in Addis Ababa 1920-1936, trading in skins and hides, part-time journalist for „Daily Mail", farmer after having been given „Mulu Farm" by Haile Selassie; leaves Ethiopia with Emperor Haile Selassie in 1936 for Bath, England; 1940/41 Chief Political Adviser of the Emperor; Brigadier, R.A.O.G. Mission in Ethiopia 1940 – 1942, Commander of "Mission 101"; CBE 1942; leading position in Addis Ababa Municipality and Director General of Ethiopian Ministry of Interior - 1949; retired to „Mulu-Farm" until his death in 1972
N 09° 03.439 ' E 038° 42.917'

3) MATTHEW Austin Frederic	* 18 II 1882	+ 18 I 1969

Anglican Chaplain to Ethiopia 1928-1951, Canon of Khartoum Cathedral 1957

4) LANGDON James Bertram	* 9 II 1893	+ 10 XII 1973
5) Mc GILLIVRAY Freda Ann née ROBINSON	* 1932	+ 1968
6) DUNBAR Justin	* 13 VIII 1974	+ 19 VIII 1974
7) RAYNER Faith	* Southsea 13 VII 1936	+ A.A. 27 IV 1968
8) LABUSCHAGNE Pete	* 20 VII 1923	+ 5 VI 1975
9) BARRY Mary	* 11 XI 1889	+ 30 I 1967
10) ABBOTT Dr. Olga Constantinova	* 1890	+ 26 III 1982
11) PORZECKI Major John Randolph	* 1909	+ 10 XI 1966
12) ROUX Pierre Jacques	* Marseille 9 IX 1915	+ 22 VI 1994
13) MILLICHAP Barbara Edith		+ IV 1966
14) MEAKINS Andrew R.	* 29 IV 1953	+ 23 XI 1996
15) YOUNG Simon Forbes	* II 1927	+ 3 III 1966
16) NORRIS Bertram	* Reading	+ 3 II 1965
17) BLAKE Nora Mary	* 3 VIII 1900	+ 26 VIII 1976
18) BRENNAN John Thomas	* 13 XII 1918	+ 3 XII 1964
19) JANES Helen	* 12 XI 1931	+ 26 II 1972

[57] See EAE, vol. 4, entry Sandford, Christine.
[58] See EAE, vol. 4, entry Sandford, Daniel.

20) ANDERSON Nicholas		+ 16 XI 1964
21) SQUIREBECK Alan	* 4 VI 1923	+ 2 IX 1964
22) Mc CURRY Hilda		+ 17 XI 1962
23) LISTER Gouglas Georges	* 20 IV 1917	+ 12 VII 2005
LISTER Esther Faucher	* 2 I 1918	+ 17 III 2006
24) WALKER Harry Owen	* 17 IX 1912	+ 27 VIII 1962
25) MARSHALL Innes	* 1924	+ 1992
26) MARSHALL James	* 1924	+ 1996
27) HAUGHTON Mike		+ 29 VII 1962 *killed flying*
28) CRAMER Leslie Henry	* London 17 V 1905	+ A.A. 28 I 1992
29) HAMLIN O.B.E. Dr. Reginald	* New Zealand 1908	+ A.A. 5 VIII 1993

Founder of the Fistula Hospital Addis Ababa, N 09° 03.432' E 038° 42.927'

30) GLADSTONE George	* 28 IV 1931	+ 30 III 1962
31) HALEWOOD Eileen	* 8 XI 1907	+ 12 IX 1961
32) FITZHERBERT Margaret	* 31 XII 1906	+ 27 X 1971
33) FITZHERBERT Anna Rachel	* 28 VI 1877	+ 12 VI 1961

Grave	Name	Rank	Regiment		
8E4	ABDALLA Mohamed Abdul Rahim	Private	East African Army Corps	* ?	+ 22 VI 1941
8F1	ABDUL MALIK Mian	Private	East African Army Serv.C.	* ?	+ 8 V 1941
8F2	ABECHER Sabul	Private	Nigeria Regiment RWAFF	* ?	+ 22 VI 1941
2B4	ADAMS Edward Charles	Air Sgt.	South African Air Force	* 1918	+ 12 IX 1940
8F8	ADUGA Dere	Private	Afr. Pioneer C. (East Afr.)	* ?	+ 23 VII 1941
8E6	ALABU Isa	Private	King's African Rifles	* ?	+ 15 IX 1941
7D11	ALFRED Lloyd	Driver	East Afr. Army Serv.Corps	* ?	+ 30 XI 1941
8G2	ALI Bin Abdalla	Private	East Afr. Army Serv. Corps	* ?	+ 28 VIII 1941
8G1	ALI Gingo	Private	East Afr. Army Serv. Corps	* ?	+ 23 XI 1941
8E9	ALI Issala	Private	Gold Coast Rgt., R.W.A.F.F.	* ?	+ 13 IX 1941
8G8	ALIKI Adamu	Private	King's African Rifles	* ?	+ 15 IV 1942
2F10	ALLEN Sidney John	Trooper	Kenya Regiment	* 1918	+ 25 III 1941
8E8	AMADU Grunshi	Private	Gold Coast Rgt., R.W.A.F.F.	* ?	+ 28 VII 1941
5E9	AMUAYI Eshimdu	Private	King's African Rifles	* ?	+ 2 XII 1941
2G16	ANDERSON Joseph	Warr.Off. Cl.I	Royal Northumberland Fus.	* ?	+ 25 V 1941
5C12	ANTON Omolo Onj.	Driver	East Afr. Army Serv.Corps	* ?	+ 3 VIII 1942
8F9	APINGA Kusasi	Private	Gold Coast Rgt., R.W.A.F.F.	* ?	+ 30 VIII 1941
2B1	ARCHER Raymond L.	Trooper	Kenya Regiment	* 1921	+ 10 V 1941
2B3	ARMSTRONG Edward George	Lieutenant	South African Air Force	* ?	+ 12 IX 1940
2D8	ARMSTRONG Joseph James	Private	S. Afr. Res. Mechannical Tr.	* ?	+ 24 VIII 1941
8E3	ASHIRU Alimi	Private	Nigeria Regiment, R.W.A.F.F.	* ?	+ 30 IV 1941
5B12	ASHIKEHEYE Mwangobara	Corporal	East Afr. Corps of Military Pol.	* ?	+ 17 VI 1942

7D4	ASILIMINGA Frafra	Private	Gold Coast Rgt., R.W.A.F.F.	* ?	+ 4 IX 1941
5E3	AUSTIN Somba	Private	King's African Rifles	* ?	+ 14 IX 1941
5F4	BABA Abanda	W.O. Class II	Nigeria Regiment, R.W.A.F.F.	* ?	+ 14 VI 1941
2C12	BAGNALL William	Signalman	Royal Corps of Signals	* 1919	+ 4 XI 1941
2F18	BARRETT Cecil Victor Lancelot	Captain	East Lancashire Regiment	* 1906	+ 7 I 1942
2B19	BARRY Hamilton Brownlee	Lance Bomb.	South African Artillery	* ?	+ 23 IV 1941
2D3	BARTON Richard James	Major	Royal Army Ordnance Corps	* 1910	+ 11 X 1941
7B5	BAYI Grunshi	Private	Gold Coast Rgt., R.W.A.F.F.	* ?	+ 11 X 1941
2A5	BAZELEY John Selwyn Standish	Pilot	Royal Air Force Volunteer Res.	* 1911	+ 27 XI 1941
2A3	BEES George Henry	W.O. Class II	Welsh Regiment	* 1903	+ 14 XI 1942
8G3	BIMA Hassan	Corporal	Nigeria Regiment, R.W.A.F.F.	* ?	+5 VI 1941
2A10	BIRCHENOUGH Michael John	Trooper Car Regi- ment	Southern Rhodesia Armored	* 1914	+ 30 I 1942
7C3	BIRUKIGWA Misale	Private	East Afr. Mil. Labour Corps	* ?	+ 17 VI 1941
4A10	BLACK Frank Milner	Lieut. Colonel	Hampshire Regiment	* 1896	+ 18 IX 1943
4B10	BLACKMOOR Ernest James	Bombar- dier	Royal Artillery	* 1914	+ 27 VIII 1943
2D4	BLOXAM Richard	Private	Imperial Light Horse, S.A.F.	* 1906	+9 V 1941
2F12	BREMNER George	Private	Cape Corps, S.A. Forces	* 1906	+ 27 VII 1941

2E2	BRISCOE Arthur Wellesley Dooley	Captain	Transvaal Scottish, S.A. Forces	* 1911	+ 22 IV 1941
8F10	BUKARE Issalla	Private	Gold Coast Rgt., R.W.A.F.F.	* ?	+ 24 VIII 1941
2A7	BULL Leon Emile	Sergeant	Royal Australian Air Force	* 1918	+ 27 XI 1941
2B2	BURNS George Clark	Private	Natal Mounted Rifles, S.A. F.	* 1920	+ 14 V 1941
5C8	BWOSIAMO Ekitipai	Private	East African Army Res. Corps	* ?	+ 18 X 1941
2B15	CAMPBELL William Alexander	Sergeant	Royal Sussex Regiment	* ?	+ 25 V 1941
7D9	CHANGWOKY Kusibon	Private	East African Army Service C.	* ?	+ 23 X 1941
2B9	CHAPMAN Arthur Sutherland	Sergeant	Kenya Regiment	* ?	+ 10 V 1941
5E8	CHILUKA Fraser	Private	East African Army Service C.	* ?	+ 22 XI 1941
5B7	CHRISTOPHER Male	Private	East African Army Service C.	* ?	+ 4 IV 1942
2E11	CLARK Matthew	Gunner	South African Artillery	* 1910	+ 19 IV 1941
2F8	CLARKE Ernest Charles	Leading Aircraft-man	Royal Air Force	* ?	+ 25 VIII 1940
5F8	CLAUDIO Masombe	Private	East Afr. Corps of Milit. Police	* ?	+ 9 V 1941
2C7	COOMBE Anthony Fleming	Major	Royal Engineers	* 1915	+ 18 X 1941
2B13	CRESWELL Richard Martyn	Captain	King's African Rifles	* 1902	+ 19 V 1941
2D9	DAMANT Frederic Hugh Ainslee	Air Mechanic	South African Air Force	* 1921	+ 24 VIII 1941
2D17	DAVIDSON D.J.	Private	Royal Natal Carbineers, S.A.F.	* 1921	+22 IV 1941

2D13	DE SWARDT Harold	Private	Duke of Edinburgh's Own Rifles, South African Forces	* ?	+17 IV 1941
6A7	DIKOA Ali	Private	Nigeria Regiment, R.W.A.F.F.	* ?	+ 15 V 1941
4B7	DODD John	W.O. Class II	Worcestershire Regiment	* 1906	+ 13 VI 1944
4B5	DOIG Andrew	Craftsman	Royal Electrical and Mechanical Engineers	* 1904	+ 28 VIII1944
4A6	DRAYTON Jammes Allan	Sergeant	Royal Corps of Signals	* 1916	+ 25 IV 1944
2C19	DU PLESSIS Frans Jacob	Sapper	South African Engineer Corps	* 1904	+ 9 IV 1941
4A1	DU TOIT Petrus Gerhardus	Private	South African Reserve Mechanical Transport	* ?	+ 2 V 1941
8F12	DUBAT Dagat	Private	King's African Rifles	* ?	+ 26 IX 1941
2F16	DUDLEY Leighton R.	Lieutenant	South African Air Force	* 1917	+ 13 III 1941
2D16	ELLIS Albert Edward	Private	Duke of Edinburgh's Own Rifles, S.A. Forces	* ?	+ 22 IV 1941
2C15	ENGLISH Stratford Wilson	Major	South African Artillery	* 1913	+ 19 VI 1941
5F3	ERENESTI Rwomweja	Private	EastAfricanArmy Serv.C	* ?	+ 25 VI 1941
5C9	ERIZIMASI Mayanja	Private	East African Army Serv. C.	* ?	+ 25 V 1941
2F1	EVANS Claude Patrick	Lance Corporal	South African Medical Corps	* 1917	+ 8 IV 1941
5D2	EZERA Kakonge	Private	King's African Rifles	* ?	+ 13 VII 1941
8G13	FARRARHARJI Mohamed	Private	East African Army Serv. C.	* ?	+ 15 X 1941
2E16	FAULKNER Charles Edward	Corporal	South African Engineer Corps	* ?	+ 30 V 1941
2F13	FERNANDEZ George	Private	Indian and Malay Corps South African Forces	* ?	+ 6 III 1942

2F4	FERREIRA Marthinus Gert Thomas	Lieutenant	South African Air Force	* 1922	+ 10 IV 1941
4A2	FLEMMER Wilfred Anthony	Private	Transvaal Scottish, S.A. Forces	* 1918	+ 27 III 1941
6A2	FRANCIS Govinda	Driver	East African Army Serv. C.	* ?	+ 19 I 1942
5F10	FRANKLIN	Sapper	Weast African Engineers, R.W.A.F.F.	* ?	+ 27 V 1941
2F15	FRICLAC John	Private	Indian and Malay Corps South African Forces	* ?	+ 13 II 1942
5B9	FRIDADI Mukasa	Private	East African Army Serv. C.	* ?	+ 14 V 1942
2A21	FRY Freek	Private	Cape Corps, S.A. Forces	* 1921	+ 30 X 1941
6A12	GARDEN Mapiri	Private	Northern Rhodesia Regiment	* ?	+ 3 VIII 1941
2A19	GAY-ROBERTS Edmund Adrian Compton	Sergeant	Rhodesia Regiment	* 1915	+ 27 V 1941
2D7	GEUSTYN Pieter Johannes	Gunner	South African Artillery	* 1914	+ 26 X 1941
5B3	GILASIANO Chaweza	Private	King's African Rifles	* ?	+ 13 III 1942
2C4	GILES Gowan Arbuthnott	Captain	South African Air Force	* 1899	+ 3 VI 1941
2A9	GILLESPIE George William	Signalman	Royal Corps of Signals	* 1918	+ 27 XII 1941
4B8	GLOVER Frederick	Sergeant	Coldstream Guards	* 1918	+ 7 IV 1943
2D10	GOBLE Everard N.	Private	Natal Mounted Rifles, South African Forces	* 1905	+ 9 VI 1941
2C1	GOLDSTONE Henry Benjamine	Lieutenant	South African Engineer Corps	* 1917	+ 31 V 1941
2F5	GRANT Ronald	Air Sergeant	South African Air Force	* 1913	+ 10 IV 1941
2E8	GUDGIN Peter Thom.	Lieutenant	Royal Norfolk Regiment	* 1919	+ 9 VIII 1941

2E9	HALE James George Car Regiment	Trooper	Southern Rhodesia Armoured	* ?	+ 16 XI 1941
5F2	HARRISION Kwami Adum	Driver	West African Army Service Corps, R.W.A.F.F.	* ?	+ 28 VII 1941
Sp.M.	HARVEY Evrill Witham	Private	Technical Service Corps, S.A. Forces	* 1901	+ 14 V 1941
2F7	HARVEY Noel Cortney	Captain	South African Air Force	* ?	+ 15 III 1941
8F11	HASSANI Ramazani	Private	East African Army Serv. C.	* ?	+ 12 IX 1941
2D11	HAYTER Arthur Roy	Sergeant	Rhodesia Regiment	* 1918	+ 10 VI 1941
7B7	HAZIWELO Gondwe	Private	King's African Rifles	* ?	+ 18 VII 1941
2E17	HIGGINS Albert James	Sergeant	Royal Army Service Corps	* 1919	+ 2 VI 1941
2C6	HODGKISS George Albert	Sapper	South African Engineer Corps	* 1916	+ 2 V 1941
2B11	HOGG Guy Wilfred	Private	Natal Mounted Rifles, S.A. F.	* 1919	+ 13 V 1941
4A5	HOWARD Norman	Sergeant	Royal Corps of Signals	* 1911	+22 X 1942
2A16	HOWITSON John	Lieutenant	South African Air Force	* 1920	+ 24 IV 1941
2A6	HUBEN Henry James	Corporal	Royal Corps of Signals	* 1919	+ 24 XII 1941
2C8	HURLY Leslie Stanley	Lance Corp.	South African Engineer Corps	* 1902	+ 14 V 1941
8G5	HUSSEINI bin Asmani	Private	East African Army Serv. C.	* ?	+ 18 X 1941
8G10	IDI Kagaruki N.	Private	Pioneer Corps	* ?	+ 5 II 1942
8G6	IDI Katsina	Sapper	West African Engineers, R.W.A.F.F.	* ?	+ 27 V 1941
2E19	IMPEY Charles Lennox	Gunner	South African Artillery	* 1904	+ 26 III 1941

5A5	JAMES Misikisi	Private	King's African Rifles	* ?	+ 19 IX 1941
8E10	JANUARY Nyepeliwa	Private	King's African Rifles	* ?	+ 4 VI 1941
2F2	JARRETT Stanley Leonard	W.O. II	Kenya Regiment	* ?	+ 6 IV 1941
7A7	JATO Kologo	Corporal	Gold Coast Regiment, R.W.A.F.F.	* ?	+ 12 X 1941
2C13	JONES John Harris	Air Mechanic	South African Air Force	* ?	+ 13 VII 1941
8G11	JUMA Hassani	Private	East African Army Serv. C.	* ?	+ 5 II 1942
7A10	KABWATA Tiriban	Private	African Pioneer Corps (East Africa)	* ?	+ 27 V 1942
8E1	KANO Sali	Private	Nigeria Regiment, R.W.A.F.F.	* ?	+ 9 VIII 1941
2D14	KARG Nevillo	Sergeant	Duke of Edinburgh's Own Rifles, S.A. Forces	* 1919	+ 17 IV 1941
5E7	KATEMA Kamando	Private	King's African Rifles	* ?	+18 XI 1941
5F6	KATUTO Ndambuki	Private	East African Army Serv. C.	* ?	+ 8 VI 1941
2A18	KELLY Francis Will.	Sergeant	South African Air Force	* 1918	+ 11 VI 1941
5B1	KENYAN Ladyeri	Lance Corp.	East African Army Serv. C.	* ?	+ 11 II 1942
5E4	KHOFI Kamfula	Private	King's African Rifles	* ?	+ 18 XI 1941
5A10	KIBEY	Private	King's African Rifles	* ?	+ 5 II 1942
7C11	KILARIO Kesi	Private	King's African Rifles	* ?	+ 1 V 1941
7B6	KILONZO Ndiso	Private	East African Army Serv. C.	* ?	+ 15 X 1941
7A13	KIMANI Kisebe	Private	East African Army Serv. C.	* ?	+ 21 I 1942
5A4	KIMANI Nyumu	Private	East African Army Serv. C.	* ?	+ 8 XII 1941

7C6	KIMULI Muthama	Private	EastAfrican Army Serv. C.	* ?	+ 16 VII 1941
7D1	KIPKIOS Omimo	Private	King's African Rifles	* ?	+ 7 IX 1941
5C10	KOPKOECH A. Mambai	Private	East African Army Serv. C.	* ?	+ 18 X 1941
5E12	KIPKOSKE Arap Langat	Private	King's African Rifles	* ?	+ 28 VIII1941
7D5	KIPKURGUT Maritim	Private	King's African Rifles	* ?	+ 14 IX 1941
7A4	KIPTANUI Rop	Private	King's African Rifles	* ?	+ 17 X 1941
2A8	KIRTON Walter	Captain	Royal Army Ordnance Corps	* 1892	+ 22 XII 1941
7D10	KITONGA Kioko	Private	East African Army Serv. C.	* ?	+ 5 I 1942
7B2	KOBINA Abeka	Driver	Gold Coast Regt, R.W.A.F.F.	* ?	+ 9 VI 1941
7D7	KODJO Ansah	Private	Gold Coast Regt, R.W.A.F.F.	* ?	+ 25 IX 1941
8G7	KONTAGORA Audu	Private	Nigeria Regiment, R.W.A.F.F.	* ?	+ 25 V 1941
7D3	KUTUBA Masuuki	Private	East Afr. Military Labour C.	* ?	+ 8 IX 1941
5F11	KWASI Bosomtwe	Sapper	West Afr. Eng., R.W.A.F.F.	* ?	+ 27 VIII1941
7B4	KYANDE Namata	Private	Nigeria Regiment, R.W.A.F.F.	* ?	+ 11 VI 1941
4B4	LAMPITT Donald Ernest	Sergeant	Royal Corps of Engineers	* 1923	+ 25 VI 1946
5A1	LAUSI Ngupe	Private	East Afr. Military Labour C.	* ?	+ 28 XI 1941
4B6	LEEK Lewis	Sergeant	Royal Warwickshire Regiment	* 1914	+ 12 VI 1944
2E13	LEVY Astor	Staff Sgt.	S.A. Reserve Mech. Transport	* 1920	+ 16 XII 1941
2E18	LEWIS Thomas	Corporal	Cape Corps, S.A. Forces	* ?	+ 6 II 1942

5B6	LIRUMA Tero	Private	East African Army Serv. C.	* ?	+ 3 IV 1942
5F12	LODI Sande	Private	King's African Rifles	* ?	+ 5 IX 1941
7D8	LUALANG Lolomunyie	Private	East African Army Serv. C.	* ?	+ 13 X 1941
5A3	LUKA Oto Ocuto	Private	East African Army Serv. C.	* ?	+ 3 II 1942
5B4	LUSIMBA Mohatia	Private	African Pioneer C. (East Afr.)	* ?	+ 24 III 1942
2B17	Mac DONALD Colin Lorne	Mimbashi (Major)	Sudan Defence Force	* 1913	+ 1 IV 1941
5B8	MACHESO Sulumuwa	Private	King's African Rifles	* ?	+ 24 IV 1942
2B8	MACLEAN Jacobus Peter	Sergeant	East African Army Serv. C.	* ?	+ 21 V 1941
2A11	Mac SWEENEY Timothy	Sec. Lieut.	Royal Corps of Signals	* 1916	+ 2 III 1942
7C9	MAJE Agot	Private	East Afr. Military Labour C.	* ?	+ 28 VII 1941
7B3	MAKAU Mauange	Private	East African Army Serv. C.	* ?	+ 22 V 1941
7A11	MAKAU Nindi	Private	East African Army Serv. C.	* ?	+ 13 II 1942
5E10	MAKLEGA Matinde	Private	King's African Rifles	* ?	+ 8 XI 1941
5E2	MAKULI Maro	Private	King's African Rifles	* ?	+ 8 XI 1941
5C1	MANGI Kamau	Private	East African Army Serv. C.	* ?	+ 11 VII 1942
2C11	MANN William Edmund	Aircraft-man 1st Class	Royal Air Force	* 1918	+ 25 XI 1941
2B7	MANNING Michael	Lieutenant	General List	* ?	+ 21 V 1941
2A13	MANSFIELD Charles Beric	Inspector	British South African Police	* 1920	+ 8 V 1942
6A8	MARWA Kimai	Private	King's African Rifles	* ?	+ 6 VII 1941

6A10	MATIYA Lokoto Okello	Sergeant	King's African Rifles	* ?	+ 27 VIII 1941
8F13	MAURIDI Mwarabu	Corporal	East African Army Serv. C.	* ?	+ 1 X 1941
7C2	MBATSETSE Dogo	Private	Nigeria Regiment, R.W.A.F.F.	* ?	+ 13 VI 1941
2D6	Mc GREGOR George	W.O. Class I	East African Army Serv. C.	* ?	+ 26 VI 1941
2C5	Mc LEWEE Charles James	W.O. Class II	Transvaal Scottish, South African Forces	* ?	+ 9 IV 1941
2D12	Mc MENAMIN John Gerald	Lieut. Colonel	Royal Natal Carbineers, S.A.F.	* 1902	+ 22 IV 1941
2C2	Mc WILLIAM Maurice	Flight Sgt.	South African Air Force	* 1920	+ 3 VI 1941
2F3	MEASURES Herbert Thomas	Sec. Lieut.	General List	* 1915	+ 27 VII 1941
2B10	MICHIE David Charles	Private	Natal Mounted Rifles, S.A. F.	* 1922	+ 13 V 1941
5F9	MIKAELI Pondamali	Private	King's African Rifles	* ?	+ 14 XI 1941
5D6	MIZULAIMU Musoke	Private	East African Army Serv. C.	* ?	+ 22 VIII 1941
7C8	MOLI Mutua	Private	East African Army Serv. C.	* ?	+ 14 VII 1941
2F11	MOONSAMY Ellappew	Private	Indian and Malays Corps, South African Forces	* ?	+ 30 I 1942
2E5	MOORE Gordon Charles	Sergeant	Royal Air Force	* 1914	+ 31 III 1941
2B6	MORLEY Chester Stanley	Captain	General List	* ?	+ 2 VI 1941
7A8	MUGUILYO Sihume	Lance Corp.	East African Army Serv. C.	* ?	+ 31 VII 1942
2F6	MULLER James Bernardus	Sergeant	Cape Corps, S.A. Forces	* ?	+ 29 VI 1941
7B8	MUNTU Muthama	Private	Afr. Pioneer C. (East Afr.)	*?	+ 6 X 1941
5C3	MUNUBE Kasuki	Private	East African Army Serv. C.	* ?	+ 18 VII 1941

2E4	MURRAY Edward Alexander	Corporal Military Police	South African Corps of Military Police	* ?	+ 1 V 1941
5D11	MUSAILI Muiba	Private	East African Army Serv. C.	* ?	+ 7 X 1941
5D4	MUSSA Kayogola	Private	King's African Rifles	* ?	+ 28 VIII 1941
7C4	MUSTAFA Allaguemo	Private	Nigeria Regiment, R.W.A.F.F.	* ?	+ 6 VI 1941
5B10	MUSTAFA Majora	Private	King's African Rifles	* ?	+ 27 XI 1941
5D7	MUTHANGA Ndiri	Private	East African Army Serv. C.	* ?	+ 7 IX 1941
7A1	MUTI Sila	Private	East African Army Serv. C.	* ?	+ 7 X 1941
5E11	MUTISO Muanza	Private	East African Army Serv. C.	* ?	+ 22 XII 1941
5C5	MUTISYA Ndolo	Driver	East African Army Serv. C.	* ?	+ 17 VII 1941
5B2	MUTUA Ingati	Private	King's African Rifles	* ?	+ 11 III 1942
7A6	MUTUA Nzau	Private	East African Army Serv. C.	* ?	+ 5 IX 1941
7A5	MUTUGI Ndegwa	Private	East African Army Serv. C.	* ?	+ 22 XI 1941
7C15	MWALALI Mutulu	Private	East African Army Serv. C.	* ?	+ 10 VIII 1941
8E7	MWAMADI Ndala	Private	King's African Rifles	* ?	+ 15 IX 1941
7A9	MWANGANGI Kioko	Lance Corp.	East Afr. Corps of Milit. Police	* ?	+ 25 VI 1942
6A3	MWIRU Wangama	Private	East Afr. Reconnaissance Rgt.	* ?	+ 17 IX 1941
7A12	NAMYENGE Khabarwa	Private	East Afr. Army Medical Corps	* ?	+ 4 II 1942
5A12	NASSRO Mabula	Private	East Afr. Corps of Milit. Police	* ?	+ 23 I 1942

7C5	NDANA Malonla	Private	King's African Rifles	* ?	+ 9 VII 1941
7B1	NDANGA Gaitha	Private	East Afgr. Military Labour C.	* ?	+ 14 VI 1941
2E15	NEL Alwyn Francis	Gunner	South African Artillery	* ?	+ 21 VI 1941
5C6	NEMETE Damufarira	Private	East African Army Serv. C.	* ?	+ 21 X 1941
2A15	NEWMARK Brian Louis	Serjeant	Kenya Regiment	* ?	+ 4 IV 1942
5D12	NGAIRUWA Stephano	Private	East African Army Serv. C.	* ?	+ 17 X 1941
7D6	NGURU Mairuna	Private	Nigeria Regiment, R.W.A.F.F.	* ?	+ 23 VII 1941
5C7	NZIOKI Muli	Private	East African Army Serv. C.	* ?	+ 21 X 1941
6A9	NZUKU Mwambai	Private	East Afr. Military Labour C.	* ?	+ 10 VIII 1941
2A14	O'BYRNE Edward	Constable	British South African Police	* 1917	+ 7 VIII 1941
5A2	OMUDU Nganga	Private	East Afr. Army Ordnance C.	* ?	+ 2 XII 1941
7C1	OPARACHA John	Sergeant	Nigeria Regiment, R.W.A.F.F.	* ?	+ 22 IV 1941
5E5	ORARIO Othieno	Private	African Pioneer C. (East Afr.)	* ?	+ 25 X 1941
5D5	ORENI Obala	Private	King's African Rifles	* ?	+ 25 VIII 1941
5B5	OUMA Obambo	Private	African Pioneer C. (East Afr.)	* ?	+ 1 VIII 1942
5C11	OYOO Ngoto	Private	African Pioneer C. (East Afr.)	* ?	+ 9 X 1941
4B9	PEARCE Clifford Fredericdk	Private	Duke of Edinburgh's Own Rifles, S.A. Forces	* 1912	+ 8 IV 1941
2D2	PELL A.C.	Corporal	South African Artillery	* 1915	+ 15 VIII 1941

5A7	PETRO Nyalandi	Private	East African Army Serv. C.	* ?	+ 20 I 1942
2E14	POTGIETER Abel Hendrik	Staff Sgt.	East African Army Serv. C.	* 1894	+ 19 X 1941
2D1	POTGIETER Johannes Hermanus	Sergeant	South African Engineer C.	* ?	+ 14 VIII 1941
4A8	PREEDY Harry	Corp. of Horse	Life Guards	* 1916	+ 17 II 1944
2B14	PRICE Norman	Serjeant	Rhodesia Regiment	* ?	+ 25 V 1941
7C13	PUGUONI Frafra	Private	Gold Coast Rgt., R.W.A.F.F.	* ?	+ 25 VIII 1941
8F5	RAJABU Mhoja	Private	King's African Rifles	* ?	+ 5 VIII 1941
2E3	RALLS Frederick Hamilton	Private	Transvaal Scottish, S.A. Forces	* ?	+ 22 IV 1941
8E2	RAMADHANI Bwakiri	Driver	East African Army Serv. C.	* ?	+ 26 XII 1941
5D8	RAMAN Bin Aporino	Trooper	East Afr. Reconnaissance Rgt.	* ?	+ 16 IV 1941
8G4	RAMATHANI Hamisi	Lance Corp.	King's African Rifles	* ?	+ 27 IX 1941
2B18	RASS Abraham	Corporal	Cape Forces, S.A. Forces	* ?	+ 1 XI 1941
2F17	REYNOLDS-BALL Reginald Chudleigh	Trooper	Kenya Regiment	* ?	+ 25 III 1941
2E7	ROBERTS Reginald France	Sergeant	Hampshire Regiment	* 1913	+ 7 XII 1941
2D19	ROGERS Harold Edward	Sec. Lieut.	Border Regiment	* 1918	+ 21 III 1941
2D18	ROGERS John Lewis Tannett	Captain	Duke of Cornwall's Light Infantry	* 1908	+ 21 III 1941
2E6	ROWAN Trevor Aubrey	Corporal	Duke of Edinburth's Own Rifles, S.A. Forces	* 1914	+ 12 VII 1941
2C10	ROWE Kenneth Howard	Captain	King's African Rifles	* ?	+ 31 V 1941

2C17	RUDD Christian Tiberius	Sapper	South African Engineer Corps	* ?	+ 20 V 1941
6A4	SALIMI Bin Saidi	Private	East African Army Serv. C.	* ?	+17 XII 1941
8F6	SAMBURA B. Balozi	Private	East Afr. Military Labour C.	* ?	+ 12 VIII 1941
7C12	SAMUEL Buabin	Private	Gold Coast Rgt., R.W.A.F.F.	* ?	+ 27 VIII 1941
5B11	SAPIYAN Gombe Muluwa	Private	King's African Rifles	* ?	+ 27 XI 1941
2C18	SAYERS James Philip	Gunner	South African Artillery	* ?	+ 9 IV 1941
2D15	SCRIMGEOUR Arnold Robert Arthur	Private	Duke of Edinburgh's Own	* ?	+ 17 IV 1941
7A2	SEIDU Wongara	Private	Gold Coast Rgt., R.W.A.F.F.	* ?	+ 12 VII 1941
5E1	SHABAN Paulo	Private	East African Army Serv. C.	* ?	+ 11 XI 1941
2D5	SHIPTON John Edward	Gunner	South African Artillery	* 1908	+ 8 VII 1941
8F4	SHOMARI Mussa	Private	East Afr. Military Labour C.	* ?	+ 1 V 1941
7A3	SIBANDA Luckas	Driver	East African Army Serv. C.	* ?	+ 12 VII 1941
7C7	SIENGO Ngui	Private	King's African Rifles	* ?	+ 25 VII 1941
4A7	SIMPSON Thomas Gordon	Sergeant	Royal Corps of Signals	* 1917	+ 29 XI 1942
2A17	STEYN Eric John	Lieutenant	South African Air Force	* ?	+ 11 VI 1941
2B5	STEYN Johannes Phillipus	Sapper	South African Engineer Corps	* ?	+ 4 VII 1941
2E10	STOTT Allan Rowland	Sergeant	Royal Natal Carbineers, S.A. Forces	* ?	+ 22 IV 1941
2C16	SUCKLING Edward William	W.O. Class II	Kenya Regiment	* ?	+ 17 II 1941

5F5	SUNDAI	Sapper	West African Eng., R.W.A.F.F.	* ?	+ 3 VI 1941
2C14	SUTHERLAND Richard Edward	Signalman	Royal Corps of Signals	* 1920	+ 25 VII 1941
5C4	SWEDI Bin Juma	Private	East African Army Serv. C.	* ?	+ 17 VII 1941
5A8	THEIR Gapero	Corporal	East African Army Serv. C.	* ?	+ 26 XII 1941
4A3	THOMAS A.	Corporal	Indian and Malay Corps, S.A.F.	* ?	+ 17 XII 1941
5F7	TIPOTI Malufumba	Private	Northern Rhodesia Regiment	* ?	+ 19 VI 1941
7C14	TOM Gia	Private	Gold Coast Rgt., R.W.A.F.F.	* ?	+ 25 VIII 1941
6A11	TUJIWENE Nyagawa	Private	East Afr. Military Labour C.	* ?	+ 21 I 1942
4A9	TWEEDIE Graham Calderwood	Pilot	Royal Air Force Volunteer Reserve	* 1921	+ 6 X 1943
5A11	USINGO Sierompre	Private	King's African Rifles	* ?	+ 3 V 1942
2F14	VAN BRIESIS J.	Private	Cape Corps, S.A. Forces	* ?	+ 26 XI 1941
2E12	VAN DER LINDE Piet Ernest Johannes	Sapper	South African Engineers	* ?	+ 30 VII 1941
2A20	VAN SCHOOR William Adrian	Private	South African Reserve Mechanical Transport	* ?	+ 7 VI 1941
2B12	VENTER Albertus Stephanus	Lieutenant	South African Air Force	* ?	+ 3 VI 1941

5A9	WAMBUA Masila	Private	East African Army Serv. C.	* ?	+ 25 XII 1941
7A14	WARE Didone	Private	East African Army Serv. C.	* ?	+ 19 I 1942
6A5	WAWIRU Kimasisio	Private	East African Army Serv. C.	* ?	+ 19 I 1942
2A12	WESTERN Bertram Charles Maximilian	Lieut. Col.	East Lancashire Regiment	* 1887	+ 21 IV 1942
4B11	WHALLEY Richard Cyril Rae	Major	Royal Engineers	* 1896	+ 11 VI 1944
8G12	WILLIAM Kiri	Private	King's African Rifles	* ?	+ 7 I 1942
4A4	WILLIAMSON John Dunlop	Major	King's African Rifles	* 1906	+ 17 II 1943
2F9	WILTON Robert Neville	Sergeant	East African Artillery	* ?	+ 17 VIII 1940
2A4	WITTY Basil Baxter	Pilot Officer	Royal Air Force*1915		+ 12 XII 1940
2C3	WRIGHT James	Sec. Lieut.	Border Regiment	* 1916	+ 31 V 1941
6A6	YOWANA Lubega	Private	East African Army Serv. C.	* ?	+ 23 VI 1941
8G9	YUDA Misi	Private	King's African Rifles	* ?	+ 16 III 1942
7C10	ZABERMA Altini	Private	Nigeria Regiment, R.W.A.F.F.	* ?	+ 1 VIII 1941
2E1	ZIETSMAN Louis	Private	Royal Natal Carbineers, S.A. F.	* 1919	+ 22 IV 1941
7D2	ZONGO Kanjarga	Private	Gold Coast Rgt., R.W.A.F.F.	* ?	+ 2 IX 1941

Three French Soldiers are also buried here, their graves markled by white crosses and the inscription "Mort pour la France". They were the crew of a French aircraft of 1st French Bomber Flight (French Squadron in Aden) attached to the 8th Bomber Squadron in Aden, which was shot down by Italian fighter planes while participating in a bombing raid on an Italian position guarding the railway bridge over the Awash River. A fourth crew member was wounded and taken prisoner.[59] Their graves are marked by white crosses and can easily be spotted among the Commonwealth War graves.

HOLLAND	Sergent	+ 9 IX 1940
LEBATO de FORIA	Sgt. Chef	+ 9 IX 1940
RITOUX-LACHAUT	Capitaine	+ 9 IX 1940

Tomb of capitaine Ritoux-Lachaut

[59] Communication by Colonel Luc de Revel, Defence Attaché, Embassy of France Addis Ababa, 19 II 2009.

4. THE CEMETERY OF THE HOLY TRINITY CATHEDRAL

Location: N 09° 01.846' E 038° 45.929'; follow the road behind the Parliament Building
Altitude: 2433 m

There are two graves in the small cemetery surrounding the Holy Trinity Cathedral of interest to tourists:

David Hall (* Jaffa / Palestine 7 V 1877 + Addis Ababa 4 III 1971)
Location: N 09° 01.831' E 038° 45.945'
The son of Moritz Hall and of Wälättä Iyäsus (Katharina Hall) settled in Ethiopia after World War I and soon engaged in major business operations, inter alia founding the popular Saint George Brewery still existing today. Counsellor of State during the reigns of Menelik II and Haile Selassie, he undertook a secret mission to Germany in 1935 to buy arms for use against the Italian army. During the Italian occupation, Hall lived in Palestine. After WW II Hall returned to Ethiopia as administrator of enemy (Italian) property. Halls' tomb is located in the cemetery at the right when approaching the cathedral. His grave bears the inscription from Psalm 13: "Ich hoffe aber daß Du gnädig bist mein Herz freut sich daß Du so gerne hilfst."

Tomb of David Hall

Sylvia Pankhurst [60](Manchester 5 V 1882 + Addis Ababa 27 IX 1960)
Location: N 09° 01.855' E 038° 45.957'

The famous British suffragette and author, who together with her mother Emmeline was active in the Women's Social and Political Union (WSPU), founded in London in 1903. Belonging to a radical branch of the movement, she rejected the concept of marriage. Editor of "The Woman's Dreadnought". A pacifist and anti-fascist, she since 1936 devoted her life to Ethiopia, publishing "New Times and Ethiopian News" opposing the Italian Fascist invasion of Ethiopia. Invited by Emperor Haile Selassie to settle in Ethiopia, she moved to Addis Ababa in 1956 publishing the "Ethiopian Observer", continuing to work for her adopted country. By order of the Emperor, who attended her funeral, she was buried in a grave monument facing Holy Trinity Cathedral.

Tomb of Sylvia Pankhurst

[60] See EAE, vol. 4, entry Pankhurst, Sylvia.

5. THE BRITISH EMBASSY CEMETERY

Administered by:
Embassy of the United Kingdom of Great Britain and Northern Ireland, Fikre-mariam Abatechan Street, Woreda 16, Kebele 06, Addis Ababa, Tel. 00 251 11 6612354

The small cemetery situated at the Eastern perimeter wall of the 45 hectares British Embassy Compound is not normally accessible to the public. It has five graves, the oldest dating back to 1918. On Remembrance Day a wreath is placed by Her Britannic Majesty's Ambassador to Ethiopia, the Defence Attaché of the British Embassy and the Anglican Bishop for the Horn of Africa.

British Embassy Cemetery, Remembrance Sunday, 9 November 2008 From left to right: Colonel RNHA deV (Sandy) Wade OBE, Bishop Andrew Proud, H.M. Ambassador Norman Ling

Buried here are W. A. M. Wakemann (* 24 X 1872 + Addis Ababa 17 XI 1918), 1st Assistant Surgeon British Legation Addis Ababa, a victim of Spanish influenza.

Arthur Anthony John Rey ("Tony") (* 5 I 1917 + Addis Ababa 13 II 1920) and Roderick Fernand James Rey (* 5 VII 1912 + Addis Ababa 13 III 1920) were sons of Charles F. Rey[61], traveller and author of "Unconquered Abyssinia" (1923), "In the Country of the Blue Nile, The Romance of the Portuguese in Abyssinia" (1929) and "The Real Abyssinia" (1932).

[61] See EAE, vol. 4, entry Rey, Charles.

According to a small bronze plaque, *"these three graves were consecrated on Sunday, January 2nd, 1927, by the Rev. J.A.Cheese in the presence of H.M. Minister and staff".*

Andre John Mesnard Melly (* 9 X 1894 + Addis Ababa 5 V 1936), leader of the British Ambulance Service in Ethiopia, was killed while rescuing wounded in Addis Ababa during the riots of May 1936. The circumstances of his death are recounted by Nicholas Raskin, Telegram from Guernica: The extraordinary Life of George Steer, War Correspondent, 2003.

Philip Photius Constantine Zaphiro[62] – originally Zaphiropoulos (* 28 II 1879 + Addis Ababa 29 VIII 1933) had started his career as medical dispenser in Harar. He was an ornithologist, working for Captain John Harrington, first British Minister to Ethiopia (1898-1909), and later for the British East Africa protectorate (1904-1911) on the demarcation of the Kenya/Ethiopia border in the area of what is now the border town of Moyale. He was first interpreter at the British Legation under Minister Wilfred Thesiger (1909-1920) with the title of Abyssinian secretary, and became Vice Consul in 1915; he served as Oriental Secretary of the British Legation from 1921 until his death in 1933.

In 1943 this little piece of land became a cemetery, as can be read on another bronze plaque: *"This plot was consecrated by the Right Rev. L.H.Gwynne, D.P. Lord Bishop of Egypt and the Sudan on the 14th April 1943 to be a place of burial."* It was however not used for burials after World War II, when – apparently as of 1947 – British and Commonwealth citizens were buried in the civilian part of the Commonwealth War Graves Cemetery in Gulele.

[62] See EAE, vol. 5, entry Zaphiropoulos (Zaphiro).

6. THE JEWISH CEMETERY

Location: N 09° 02.645' E 038° 44.175'
Altitude: 2493 m
Guardian: Mr. Muluneh Teffera, Tel. 011 – 276 90 92 or mobile 0911 – 43 09 03

The Jewish Community of Addis Ababa was made up of Beta Israel, known as "Falasha", as well as some Jewish traders from the then British colony of Aden and Yemen. As Johannes Launhardt points out, "the legal organising of the Jewish Community in Addis Ababa took quite some time." A Provisional Committee of the Jews of Addis Ababa was set up on 15 January 1924. "In the Jewish world, however, 19 September 1936 is taken usually as the date of birth of the Jewish Community in Ethiopia's capital. On this day an order, concerning their community, was issued by R.. Graziani, the Italian Viceroy in Ethiopia."[63]

The Jewish cemetery, with the official address Addis Ketema, Kebele 14 / 21 is situated in Burkina Faso Street. It used to be referred to as the Jewish Cemetery in Gulele, but due to a change of boundaries of Addis Ababa's sub-districts it is, as far as administration is concerned, no longer located in Gulele district.

The easiest way to reach it is by taking Arbanyoch (Patriots) Street to Ambo. When you see a 6-storey pink building to your left, continue for 200 m, turn left, and after roughly 100 m you will find on the right a gate painted in grey, with a little Star of David on its left side. You have arrived at the Jewish cemetery, set in a little Eucalyptus forest.

It is suggested to call the guardian of the cemetery well in advance; Mr. Teffera is very helpful in guiding you around the cemetery – and remember: as he does not receive a regular salary – his mother receives 180 Birr (11 Euro) from the Jewish Community - a generous "schai" (tea-money or baksheesh) is highly appreciated.

According to the guardian, who also acts as keeper, gardener and gravedigger, the cemetery was established in 1948, his late father having been the first guardian. The land – 3806 m2 according to the guardian - was given by Emperor Haile Selassie I to the Jewish Community. The oldest tomb (N 09° 02.665' E 038° 44.144') with a practically illegible inscription dates back to 1942 according to the Ethiopian calendar, or 1950 according to Georgian calendar; these data seem correct, as there are Jewish graves in the international part of the Gulele cemetery preceding 1950. He assumes the number of burials to be around 5000, a figure which seems very high, as the number of tombs does not even reach 1/10 of that figure. Mr. Teffera does unfortunately not have a tomb register; he however keeps correspondence from the 1990s with the American Joint Distribution Committee office in Addis Ababa, which was obviously covering the expenses of running the cemetery.

The cemetery is mainly consisting of tombs of Falashas with an Amharic inscription. On the right side, you will find the small Ferendji section of the cemetery, with a dozen or so tombs with English, Italian or Hebrew inscriptions of European, American and Aden or Yemeni Jews.

The first tomb is of Dr. Karl Pollak (* Vienna/Austria 20 V 1906 died Addis Ababa 24 VI 1980), located at N 09° 02.666' E 038° 44.162'; he was a business-

[63] Johannes LAUNHARDT, Evangelicals in Addis Ababa 1919 – 1991, Berlin-Hamburg-Münster 2004, pp. 19- 22.

man who had settled in Addis Ababa after World War II. Whereas at the end of 2006 his tomb was still in a relatively good condition, by March of 2009 it was beginning to fall apart.

The tomb of Austrian businessman Dr. Karl Pollak

The next tomb is of Lewis Edward Greenwald, son of D. Lewis Greenwald (* New York 19 IX 1947 died Bahir Dar 18 I 1975) who might have drowned in Lake Tana or died of malaria or in a car accident. The third tomb with a Latin inscription is of Giuseppe Wax fu Nelson (died Addis Ababa 22 VI 1952). There are five other tombs of adults and one tomb of a child (died 1971) with Hebrew inscriptions, all of them of Jews from Aden. One tomb is of Mrs. Yephet Menagem, who died on 28 XI 1948 (?), another of Shmuel Salem, who died on 17 III 1966, another of Rina Nazrak. A little further on, we find the tombs of two brothers, Shlomo Ben Yaphet Yaacov (died 23 XII 1976) and Israel Ben Yaphet Yaacov (died 7 XII 1968)[64]. The photos and their bronze frames which once adorned these tombs have long gone. Several pits indicate that tombs have been transferred to Israel.

[64] The author is grateful to H.E. Mr. Oded Ben-Haim, ambassador of the State of Israel to Ethiopia, for having studied the tomb inscriptions on 22 II 2009.

Although the area of the Adeni Jewish tombs and the three European / American graves is very small and graves not very old, the ambience somehow recalls the old Jewish cemeteries of Prague or Cracow.

Neither Prague nor Cracow, but Addis Ababa: a grave in the Jewish Cemetery

As the Jewish Community of Addis Ababa – particularly of Aden Jews – is dwindling in size, only the future will tell whether the cemetery will survive or turn into an object of real estate speculation.

Recht und Politik in Afrika – Law and Politics in Africa
hrsg. von Prof. Dr. h.c. Heinrich Scholler (Universität München)

Heinrich Scholler
Recht und Politik in Äthiopien
Von der traditionellen Monarchie zum modernen Staat
A Historisch: 1. Ser'ata Mangest (m. Bairu Tafla); 2. The Ethiopian community in Jerusalem 1850 – 1914; 3. Ancien Regime und Regierung; 4. Herrschaft und Reich – die Entwicklung von der Reform zur Revolution; 5. Fechter; 6. German World War I aims in Ethiopia; 7. Die Rezeption des westlichen Rechts; 8. Die Entwicklung der Rechtsordnung nach 1974; 9. Phasen der äthiopischen Revolution; B Allgemein: 1. Prinzipien und Grundstrukturen der neuen Verfassung; 2. Societal Script und Verfassungsrecht; C. Besonderes: 1. Die neue Verfassung und ihre Auswirkungen auf die Rechtsordnung; 2. Menschenrechte und Minderheitenschutz; 3. Law Faculty; 5. Special Court und Rechtsentwicklung; 6. Recht und Sprichwort; 7. Open Air Courts in Popular Paintings
Bd. 2, 2008, 312 S., 29,90 €, br., ISBN 978-3-8258-7789-7

LIT Verlag Berlin – Münster – Wien – Zürich – London
Auslieferung Deutschland / Österreich / Schweiz: siehe Impressumsseite